# The Cultural Politics of Talent Migration in East Asia

As the world globalises, more people than ever are on the move, including the many professional, managerial and entrepreneurial elites – often referred to as 'international talent' – who circulate between cities in response to career and business opportunities. While much has been written about the economic motivations behind these mobilities, less is known about the everyday experiences and encounters of highly skilled transnational migrants, who, with the rise of Asia as an economic powerhouse and cultural magnet, are not only increasingly Asian in composition but also rapidly attracted to the globalising cities in Asia.

This book demonstrates how the migratory moves of transnational elites are not only implicated in the reality of multiple belongings, but are also intertwined with the broader cultural politics of specific places. By exploring the interfaces of contact and their diverse subjectivities from race and gender to class and nationality, this collection as a whole – with papers examining talent moving among cities in China, Taiwan, Singapore, Japan, Britain and Canada – paints a decidedly complex picture of how talented migrants inhabit the world in 'more-than-rational' ways. Through the lens of the everyday, this book uncovers the ways in which 'cosmopolitanisms' are forged in different localities and offers new insights into cities as transnational spaces of encounter in the 21st century.

This book was originally published as a special issue of the *Journal of Ethnic and Migration Studies*.

**Brenda S.A. Yeoh** is Professor (Provost's Chair) in the Department of Geography, and Dean of the Faculty of Arts and Social Sciences, at the National University of Singapore. She is also Research Leader of the Asian Migration Cluster at the NUS Asia Research Institute.

**Shirlena Huang** is Associate Professor in the Department of Geography and a Vice Dean of the Faculty of Arts and Social Sciences at the National University of Singapore.

# The Cultural Politics of Talent Migration in East Asia

*Edited by*
**Brenda S.A. Yeoh and Shirlena Huang**

LONDON AND NEW YORK

First published 2013
by Routledge
2 Park Square, Milton Park, Abingdon, Oxon, OX14 4RN

Simultaneously published in the USA and Canada
by Routledge
711 Third Avenue, New York, NY 10017

First issued in paperback 2017

*Routledge is an imprint of the Taylor & Francis Group, an informa business*

© 2013 Taylor & Francis

This book is a reproduction of the *Journal of Ethnic and Migration Studies*, volume 37, issue 5, with the exception of Chapter 5, which was originally published in the *Journal of Ethnic and Migration Studies*, volume 31, issue 2. The Publisher requests to those authors who may be citing this book to state, also, the bibliographical details of the special issue on which the book was based.

All rights reserved. No part of this book may be reprinted or reproduced or utilised in any form or by any electronic, mechanical, or other means, now known or hereafter invented, including photocopying and recording, or in any information storage or retrieval system, without permission in writing from the publishers.

*Trademark notice*: Product or corporate names may be trademarks or registered trademarks, and are used only for identification and explanation without intent to infringe.

*British Library Cataloguing in Publication Data*
A catalogue record for this book is available from the British Library

Typeset in Times New Roman
by Taylor & Francis Books

**Publisher's Note**
The publisher would like to make readers aware that the chapters in this book may be referred to as articles as they are identical to the articles published in the special issue. The publisher accepts responsibility for any inconsistencies that may have arisen in the course of preparing this volume for print.

ISBN 13: 978-1-138-10944-5 (pbk)
ISBN 13: 978-0-415-52813-9 (hbk)

# Contents

| | |
|---|---|
| *Citation Information* | vii |
| *Notes on Contributors* | ix |

1. Introduction: Fluidity and Friction in Talent Migration
   *Brenda S.A. Yeoh and Shirlena Huang* — 1

2. Cosmopolitanism at Work: Labour Market Exclusion in Singapore's Financial Sector
   *Junjia Ye and Philip F. Kelly* — 9

3. Servicing British Expatriate 'Talent' in Singapore: Exploring Ordinary Transnationalism and the Role of the 'Expatriate' Club
   *Jonathan V. Beaverstock* — 26

4. Identity Politics and Cultural Asymmetries: Singaporean Transmigrants 'Fashioning' Cosmopolitanism
   *Elaine Lynn-Ee Ho* — 46

5. Singaporean and British Transmigrants in China and the Cultural Politics of 'Contact Zones'
   *Brenda S.A. Yeoh and Katie Willis* — 64

6. Global Nightscapes in Shanghai as Ethnosexual Contact Zones
   *James Farrer* — 81

7. Shanghai Rush: Skilled Migrants in a Fantasy City
   *Yen-Fen Tseng* — 99

8. Making Careers in the Occupational Niche: Chinese Students in Corporate Japan's Transnational Business
   *Gracia Liu-Farrer* — 119

9. 'The Moon Back Home is Brighter'?: Return Migration and the Cultural Politics of Belonging
   *Sin Yih Teo* — 138

10. A Ritual Economy of 'Talent': China and Overseas Chinese Professionals
    *Xiang Biao* — 154

*Index* — 172

# Citation Information

The following chapters were originally published in the *Journal of Ethnic and Migration Studies*. When citing this material, please use the issue information and original page numbering for each article, as follows:

**Chapter 2**
Cosmopolitanism at Work: Labour Market Exclusion in Singapore's Financial Sector
Junjia Ye and Philip F. Kelly
*Journal of Ethnic and Migration Studies*, volume 37, issue 5 (May 2011) pp. 691-707

**Chapter 3**
Servicing British Expatriate 'Talent' in Singapore: Exploring Ordinary Transnationalism and the Role of the 'Expatriate' Club
Jonathan V. Beaverstock
*Journal of Ethnic and Migration Studies*, volume 37, issue 5 (May 2011) pp. 709-728

**Chapter 4**
Identity Politics and Cultural Asymmetries: Singaporean Transmigrants 'Fashioning' Cosmopolitanism
Elaine Lynn-Ee Ho
*Journal of Ethnic and Migration Studies*, volume 37, issue 5 (May 2011) pp. 729-746

**Chapter 5**
Singaporean and British Transmigrants in China and the Cultural Politics of 'Contact Zones'
Brenda S.A. Yeoh and Katie Willis
*Journal of Ethnic and Migration Studies*, volume 31, issue 2 (March 2005) pp. 269-285

**Chapter 6**
Global Nightscapes in Shanghai as Ethnosexual Contact Zones
James Farrer
*Journal of Ethnic and Migration Studies*, volume 37, issue 5 (May 2011) pp. 747-764

**Chapter 7**
Shanghai Rush: Skilled Migrants in a Fantasy City

CITATION INFORMATION

Yen-Fen Tseng
*Journal of Ethnic and Migration Studies,* volume 37, issue 5 (May 2011) pp. 765-784

**Chapter 8**
Making Careers in the Occupational Niche: Chinese Students in Corporate Japan's Transnational Business
Gracia Liu-Farrer
*Journal of Ethnic and Migration Studies,* volume 37, issue 5 (May 2011) pp. 785-803

**Chapter 9**
'The Moon Back Home is Brighter'?: Return Migration and the Cultural Politics of Belonging
Sin Yih Teo
*Journal of Ethnic and Migration Studies,* volume 37, issue 5 (May 2011) pp. 805-820

**Chapter 10**
A Ritual Economy of 'Talent': China and Overseas Chinese Professionals
Xiang Biao
*Journal of Ethnic and Migration Studies,* volume 37, issue 5 (May 2011) pp. 821-838

# Notes on Contributors

**Jonathan V. Beaverstock** is Professor of Economic Geography in the School of Geography and the Director of the Integrating Global Society Research and Knowledge Transfer Priority Group at the University of Nottingham, UK. He is also an Honorary Professor at the University of Otago, New Zealand and has held visiting professorships at the University of Ghent, Belgium, the University of Western Sydney, Australia and the National University of Singapore, Singapore.

**James Farrer** is Professor of Sociology and Global Studies at Sophia University, Tokyo, Japan.

**Elaine Lynn-Ee Ho** is Assistant Professor at the National University of Singapore.

**Shirlena Huang** is Associate Professor in the Department of Geography and a Vice Dean of the Faculty of Arts and Social Sciences at the National University of Singapore.

**Philip F. Kelly** is Professor of Geography and Director of the Centre for Asian Research at York University, Toronto, Canada.

**Gracia Liu-Farrer** is Associate Professor of Sociology at the Graduate School of Asia-Pacific Studies, Waseda University, Japan.

**Sin Yih Teo** is Doctoral Candidate in the Department of Geography at the University of British Columbia, Canada.

**Yen-Fen Tseng** is Professor of Sociology at National Taiwan University.

**Katie Willis** is Professor of Human Geography at Royal Holloway, University of London, UK.

**Junjia Ye** is Postdoctoral Research Fellow in Urban Geography at the Max Planck Institute for the Study of Religious and Ethnic Diversity. She is also Visiting Research Fellow at the Asia Research Institute at NUS.

**Brenda S.A. Yeoh** is Professor (Provost's Chair) in the Department of Geography and Dean of the Faculty of Arts and Social Sciences at the National University of Singapore. She is also Research Leader of the Asian Migration Cluster at the NUS Asia Research Institute.

**Xiang Biao** is Lecturer at the Institute of Social and Cultural Anthropology and COMPAS, University of Oxford, UK.

# Introduction: Fluidity and Friction in Talent Migration

**Brenda S.A Yeoh and Shirlena Huang**

In an article in *The Australian*,[1] demographer Bernard Salt (2008) reports what global human-resource directors based in Singapore had to say in describing the attributes of 'the perfect global corporate citizen': this virtual being who 'floats effortlessly between cities' should be between 35 and 38 years of age, speak no fewer than three languages, and be single with no children. Apparently, having a partner (and especially a wife) and children in tow amounts to 'a recipe for disaster', as family appendages require support infrastructure in host cities and, if this is not well-developed, the moveability (i.e. relocation potential) of the talented corporate citizen will be adversely affected. Instead, as Salt writes: '… the perfect global citizen [must] be prepared to offer a personal commitment to the corporation that simulates marriage. No need for a partner because partners only cause trouble'.

The earlier academic literature on the mobility of the professional, managerial and entrepreneurial elite—increasingly valorised given the intensification of economic globalisation processes and the global war for talent—had also tended to reflect a similar ideological construct of these 'talent workers'.[2] Emphasis on the hyper-mobility of these elite transnational subjects—always on the move, perpetually in transit, repeatedly unmoored, forever part of the 'space of flows'— led to depicting them as mobile individual careerists responding purely to corporate logic and circulating in an intensely fluid world of intra- and inter-firm transfers and career mobility. In more recent times, however, the emerging scholarship on highly skilled economic migrants has attempted to move beyond assumptions of hyper-mobility and cosmopolitan sophistication to portray them as embodied bearers of culture, ethnicity, class or gender (Conradson and Latham 2005a; Bailey 2010; Fechter and Walsh 2010). Feminist geographers, for example, have emphasised the need to unpick masculinist assumptions about professional migration and to examine gender-differentiated power geometries at work in the labour market and the workplace, as well as patriarchal ideologies and the gendered power relations within the household and the reproductive sphere in shaping who moves and who stays (Iredale 2005; Kofman and Raghuram 2005, 2006; Nagel 2005; Raghuram 2000; Yeoh and Willis 2005). In a different vein, Michael Smith (2001) stresses the need to consider transnational actors—including elite migrants—as transnational subjects in a continual flurry of border-crossing and place-making activities; they are not necessarily transgressive bearers of new social subjectivities or cosmopolitan ideals, or those who have successfully disentangled themselves from the discursive or material webs spun by the state, capital or powerful others.

A second related move in the emerging literature is to counter earlier assumptions that transnational elites are perpetually 'rootless merchant sojourners' (Cheah 2001: 135), 'cosmopolitans' who are 'basically indifferent to where they lived', or 'cosmopolites' who are 'habitants of a vast universe' (Robbins 1998: 3); they transcend processes of 'transculturation' in specific places and play out their politics of identity and belonging on a different stage from that of the individual city in which they are, even if it were only for the moment, located. Often, they are portrayed if not as 'astronauts', then as 'frequent flyers' who are insufficiently 'grounded' to be involved in the localised politics of place-making in the co-presence of others. Yet, as Ley (2004: 151) has argued, 'the expansive reach and mastery imputed to global subjects [referring to transnational businessmen and cosmopolitan professionals], their flight from the particular and the partisan, their dominance and freedom from vulnerability, are far from complete'. More specifically, Yeoh and Willis (this volume) argue for the importance of examining cultural politics implicated in the construction of 'contact zones' by highly skilled transnational migrants. Rather than seeing them as experiencing the globe as an abstract 'space of flows', these migrants must be recognised for their ineluctable involvement in a multiplicity of place-specific and everyday transactions with others within the globalising city. While they may not be moored permanently in one place as longer-term migrants are, or constitute a significant presence like their lower-skilled counterparts do, their embodied relations and encounters with different urban contexts and citizens, however brief, nonetheless are capable of producing new social and cultural situations of a political sort.

In this book, the papers exactly move away from portraying transnational elites as 'knowledge nomads' who inhabit a completely frictionless space by virtue of their privileged positionings within processes of globalisation and in contradistinction to their lower-skilled counterparts (Willis *et al.* 2002). Instead they show that, while economic relations and rationalities are fundamental to the phenomenon of talent migration, they are folded into broader culturing processes at work. More specifically, we collectively argue that the migratory moves of the talented and skilled have to be understood within a broader cultural politics—both in terms of a politics of moving (and belonging) and a politics of place.

## The Cultural Politics of Moving and Belonging

The complexity of moves that transnational elites make on the global stage is somewhat akin to chess pieces making strategic moves across a chessboard criss-crossed with visible and invisible gridlines and rules, sometimes in forwarding a carefully thought-out plan of action, sometimes in unexpected retreat, and with significant pauses in between moves. The (in)flexibility and provisionality of these moves are reflected in the increasingly obvious inadequacy of the 'immigration/emigration' dyad and the expanding terminology necessary to describe these moves, including 'step migration', 'return migration', 'multiple migration', 'sojourning', 'circulation' and multidirectional '(hyper)mobilities'. Transnational migratory moves are hence *negotiated* moves, as mobile sensibilities are shaped not just in response to corporate logic or economic rationalities alone but also in the context of social-cultural-political considerations operative at family-community-country scales (see also Ley and Waters 2004).

Ley and Kobayashi (2005) underscore the range of non-pecuniary reasons for which Chinese transnationals choose to straddle their lives, and shuttle between Hong Kong and Vancouver, even as they seek to juggle their businesses in Asia with their aspirations to a better 'quality of life' in Canada. In examining the 'return migration' of skilled migrants from Canada to China and 'the tensions between integration and transnationalism, between flexibility and rootedness, and between citizenship and nationalism',[3] Teo (this volume) illustrates the provisionality of moving or not moving —a common refrain being 'We will see; we will talk about it again; who knows what may happen in the future?', as people choose 'not to choose'. Further illustrations include the unexpected route, as seen in moving from Beijing to Shanghai via a stint in Vancouver in order to avoid the complications of *guanxi*,[4] the 'grounding' effects of children's educational aspirations, and 'face' issues in contemplating returning home without ostensible achievements. In a similar vein, Tseng (this volume) explains why many Taiwanese want to work and live in Shanghai—and only Shanghai—for a host of reasons (including the priority given to Shanghai's infrastructure, which can support a lifestyle suited to international families, 'including comfortable apartment flats, grocery stores stuffed with Western food, and English-speaking schools at all levels') which defy notions of *homo economicus* behaviour. Likewise, Ho (this volume) demonstrates how Singaporean transmigrants' desire for self-development and exploration may underlie their move to London even at the opportunity cost of a lower standard of living.

Shifting the perspective from that of the individual migrant to the state, Xiang (this volume) shows how the Chinese government woos and engages with overseas Chinese professionals (OCPs) not only through economic rationalities but also through mounting a 'ritual economy' replete with spectacle and show. What appears to be seemingly a political ritual acquires strong mobilising and legitimating power and, as Xiang argues, is particularly effective in producing new subjectivities, incorporating OCPs into the established political order, and developing new social and political relations across national borders. The economic, cultural and political are all inextricably stitched together in the performance of the 'ritual economy', even though the threads used in the suturing are invisible at first sight.

Inasmuch as 'moving' is negotiated within multiple life domains, decisions to 'stay' after the move, and the contemplation of different kinds of 'belonging' are equally embedded in social-cultural-political matrices. Teo (this volume) writes that among the Chinese migrants in Vancouver, adopting formal Canadian citizenship (*ruji*) is often a pragmatic decision shaped by settlement experiences and quite differentiated from 'national identity', which is 'not so much an issue of citizenship as feelings of attachment to a country they grew up in'. Tseng (this volume) puts it differently, arguing that the easy association of skilled migrants with 'a global identity' is a myth and that 'with the exception of those at the top rank, most skilled migrants *cannot afford* to be rootless, for a number of valid economic and social/cultural reasons'. Liu-Farrer (this volume) and Ho (this volume) both demonstrate the significance of cultural capital in accessing specific labour markets. For example, Liu-Farrer explains that Chinese student migrants are able to stay on in corporate Japan, despite its ethnic and cultural homogeneity, primarily by exploiting what she calls an 'immigrant occupational niche', which depends on the migrants possessing recognisable educational credentials from Japanese higher education, demonstrating fluency in both Japanese and Chinese, and being in a position to understand and 'bridge' both societies in order to assist their companies to expand transnational business. At the same time, while career mobility and advancement require becoming a Japanese citizen as a show of 'true commitment', most of the Chinese migrants surveyed aspire to return to China as 'pseudo-expats', primarily because of the impression that 'Japan is for the Japanese' and sometimes for pragmatic reasons such as a desire to raise their children in China, which is seen to be academically and morally superior to Japan.

## The Cultural Politics of Place and Identity

The complexity of multi-local moving and belonging is very much emplaced in particular localities. For transnational elites, these localities are often (though not always) global cities of the world which appear to be the most successful in securing the greatest quantities and qualities of these flows. Even as significant numbers of transnational elites are drawn to established global cities such as London, New York and Tokyo for work, cities such as Shanghai and Singapore have emerged as major contact zones of global capitalism in the last two to three decades as governments have put in place policies—including the redevelopment of the built and cultural environments of their major cities—aimed not only at the attraction of the very best of international talent to their shores, but also at the transnational reincorporation of their overseas nationals to the home polity (Guarnizo and Smith 1998; Yeoh and Lai 2008). The most successful of these 'talent-harnessing places' are argued to be the 'kinds of places that … [allow] people to be themselves and to validate their distinct identities' (Florida 2005: 7).

In this increasingly managed and diverse geography of global cities, cultural factors (especially in terms of lifestyles, subcultures and leisure activities) are argued to be particularly important influences in the way these cities are perceived by transnational elites, with class, gender and regional origins acting as 'critical determinants of migrants' destination, attainment and transnationality' (Guarnizo and Smith 1998: 14). Tseng (this volume) examines how Shanghai has been successful in attracting Taiwanese skilled migrants (both male and female) because it has become fashioned in their minds as a fantasy city of sorts, 'a present-day gold rush destination—a place to fulfil modern economic goals and postcolonial cultural dreams' and one that facilitates their pursuit of a cosmopolitan (read 'internationalised') lifestyle. By focusing on Shanghai's rapidly developing international-style clubbing scene, Farrer (this volume) also highlights how the city's exciting global nightscapes have contributed to its allure for a wide range of racially and sexually heterogeneous foreign talent, particularly Japanese and American. But it is not only the foreigners who consider the politics of place in terms of cultural factors. The papers by Teo and Xiang (both in this volume) clearly show that, inasmuch as the People's Republic of China (PRC) has marketed particular places (such as science parks and special development zones) and developed specific policies and programmes (tied to material rewards and political rituals) to proactively and aggressively forge new relations with their 'overseas talents' located in North America, Europe and Australia to attract them 'home', potential return migrants assess their capacity to do so in terms of concerns such as the ability of their children to (re)adjust to China (particularly educationally), their own facility to re-establish their ties, and the Asian notion of 'face'.

It is important to recognise that transnationalism is not a set of 'abstracted, dematerialised cultural flows' but is instead grounded on 'the concrete, everyday changes in people's lives' (Ong and Nonini 1997 cited in Jackson *et al.* 2004: 10). As such, research has increasingly begun to examine the ways in which the 'multiplicity of involvements' is sustained by 'transmigrants ... in both home and host societies' (Basch *et al.* 1996: 7) at the *everyday* level (see Conradson and Latham 2005a). While the social relations and networks of people 'on the move' are likely to be different from those who do not move (Conradson and Latham 2005b), their daily geographies are, for the most part, rather ordinary. The complexities of transnational relations to place are rooted in and routed through particular transnational spaces within which transmigrant elites move. Arguably, despite the heterogeneity of global cities, globalisation has enabled transnational elites to move through these cities 'with relative ease upon landing... [by] using the categories of spaces learned already in similar settings' (Farrer, this volume). The particular transnational sites within which transmigrant elites establish social and professional networks in global cities may range from workplaces to social spaces such as overseas clubs, expatriate clubs, bars and nightclubs.

Even as they move through these spaces, 'the cosmopolitan figure [is said to] demonstrate an "orientation, a willingness to engage with the Other"' (Molz 2005: 519, citing Hannerz 1990) over and above those who share the same roots (co-ethnics and citizens) and (transnational) routes as they do. Many of the papers in this book (see particularly those by Beaverstock, Farrer, Ho, Liu-Farrer, and Ye and Kelly) reveal not only that the everyday negotiations within such sites in each city need to be learnt and contextualised within the opportunities and constraints of the particular cultures within which transnational elites operate, but that these localities are racially and nationally marked by the practices and prejudices of embodied cosmopolitanism. Operating appropriately at the everyday level within these fractious landscapes is as much about understanding the cultural politics in the workplace as it is about learning to utilise social spaces to develop economic relationships and opportunities: the economic and the social cannot be bifurcated. For example, Ho (this volume) highlights the complex ways in which difference is encountered and negotiated by Singaporean transmigrants in London. She demonstrates how Singaporeans selectively acquire and mobilise cultural traits and bodily codes of behaviour as part of the basket of 'working and socialising norms' to facilitate their everyday negotiations of 'difference' and 'outsideness' in both their British (read 'English') work environments and spaces of social interaction such as pubs. It is also clear from Ho's paper—and also the paper by Ye and Kelly (this volume) that looks at negotiations of cosmopolitanism in Singapore—that Singaporeans' 'purported form of cosmopolitan savvy' is a slippery concept that 'oscillates' uneasily between a post-colonial hang-up of 'white' or 'Western' superiority and a desire to master its performance on the one hand, and a sense of ambivalence towards whiteness and a celebration of Singapore's progressive multicultural stance on the other. Similarly, a competition between a dominant but declining Global Whiteness and a rising Global Chinese racial identity was identified by Farrer (this volume) in the (sexual) interactions between the different groups of foreigners and mobile citizens of the PRC.

The papers by Farrer and Liu-Farrer (both in this volume) also bring to the fore the *gendered* nature of transnational global spaces. In examining some of the everyday realities of employment that shape PRC student migrants' career mobility in Japan, Liu-Farrer shows how some Chinese women have chosen to be self-employed to avoid the gendered cultural norms of the Japanese workplace (such as promotion ceilings, wage differentials, or the expectation of women colleagues serving tea to their male counterparts). Farrer's ethnography of Shanghai's global nightscapes reveals specific positionings for men and women in these spaces: while white men experience 'their embodiment of national and racial characteristics as a sexual bonus, as do some transnational Asian men and women, …white women experience the most distressing forms of desexualisation'. As such, the patterns and dynamics of the mobility embodied in the quotidian life-worlds of the many different groups of transnational talent clearly support the notion that they are embodied social actors who are geographically placed and socially positioned.

## Conclusion

The papers in this book focus on a range of talents—in terms of occupation, nationality, ethnicity and gender—flowing in and out of Asia, the world's fastest-growing economic region even in this period of economic slowdown. The diversity of flows in terms of origins and destinations represented in the papers examined in this collection —with talent moving amongst places in the PRC, Taiwan, Singapore, Japan, Britain and Canada—present important case studies of the discursive constructions and grounded practices of the cultural politics of talent mobility (moving, transiting, returning, etc.) from an Asian perspective, as well as the cultural politics played out among different groups of talent in transnational spaces of encounter which allow for 'multiple points of contact, alliances and conflicts' (in the words of Farrer, this volume).

The various case studies also reveal the complex ways in which hyper-mobile talent negotiates the power asymmetries of race and nationality between 'host' and 'migrant'. Even in supposedly cosmopolitan settings (e.g. of work and leisure spaces in global cities), there appears to be an expected set of culture-specific behaviours—often tied to a set of ethnic, gendered, linguistic and other embodied norms—to which talents are expected to conform, and which challenge the idea of a seamless transnational capitalist class. The complex negotiations that returning global talent (as in the case of returning PRC transmigrants) has to undertake in grappling with the 'layered nuances' of their identities as 'citizens' versus 'nationals' also call into question the universality of the cosmopolitan ideal.

Finally, the papers show that employing the lens of 'the everyday' not only helpfully uncovers the ideological, cultural and material ramifications of transnational border crossings on global talent, but also renders a clear portrayal of those talented individuals who do not live their day-to-day lives in reified worlds but who in fact navigate their 'professional, social and cultural life-worlds' (to quote Beaverstock, this volume) under very ordinary circumstances. Indeed, the analyses reinforce the usefulness of focusing on 'banal geographies' as a means to better uncover the multiple subjectivities and differentiated power geometries operating in the transnational work and social spaces in which international talent moves and is located. The analyses also highlight the need to avoid artificially bifurcating the lives of cosmopolitans into the economic (work spaces/life) and the social (social spaces/life)—but instead to appreciate how these are interwoven—if we are to move towards a fuller understanding of the 'ins and outs' of talent migration. Further research adopting a more holistic framework and giving focus to a wider range of case studies across Asia (and other parts of the world) should reveal even more diverse patterns of, and nuanced insights into, the phenomenon and the processes at work in the cultural politics of talent migration.

## Acknowledgements

First presented at the International Conference on 'In and Out of Asia: Globalising Cities, Migrating Talents' (jointly organised by the Asia Research Institute and the Faculty of Arts and Social Sciences, both of the National University of Singapore from 19–21 November 2007), most of the papers in this volume were initially published in the *Journal of Ethnic and Migration Studies*. We are grateful to Sharon Wok and Lin Weiqiang for providing us with editorial assistance and also to the Asia Research Institute and the Faculty of Arts and Social Sciences for providing funding and organisational support for the conference.

## Notes

1 We are grateful to Ravinder Sidhu for alerting us to the article.
2 For a brief discussion of the notion of 'talent' and 'talent migration', see Yeoh and Lai (2008).
3 For China, these tensions have intensified since the late 1970s, given major political changes which render 'expatriating' no longer traitorous but 'patriotic' (Cao 2008; Nyíri 2004).
4 *Guanxi* refers to personalised networks of influence as used in Chinese society.

## References

Bailey, J. (2010) 'Population geographies, gender and the migration-development nexus', *Progress in Human Geography* 34: 375-386.
Basch, L., Glick Schiller, N. and Blanc, C. (1996) Nations Unbound: Transnational Projects, Postcolonial Predicaments and Deterritorialized Nation-States. New York: Gordon and Breach.
Cao, C. (2008) 'China's brain drain at the high end: why government policies have failed to attract first-rate academics to return', *Asian Population Studies*, 4(3): 331–45.
Cheah, P. (2001) 'Chinese cosmopolitanism in two senses and postcolonial national memory', in Dharwadker, V. (ed.) *Cosmopolitan Geographies: New Locations in Literature and Culture*. London: Routledge, 133–70.
Conradson, D. and Latham, A. (eds) (2005a) 'Transnational urbanism: attending to everyday practices and mobilities', *Journal of Ethnic and Migration Studies*, 31(2): 227–33.
Conradson, D. and Latham, A. (2005b) 'Friendship, networks and transnationality in a world city: Antipodean transmigrants in London', *Journal of Ethnic and Migration Studies*, 31(2): 287–305.
Fechter, A.M. and Walsh, K. (2010) 'Examining "expatriate continuities": postcolonial approaches to mobile professionals', *Journal of Ethnic and Migration Studies*, 36: 1197-1210.
Florida, R. (2005) *Cities and the Creative Class*. New York and London: Routledge.
Guarnizo, L.E. and Smith, M.P. (1998) 'The location of transnationalism', in Smith, M.P. and Guarnizo L.E. (eds) *Transnationalism from Below*. New Brunswick, NJ: Transaction, 3–34.
Hannerz, U. (1990) 'Cosmopolitans and locals in world culture', *Theory, Culture & Society*, 7(2): 237–251.

Iredale, R. (2005) 'Gender, immigration policies and accreditation: valuing the skills of professional women migrants', *Geoforum*, *36*(2): 155–66.

Jackson, P., Crang, P. and Dwyer, C. (2004) 'Introduction: the spaces of transnationality', in Jackson, P., Crang, P. and Dwyer, C. (eds) *Transnational Spaces*. London: Routledge, 1–23.

Kofman, E. and Raghuram, P. (eds) (2005) 'Gender and skilled migrants: into and beyond the workplace'. Special issue of *Geoforum*, *36*(2): 133–271.

Kofman, E. and Raghuram, P. (2006) 'Women and global labour migrations: incorporating skilled workers', *Antipode*, *38*(2): 282–303.

Ley, D. (2004) 'Transnational spaces and everyday lives', *Transactions of the Institute of British Geographers*, *29*(2): 151–64.

Ley, D. and Kobayashi, A. (2005) 'Back to Hong Kong: return migration or transnational sojourn?', *Global Networks*, *5*(2): 111–27.

Ley, D. and Waters, J.L. (2004) 'Transnational migration and the geographical imperative', in Jackson, P., Crang, P. and Dwyer, C. (eds) *Transnational Spaces*. London: Routledge, 104–21.

Molz, J.G. (2005) 'Getting a "flexible eye": round-the-world travel and scales of cosmopolitan citizenship', *Citizenship Studies*, *9*(5): 517–31.

Nagel, C. (2005) 'Skilled migration in global cities from "other" perspectives: British Arabs, identity politics, and local embeddedness', Geoforum, *36*(2): 197–210.

Nyírí, P. (2004) 'Expatriating is patriotic? The discourse on "new migrants" in the People's Republic of China and identity construction among recent migrants from the PRC', in Yeoh, B.S.A. and Willis, K. (eds) *State/Nation/Transnation: Perspectives on Transnationalism in the Asia-Pacific*. London: Routledge, 120–43.

Ong, A. and Nonini, D.M. (1997) Ungrounded Empires: The Cultural Politics of Modern Chinese Transnationalism. New York: Routledge.

Raghuram, P. (2000) 'Gendering skilled migratory streams: implications for conceptualisations of migration', *Asian and Pacific Migration Journal*, *9*(4): 429–57.

Robbins, B. (1998) 'Introduction Part I: actually existing cosmopolitanism', in Cheah, P. and Robbins, B. (eds) *Cosmopolitics: Thinking and Feeling Beyond the Nation*. Minneapolis: University of Minnesota Press, 1–19.

Salt, B. (2008) 'Gen Y learns a recession lesson', *The Australian*, 11 December.

Smith, M.P. (2001) *Transnational Urbanism: Locating Globalization*. Malden, MA and Oxford: Blackwell.

Willis, K., Yeoh, B.S.A. and Fakhri, S.M.A.K. (2002) 'Transnational elites', *Geoforum*, *33*(4): 505–07.

Yeoh, B.S.A. and Lai, A.E. (2008) 'Guest editors' introduction: "talent" migration in and out of Asia: challenges for policies and places', *Asian Population Studies*, *4*(3): 235–45.

Yeoh, B.S.A. and Willis, K. (2005) 'Singaporeans in China: transnational women elites and the negotiation of gendered identities', *Geoforum*, *36*(2): 211–22.

# Cosmopolitanism at Work: Labour Market Exclusion in Singapore's Financial Sector

Junjia Ye and Philip F. Kelly

*Amid a resurgence of academic interest in the concept of cosmopolitanism in recent years, this paper explores the ways in which practices of cosmopolitanism are played out in the workplace. Singapore's financial sector is selected as a case study of a context that might be expected to exemplify a vanguard for the acceptance of difference. Not only are firms in this sector engaged in global labour markets for professional staff, but Singapore itself represents a case of explicit state-led promotion of cosmopolitanism as condition, attitude and practice. Nevertheless, interviews with financial sector professionals reveal that, while the concept of cosmopolitanism is indeed invoked in their workplaces, the realities of recruitment practice and workplace relations leave a very narrow range of personal characteristics that are deemed acceptable. Those who do not conform to these 'cosmopolitan' characteristics—based on language, clothing, bodily self-presentations, education and ethno-racial identity—appear to be excluded from access to (or upward mobility within) the financial sector workforce.*

## Cosmopolitanism as Concept

Theorisations of cosmopolitanism often invoke the eighteenth-century intellectual legacy of Immanuel Kant, who envisaged a global citizen and moral community of humanity, while at the same time peddling some decidedly racist and ignorant assessments of large segments of that humanity. David Harvey (2000, 2009) picks up on the contradiction in Kant's writings and notes that, while 'cosmopolitanism is back' on the academic agenda, the cosmopolitanisms described are often underpinned by geographical ignorance, prejudice and the exercise of power. Thus, according to Harvey, cosmopolitan pronouncements are not matched by an understanding of otherness and other places, or the actual practice of such a world-view.

Cosmopolitanism as philosophy or world-view, however, represents only one possible interpretation of the concept. Vertovec and Cohen (2003: 9) identify five other perspectives on cosmopolitanism: a socio-cultural condition of 'ethnic pluralism and cultural admixture'; a political project of supra-state governance structures and civil society organisations; a political subjectivity in which multiple loyalties are simultaneously maintained; an attitude or disposition which involves 'willingness to engage with the Other' (Hannerz 1990: 239); and a practice or competence represented by a skill at navigating different systems of meaning (Young *et al.* 2006).

Cosmopolitanism can, then, represent a world-view, a condition, a project, a subjectivity, an attitude or a practice. But in each case, Harvey's critique remains equally valid. How is cosmopolitanism actually reconciled with geographical difference? Does the actual practice of cosmopolitanism in particular places represent anything more than a perpetuation of exclusion and division? As Harvey (2000: 545) suggests, geographies of difference can often be seen as inconsistent with the universalism that cosmopolitanism easily becomes equated with:

> The rootedness of peoples in place (the geographical rootedness of the nation-state in particular) draws us rather awkwardly back to Kant's actual geographical world characterised by folly and aggression, childish vanity and destructiveness, the world of prejudice that cosmopolitanism must counteract or actively suppress in the name of human progress. It takes but a small step then to see geographies and spatialities (and local loyalties) not only as disrupters of order and of rational discourse, but as undermining universal morality and goodness. They become, as with Kant's Geography, the fount of all prejudice, aggression and evil.

This paper is concerned with the practice of cosmopolitanism in a specific place (see also Binnie *et al.* 2006; Young *et al.* 2006). If cosmopolitanism is a practice—'the cultural habitus of globalisation' as David Ley (2004: 159) calls it—and one that is grounded in lived places, then how is it practised? More importantly, Ley's deployment of Bourdieu's (1984) terminology implies that, as a habitus, cosmopolitanism also creates a metric of evaluation—a standard against which an individual's embodied cultural capital can be assessed. If so, how does cosmopolitanism get embodied—who is deemed to have it; who does not? As Young *et al.* (2006: 1689) note, 'the question is whether the production of cosmopolitan space is linked to paradoxical displacement of other forms of "disruptive" difference which need to be excluded from certain spaces'. While Young *et al.* and others have asked this question in relation to urban spaces, we address it here in relation to workplace identities and we ask who has access to certain kinds of work in the labour market. In this case, it is individuals, as much as places, who are constructed as cosmopolitan (or not) and so we argue that this has an important influence upon who is deemed to fit with certain sorts of labour market opportunity and class position.

As a case study, we use a place where one might most expect to find cosmopolitanism—the workplaces of major financial institutions in the city-state of Singapore. Not only do financial institutions draw upon some of the more globalised labour markets, but those located in Singapore are situated in a city where cosmopolitanism is explicitly promulgated by a strongly interventionist state. Ultimately, however, we suggest that the cosmopolitanism that is found in financial sector workplaces is in fact a narrow and exclusionary subjectivity and quite the opposite of the openness to otherness that the cosmopolitan ideal implies. In this way, an inability to perform a very specific global subjectivity (approaching, if not quite reaching the standard of 'the perfect global corporate citizen' described by Yeoh and Huang in the Introduction to this special issue) serves as a barrier to accessing employment in the sector for those who do not fit the mould.

The paper develops this argument in three sections. The first explores the various dimensions of cosmopolitanism in the Singaporean context and relates these ideas to the political economy of development in the city-state. The second section briefly describes the methodology used in this research, while the third critically examines workplace dynamics to explore the ways in which cosmopolitanism plays out in practice and in prejudice.

## Singapore as Cosmopolis

Cosmopolitanism is a concept that has a great deal of political currency in Singapore (Ho 2006; Yeoh 2004). The country's post-colonial genesis in the mid-1960s was marked by inter-communal violence between different ethnic, religious and linguistic communities, and the government of the People's Action Party—which has ruled ever since—has taken great care to carefully manage ethnic difference and foster national unity in the face of such divided loyalties (Chua 1998; Purushotam 1998).

The first meaning of cosmopolitanism in Singapore, then, is as a city with a cosmopolitan condition in which cosmopolitan attitudes are a necessary part of co-existence (Yeoh 2004). The active construction of such attitudes has been at the centre of the government's education, housing and community development policies. Indeed the very definition of different ethnic identities in Singapore, according to a classification into Chinese, Malay, Indian and Other, has been a part of this governmentality of cosmopolitanism.

But cosmopolitanism in Singapore has taken a slightly different turn since the late 1990s. Rather than simply an attitude fostered to enable Singaporeans to co-exist with each other, the government has also projected Singapore as an entrepôt city that forms a gateway, a crossroads or a hub (spatial metaphors abound) in global economic flows. Cosmopolitanism has become the cultural means to economic ends.

To understand why this is so, it is necessary to review Singapore's developmental trajectory. Singapore's post-colonial history is one of the world's most remarkable economic success stories. From colonial entrepôt and military base, the city-state transformed itself after 1965 into a major global centre for manufacturing—and later research and development—in the electronics industry; a shipping hub with one of the busiest container ports in the world; a growing petrochemical and biosciences cluster; and a regional centre for financial and other business services (Huff 1995; Lee and Tee 2009). The country's *per capita* income in 2006 was US$31,710 (based on purchasing power parity). Its foreign exchange reserves amount to US$120 billion, and the government's investment arm, Temasek Holdings, managed global investments in excess of US$100 billion in 2006. While the assets of Temasek (and other government-linked investment bodies) declined substantially in 2008–09 (losing one-third of its value between March 2008 and March 2009), by August 2009 total global assets had almost returned to their high point of mid-2008.

Throughout this developmental success story, the Singaporean state has played a heavily interventionist role—through the dominance of government-linked corporations, the relative weakness of domestic private capital, a carefully orchestrated system of social management and control (especially around issues of ethnic and class relations) and close collaboration with transnational capital. While other developmental states in East Asia have seen a decline in their dominance, no such diminution has occurred in Singapore (Pereira 2008).

Any extolling of Singapore's development successes must, however, be conditional because the city's competitiveness is predicated on a model of unequal incorporation into this success (Yeoh and Chang 2001). In particular, temporary foreign labour is the source of a low-cost and disenfranchised workforce that creates, but does not share in, the wealth of the economy as a whole (Yeoh 2006). In December 2008, 36 per cent of Singapore's employed labour force of 2.95 million persons were foreign nationals, living and working on visas rather than as enfranchised citizens or permanent residents of the country (Ministry of Manpower 2009). For most, this means that they live under restrictive conditions that specify the work they can do, forbid family members from accompanying them and (like foreign workers everywhere) are under threat of deportation.

For a smaller group of expatriate professionals, however, Singapore is a much more welcoming place. Since the mid-1990s, the government has viewed so-called 'foreign talent' as a fundamental necessity in seeking global competitiveness in sectors such as finance, biotechnology, electronics and academia. The Prime Minister in the late 1990s, Goh Chok Tong, expressed this in his 1997 agenda-setting National Day Rally speech, 'Global City, Best Home':

> Singapore must become a global, cosmopolitan city, an open society where people from many lands can feel at home (http://www.moe.gov.sg/media/speeches/1997/240897.htm).

The goal of becoming a cosmopolitan city is seen as both a result of attracting a talented workforce from around the world and a precondition for attracting such workers (Ho 2006):

> We must make sure that we're getting our fair share of the weird and wonderful from China, India, the West and the rest of the world. If we can do that, then we are in the running (Minister for Trade and Industry, George Yeo, *The Business Times*, 22 May 2002, cited in Yeoh 2004: 2436).

> To succeed, Singapore must be a cosmopolitan centre, able to attract, retain and absorb talent from all over the world. We cannot keep the big companies out of the local league. Whether we like it or not, they are entering the region ... Now in a globalised economy, we are in competition against other cities in the First World. Hence we have to become a cosmopolitan city that attracts and welcomes talent in business, academia, or in the performing arts. They will add to Singapore's vibrancy and secure our place in a global network of cities of excellence (Senior Minister Lee Kuan Yew; Speech at Nanyang Technological University, 15 February 2000, http://www.mita.gov.sg/ cited in Yeoh 2004: 2435).

Policies to realise this goal of becoming a global talent magnet have taken various forms. Most obviously, visa regulations for employees above a certain salary level are very lenient—such individuals and their families can live and work in Singapore with few of the restrictions imposed on the far more numerous 'foreign workers' at the other end of the labour market (Yeoh 2006).

In recent years, the government has also started to emphasise the notion of 'foreign talent' as potential immigrants to Singapore, rather than as transient employees. In this way, skilled foreigners are seen as supplementing the country's population base as well as its economic competitiveness.

> At the same time, through the years, many of our global talent have decided to become PRs and citizens, to become long-term residents in Singapore. Talent attraction not only serves the purpose of meeting our economic needs, but is also a key strategy in our population augmentation efforts (Wong 2008).

It is clear, however, in both the terminology and the legislation applied to different groups, that while 'global talent' is considered a potential source of immigrants, 'foreign workers' definitely are not.

The government has also seen the physical and social landscape as a tool for talent attraction, with cultural policy serving an important role in economic development goals:

> We also need to remake our city, so that it is vibrant, cosmopolitan and throbbing with energy (Lee 2004; cited in Rodan 2006: 180).

Several major arts centres have been constructed within the last ten years, and sites that might be described as self-conscious cosmopolitan urbanity have been cultivated

(Chang *et al.* 2004; Yeoh and Chang 2001). For example, recent additions to the Singapore River's waterfront entertainment district include the Crazy Horse nightclub franchise from Paris and the Ministry of Sound from the United Kingdom.[1] The rather straight-laced Minister for Trade and Industry, Lim Hng Kiang, assured Singaporeans that:

> Crazy Horse fills the gap in premium night entertainment for a niche group of well-heeled business travellers and regional visitors ... In the last year, night entertainment in Singapore has grown more vibrant and diversified. Later this month, one of the world's most famous clubs and a haven for lovers of electronic music, the Ministry of Sound, will open just a few doors away. The scene is set for further transformation. Over the next year, more than $60 million will be injected to develop the industry ... which is envisioned to become the region's most dynamic 24-hour waterfront entertainment belt (Lim 2005).

The point, then, is that otherness is welcomed for strategic economic purposes. In this case the opening of night clubs represents both the expansion of an economic sector and the creation of a cosmopolitan space in which well-heeled travellers and expatriates will feel at home (see Farrer, this issue, for a detailed ethnography of such nightclubs as a cosmopolitan contact zone in Shanghai).

In addition to the physical landscape, the government has also done discursive work to shape the attitudes of Singaporeans in relation to foreign talent. Cosmopolitanism has therefore been represented as a disposition that Singaporeans should have towards non-Singaporeans working among them, ultimately justified through arguments that come back to economic rationality in relation to Singapore's future development. This has been necessary work on the government's part, as subdued grumblings about the numbers of foreign employees in higher-level positions have persisted (Coe and Kelly 2002; Ho 2006; Yeoh 2006).

Cosmopolitanism is also fostered by the government in one final sense related to the practices and competencies of Singaporeans. Here cosmopolitanism becomes an identity to which Singaporeans can aspire, an identity directly related to their ability to function in global business settings. This aspirational identity was laid out by the then Prime Minister himself in a speech in the late 1990s (*The Straits Times*, 23 August 1999). He classified Singaporeans into 'cosmopolitans' and 'heartlanders'. The implication was that 'heartlanders' are rooted in place and give Singapore its distinctiveness. Their job is to accept Singapore as a cosmopolitan place. 'Cosmopolitans', meanwhile, are expected to have cosmopolitan skills—to be culturally competent in multiple linguistic and cultural systems and able to operate on a global economic stage.

Cosmopolitanism in Singapore, then, has been a condition of cultural mixture, an attitude of acceptance towards that mixture, and a set of practices or dispositions that mark a cosmopolitan identity. The state-led project of cosmopolitanism has not, however, been without its silences and contradictions. Vertovec and Cohen's (2003) versions of cosmopolitanism as a world view of global citizenship, or as a transnational political project, or as a subjectivity of multiple loyalties are all notably absent. Furthermore, while certain forms of cosmopolitanism are being fostered by the government, it is certainly not intended to interfere with either national sovereignty, nationalist sentiments or a system of one-party political univocality (Ho 2006; Yeoh and Chang 2001).

The discursive setting, then, is one in which certain forms of cosmopolitanism are valued commodities. When it hits the ground, however, cosmopolitanism is enacted in everyday settings. It is this cosmopolitanism-in-practice that we examine in the context of Singapore's financial sector after briefly reflecting on the methodology used in this study.

**Research as Cosmopolitan Encounter**

Interviews for this study were conducted by Junjia Ye. A total of 25 financial sector professionals were interviewed privately, in a semi-structured fashion, in the summer of 2005. Respondents were recruited through various social networks and were selected based on their work positions in the financial sector; all were engaged in professional or technical work as managers, executives or assistant vice-presidents. Ye made a conscious effort to speak with a diversity of participants of different genders, nationalities, ethnicities, job types and ages. It is important to note that, as a Singaporean-Chinese woman now living in Canada, Ye's positionality in interview settings was a distinctive one. The data collected, and the way they are interpreted, are a part of a knowledge production process that is inextricably bound up in the identities and performances of the interviewer and interviewees during the research encounter (Rose 1997). For example, although Ye is fluent in the Chinese dialects spoken in Singapore, the interviews were conducted in English, which undoubtedly made some respondents more forthcoming about the types of exclusions faced by Chinese-speaking employees at work. Similarly, Ye's own gender, body type and so on, likely influenced what respondents would comment on in relation to these issues.

Ye's life trajectory is also significant. As a Singaporean who has spent much of her adult life in Canada, she was undoubtedly 'read' as a fellow cosmopolitan. But having been born, raised and schooled in Singapore for 18 years, she was negotiating a relationship of closeness and distance with the city and its culture. In a sense, this established an immediate commonality with many Singaporean respondents. At the same time there were occasions when her familiarity and 'sameness' with Singaporean interviewees meant that some issues were assumed rather than spelled out. For example, one interviewee mentioned that, as a Singaporean, Ye 'should know how Chinese Singaporeans are towards Malays'. While Ye's sameness allowed this issue to surface, it also meant that, in other interviews, it was left unsaid and simply assumed.

In a variety of ways, then, the identity of the interviewer in relation to her respondents is implicated in the qualitative material presented here. The precise ways in which it affects the material collected is multidimensional, ambiguous and ultimately elusive. It does, however, seem likely that Ye's Singaporean/Canadian and feminine identities were important in eliciting qualitative data, especially given that the practices and opinions described were quite inflammatory in some instances.

## Constructions of Cosmopolitanism in Financial Services

The financial sector made up 13.1 per cent of Singapore's gross domestic product in 2008 (Government of Singapore 2009). There are over 750 local and foreign financial institutions in Singapore, employing 5 per cent of the city-state's total workforce (Lee 2004). The financial services industry represents one of the key sectors targeted as part of Singapore's post-industrial growth strategy and the city currently plays a significant regional and global role in corporate and investment banking, foreign exchange, derivatives trading, asset management, insurance and commodities trading (Beaverstock 2002; ERC 2002; MAS 1998).

As a sector with high levels of foreign ownership and one that is necessarily connected with global financial centres elsewhere, finance forms something of a vanguard in terms of cosmopolitan conditions in the workplace. The Singaporean government also actively markets the city's financial sector as an attractive place for 'global talent':

> Singapore is a cosmopolitan city—a melting pot of cultures where people of different races live, work and play harmoniously. Here, you can enjoy one of the highest standards of living in the world at relatively low cost. For families with children, you have access to a world-class education system including numerous international schools. Our healthcare services are also renowned. We have successfully integrated lush greenery into our urban developments, truly creating a city within a garden. Our vibrant arts and cultural scene and wide range of entertainment, dining and leisure options make it easy for working professionals to strike a good work–life balance. It is thus no wonder that Singapore has been ranked the best place to live if you're an expatriate, according to a study conducted by HSBC Bank International, a Jersey-based subsidiary of the world's biggest company (http://www.financeconnectsingapore.com, last accessed on 3 October 2009).

Ostensibly, then, both the city and the financial sector workplace are cosmopolitan, and evince cosmopolitan attitudes. The emphasis on Singapore's attractions for 'foreign talent' is highly strategic and the government's planning documents for financial sector development note the dependence of the sector on such foreign human capital for specialist technical and managerial expertise (ERC 2002). The website for the Credit Suisse, meanwhile, trumpets the goal of a cosmopolitan utopia in the bank's workplace:

> [Our goal is]... to achieve an inclusive workplace where everyone is treated with dignity and respect and where each individual has the opportunity to advance and succeed. Individuals of different genders, races, ages, religions, nationalities, ethnic backgrounds, sexual orientations and disabilities are thus brought together to

create a world-class team of financial services professionals (https://www.creditsuisse.com/citizenship/en/employer/diversity.jsp, accessed July 2005).

In our interviews, a number of individual respondents reflected this cosmopolitan identity and aspiration—one that transcended boundaries of ethnicity, nationality, gender and language.

> I don't rely on my ethnicity 'cos that's what a lot of these people who have these problems tend to do—they rely on their ethnicity: 'I am Indian, therefore I treat you this way'. I don't have any of these problems. I forget sometimes that I am Indian even, which is an amazing, amazing thing (Chandra,[2] Indian-Indian, male, IT executive in a British bank).

> I hope that, in spite of all [our differences], we can co-exist. I think as time goes on we will become more and more mixed through inter-marriages and cultural mixing. I hope that is what it becomes. That is who I want to be. I believe we can connect (Elizabeth, British-Caucasian, female, assistant manager for Human Resources in a Swiss bank).

Others saw a cosmopolitan disposition and practices as a strategic way of gaining advantage and advancement in the workplace:

> I can talk to different people, no problem ... if you cannot relate to those people from different cultures, then eventually ... I feel that you will be left behind. Like one step behind (Jayakumar, Singaporean-Indian, male, IT manager in a Swiss bank).

While these quotes highlight the idealistic or strategic pursuit of a cosmopolitan vision, further examination of workplace attitudes and practices reveals that this purported cosmopolitanism was often played out less as a respectful acceptance of difference, and more as conformity to a generic global subjectivity with very specific characteristics. We now turn to the various dimensions of this restrictive cosmopolitanism.

The first critical moment at which a cosmopolitan ideal is tested is during the recruitment process. A human resources professional in the financial sector explained that, as the selection process progresses, judgments on the candidates become less focused on technical skills and relate instead to bodily self-presentation, and 'international experience' represents a particular asset:

> If it comes down to the three people I have short-listed, they have all got the same sort of experience; then it becomes a question of 'How much do I like them?' When I look at you, do I like you or do you turn me off? All that you would not be able to see on paper, no matter how good you are. After the criteria are met, I will look at the companies you've worked in, then I would get a good idea because, if the company is global in nature, so you've done more than just a Singapore-based job. I would want somebody who has been out there, and going abroad to study is very good training ... learning how to budget is one thing, learn to cope, get your meals

and not eat packet noodles all the time—all that is an education! ... if you were to ask me if I would take someone who has never lived outside Singapore, and I'm a global type of business ... probably not. But there are some people who have never lived abroad but then got a very broad outlook. So I will still consider them. They must prove themselves though... (Rosalie, director of Asia-Pacific operations, XYZ Human Resources Group).

While the desire for international experience would seem to suggest that employers are looking for individuals who can move confidently across cultures and engage with difference, the question 'When I look at you, do I like you or do you turn me off?' implies that a great many other judgments are also being made. These relate to a variety of bodily attributes which, far from celebrating difference, demand a close adherence to a narrowly conceived norm.

One respondent viewed this is as a 'quite natural' desire for workforce homogeneity:

> It is quite natural. They want people who can fit into the organisation better. That means that, when you get in, we speak the same language. You know, so we can work better together and we can communicate better (Ken, Singaporean-Eurasian, male, assistant vice-president of corporate banking in a Singaporean bank).

What constitutes this 'fit' and 'common language' depends to some extent on the type of business a particular financial institution is doing, and upon the role of the individual. Nevertheless, respondents revealed a series of ways in which employees are expected to conform to a generic standard—essentially one rooted in English-language fluency, a particular style of bodily self-presentation, conservative dress codes, specific forms of masculinity and femininity and, especially, either whiteness or Chineseness. We will consider each of these in turn.

*Language Skills*

Language capabilities are a prime axis of distinction in determining acceptance in the 'cosmopolitan' workplace. In particular, English fluency and appropriate accenting are seen as essential elements of a cosmopolitan identity. This is not, it should be noted, related to the basic ability to make oneself understood and carry out professional responsibilities adequately. Instead, it relates to an ability to linguistically mark oneself as belonging to a cosmopolitan 'set':

> The senior people are very 'banana'. You can tell they are English-educated ... in fact, most of them cannot speak, read or write Chinese that well! There is a Singaporean guy who studied in Australia and he loves making fun of people in the organisation with very crappy English and he never hangs out with anyone who is Chinese-ed[ucated]. He looks down on them (Ken).
>
> My colleagues who have studied all the way in Singapore like to make fun of the way I speak English. They say that I sound so high-class with my accent because

> I have lived and studied in Canada. I guess it's a good thing! (Jesse, Singaporean-Canadian, male, marketing executive in a Swiss bank).

In this way, competence in the English language is closely equated with professional competence. Indeed, respondents who spoke French, Chinese and Malay indicated that they would do so only outside the workplace. Inside the workplace, and in social settings related to work, fluent English, spoken with appropriate cadences, accents and colloquialisms, was the marker of fitting the cosmopolitan and professional norm.

### Physical Impressions

Bodily self-presentation, dress and comportment are also important elements of workplace 'fit'. A specific set of physical characteristics are deemed desirable. Rosalie noted that:

> As much as 30 per cent [of the decision-making in hiring mid- to upper-level financial professionals] will go into how you fit into the corporate image, 30 per cent goes to the impression, another 30 per cent will be how you talk, your gestures, your posture, your dressing. Less than 10 per cent is your qualifications. I don't stress so much on the qualifications because, if you get to this stage, chances are those things are already taken for granted . . . . If I were to shortlist ten people now . . . you look at the person once they walk in through the door, confident and professionally dressed, hair nicely done up, little to no make-up for girls, you form an impression. Chunky jewellery might be OK for the advertising industry but banks deal with professionalism and hence we are more knowledge-based and conservative, so you cannot have somebody giving off the impression that they are a young rocker, punk. You want somebody out there who exudes professionalism and addresses the values of a bank!

This respondent is quite explicit about the list of characteristics that are immediately assessed in the bodily performance of job applicants: dress, jewellery, hair, make-up, gesture, posture. All are clearly linked discursively to the notion of 'professionality', but equally this correlation is conceived within a very narrow set of cultural parameters.

### Gendered Dimensions

Implicit in the previous quote are the gendered dimensions of these requirements—indeed each form of bodily performance is explicitly gendered. In this respect, our findings reiterate many of the same issues as McDowell and Court's work in the City of London about the ways in which femininity in the workplace is carefully prescribed (McDowell 1997; McDowell and Court 1994). Physical attractiveness featured commonly as a requirement of workplace integration among our respondents:

> My previous division head was all about how we physically looked to represent the bank. The women that he chose, especially, were all physically attractive. If you look at the sales women we have, there are no ugly ones. There is this one girl from marketing who is really attractive—she does the emcee-ing of our events. She dresses in low-cut tops, frilly skirts. I think she does so because, as a marketing person, it would work better if you were attractive (Ken).

> For women, you have to be on it. You have to look really good, unless you are really that great in your work and there are very few of those. Female counterparts dress perfect. They dress to impress on the trade floor, especially those with good bodies ... they can be Chinese Singaporeans or expats or whatever. Hot is hot! (Chandra).

It is important to note that the two possible ethnic identities entertained for traders in the last quote are 'Chinese Singaporean' and 'expats' (which can be taken to imply 'white'). The types of femininity expressed through bodily self-presentation and dress that are described here are clearly inconsistent with cultural expectations of Muslim women (and many others). In this sense, gendered discourses of cosmopolitan performance intersect in important ways with ethnic identities.

Men, too, are subject to expectations of bodily performance, although the requirements appear to revolve around clean-cut good health rather than explicit sexuality:

> Ideally, you'd be confident, tall and slim because that shows you take care of yourself; as a manager on the trade floor, you don't have to worry about him taking sick leave, also amount of facial hair and facial complexion ... Yes, you have to have the ability but once that is settled, they do hire for looks (Chandra).

### *Dress Codes*

Dress also features as an important element of performance for men. One respondent recounted the way in which a deviation from the workplace dress code was addressed for a Russian employee:

> People generally adhere to the dress code but there was this one guy, Nikov, from Russia, and for the first six months he was here, he only wore a pair of white sneakers even on the trade floor! So he became known as Nikov White Sneakers. He had no idea there was even a dress code but finally the boss came up to him and said 'Listen, you have a problem'. He's a big sort of guy so nobody really wants to bug him, you know. It's cool—he's changed to more proper shoes but he is still known as Nikov White Sneakers (Chandra).

In this case, action to correct the departure from the dress code was a long time in coming but, more significantly, the deviance was noted quickly and became the subject of peer gossip. Indeed, it is interesting that, while 'the boss' took six months to correct the footwear malfeasance, it was a peer group sense of the need for conformity that reacted immediately. Furthermore, the deviance from a very narrow sartorial range for the male employee was sufficient to become a lasting marker through which the Russian employee would be labelled by co-workers.

*White? Chinese?*

While various dimensions of linguistic competence and physical appearance define some elements of conformity to which the 'cosmopolitan' is expected to adhere, perhaps the most egregious form of exclusion found in ostensibly cosmopolitan workplaces relates to ethno-racial identities. Most of the respondents were employed in workplaces that were predominantly Singaporean Chinese. All of them had at least three or four foreigners as colleagues while, as one of the respondents pointed out, 'there are literally one or two Indians in the workplace and no Malays'. Not only does this ethnic composition fail to correspond with Singapore's 'cosmopolitan' ethnic composition, but some respondents also suggested more calculated ways in which these ethnic groups were excluded:

> The ethnic breakdown in my office is very strange... Mostly Chinese... I recommended this guy who had almost ten years of cash management experience... he wasn't asking for a lot of money, he can do sales, project implementation, can trade, will hit the ground running and roll out projects straight away. But they didn't hire him, I felt, because he was Indian. They don't want Malays as well (Ken).

> I found it quite interesting because the people in HR didn't realise I was of Indian origin since my name was Nelson and maybe I look Latino or South American. We were hiring and they were going through the CVs... and every time an Indian CV came through, they threw it into the bin without even looking at it (Gwen, British-Indian, female, director, British bank).

In several other instances, respondents readily pointed to cases where Malays and Indians, in particular, were excluded from employment in their financial institutions. Malays in particular are seldom seen in professional occupations in the financial sector workplace, leading to a sense that they do not fit with the 'cosmopolitan' identity:

> The Malays... I hardly see them. Because there is really [only] one of them at night and the other one in the day! Very few of them. So you hardly notice they are there. I had Malay friends who were just turned away like that. It's quite bad. I also know a lot of Indians and Malays who have told me it's damn hard (Jayakumar).

If some respondents felt that such exclusions were the product of management decisions during hiring processes, it was also clear that everyday discourses within the workplace operated to create an exclusionary environment. In particular, several respondents noted the use of humour in the workplace relating to particular ethnic groups.

> The advantage [of there being so few of them] is I like to crack a lot of *Mat*[3] jokes and Indian jokes so I don't really have to look around before I crack those jokes and I am not afraid they would reach or hurt that person who is a Malay and it comes back to me, cos they are all Chinese and they all get the joke! (Ken).

> I wouldn't call them racist jokes. I've had jokes made to and about me! I come right back with 'You English sod!' and they're cool with it! It's fine! It's not a problem. Very relaxed, very open. There are some Jewish jokes too (Chandra).

In a context where racist attitudes and practices are anathema to both workplace regulations and national laws (and political sensibilities), these kinds of statement are quite incendiary. And yet, respondents from several different institutions (and in some cases themselves from minority ethnic and national backgrounds) consistently noted the ways in which Malays and Indians in particular (and here they could be referring to nationals of Malaysia or India, or, more likely, Singaporeans of Malay or Indian ethnic origins) were deemed not to fit with the financial workplace. Humour not only highlights, but goes further to normalise and perhaps even make light of, the ethnic politics operating in the multicultural workplace.

In sum, this brief insight into the ways in which individuals present themselves, and the ways in which bodies are 'read' in the financial workplace, suggests an environment in which a cosmopolitan tolerance or celebration of difference is far from the norm. Indeed, access to the ranks of financial sector professionals appears to be limited to those who conform to a fairly narrow set of characteristics.

## Conclusion

The qualitative data presented here are not necessarily purporting to be representative, nor are they the product of detailed ethnography. They are, however, plausibly suggestive of the intolerance of diversity and the enforced conformity that actually exist in supposedly cosmopolitan workplaces.

The cosmopolitan identity that holds sway is not one based on an attitude of acceptance of diversity, but instead demands conformity to a particular style of self-presentation and to a quite limited range of characteristics. Indeed, the notion of cosmopolitanism is used as a screen that selectively filters individuals' access to the professional/technical class in the financial sector. Ideas of diversity and inclusion hence mask the intolerance and inequality that continue to pervade the global workplace. Moreover, these forms of exclusion are reproduced not simply by hiring practices implemented by managers, but also through the everyday micropolitics of the workplace manifested in humour, nicknames and gossip circulated among employees.

While cosmopolitanism is demanded of employees, it is in fact an economically grounded cosmopolitanism that has more to do with a narrow but generic global business culture than it does with acceptance of diversity. The effect, ironically, is one of exclusion rather than inclusion—a requirement to conform to a narrow set of linguistic, ethnic, and bodily norms. Failure to do so leads to exclusion from, or upward immobility within, the workplace. As Harvey (2000) suggests, the specificity of place and difference confounds the universality of the cosmopolitan ideal. The celebration of diversity in these particular workplaces turns out to conceal a systematic process of exclusion and labour market segmentation.

While we have focused on the exclusion of particular bodily characteristics from the financial sector workplace, it is also important to note that possession of the requisite forms of cosmopolitan cultural capital is not random, nor are they easily attained. In some respects, exclusions based on ethnic identity reproduce other forms of dominance, especially of Chinese Singaporeans in the country's economic system. But they also represent forms of class reproduction, as many of the personal characteristics discussed here can be seen as forms of class habitus (Bourdieu 1984). In other words, the dispositions assessed in workplace encounters are those learned through processes of socialisation and social reproduction. English-language proficiency, for example, is likely to have been acquired through private schooling and the opportunity to study overseas, both of which reflect the class positioning of families. Less tangibly, as Bourdieu also shows, the acquisition of certain forms of taste (reflected in dress, make-up, and other aesthetics) is shaped by the class context of an individual's socialisation. The point, however, is not simply that class comes with particular cultural corollaries, but rather that these cultural corollaries are in turn instrumental in reproducing class from generation to generation. Those who know the 'codes' and have been socialised or trained into the appropriate forms of behaviour and performance, are generally the ones to be found in well-paid professional and technical occupations. Furthermore, in the context described in this paper, where particular ethnic groups are largely excluded from the kinds of professional/technical job held by our respondents, and where specific forms of gendered performance are required, class is closely intersected with cultural identity.

## Notes

[1] Crazy Horse ceased operations in 2007 (Channel News Asia 2007).
[2] All respondents' names are pseudonyms.
[3] '*Mat*' is a derogatory term for Malays in Singapore.

## References

Beaverstock, J.V. (2002) 'Transnational elites in global cities: British expatriates in Singapore's financial district', *Geoforum*, 33(4): 525–38.
Binnie, J., Holloway, J., Millington, S. and Young, C. (2006) 'Introduction: grounding cosmopolitan urbanism: approaches, practices and policies', in Binnie, J., Holloway, J., Millington, S. and Young, C. (eds) *Cosmopolitan Urbanism*. London: Routledge, 1–34.
Bourdieu, P. (1984) *Distinction: A Social Critique of the Judgement of Taste*. Cambridge, MA: Harvard University Press.

Chang, T.C., Huang, S. and Savage, V. (2004) 'On the waterfront: globalization and urbanization in Singapore', *Urban Geography*, 25(5): 413–36.
Chua, B.-H. (1998) 'Culture, multiracialism, and national identity in Singapore', in Chen, K.-H. (ed.) *Trajectories: Inter-Asia Cultural Studies*. London and New York: Routledge, 186–205.
Coe, N. and Kelly, P.F. (2002) 'Languages of labour: representational strategies in Singapore's labour control regime', *Political Geography*, 21(3): 341–71.
ERC (2002) *Positioning Singapore as a Pre-Eminent Financial Centre in Asia: Main Report*. Singapore: Ministry of Trade and Industry. Online at: http://app.mti.gov.sg/data/pages/507/doc/ERC_SVS_FIN_MainReport.pdf, last accessed July 2005.
Government of Singapore (2009) *Economic Structure of Singapore, 2008*. Available online at: http://app.mti.gov.sg/default.asp?id=485, last accessed on 3 October 2009.
Hannerz, U. (1990) 'Cosmopolitans and locals in world culture', *Theory, Culture and Society*, 7(PART NO?): 237–51.
Harvey, D. (2000) 'Cosmopolitanism and the banality of geographic evils', *Public Culture*, 12(2): 529–64.
Harvey, D. (2009) *Cosmopolitanism and the Geographies of Freedom*. New York: Columbia University Press.
Ho, E. (2006) 'Negotiating belonging and perceptions of citizenship in a transnational world: Singapore, a cosmopolis?', *Social and Cultural Geography*, 7(3): 385–401.
Huff, W.G. (1995) *The Economic Growth of Singapore*. Cambridge: Cambridge University Press.
Lee, H.L. (2004) *Financial Sector: Liberalisation and Growth*. Singapore: speech by Deputy Prime Minister Lee Hsien Loong to the Association of Banks in Singapore. 17 June 2004. Online at http://stars.nhb.gov.sg/stars/public, last accessed September 2005.
Lee, Y.S. and Tee, Y.C (2009) 'Reprising the role of the developmental state in cluster development: the biomedical industry in Singapore', *Singapore Journal of Tropical Geography*, 30(1): 86–97.
Ley, D. (2004) 'Transnational spaces and everyday lives', *Transactions of the Institute of British Geographers*, 29(2): 151–64.
Lim, H.K. (2005) *Speech by Mr Lim Hng Kiang, Minister for Trade and Industry, at the official opening of Crazy Horse Paris*, Monday, 5 December 2005. Online at: http://app-stg.mti.gov.sg/default.asp?id=148&articleID=1261&surveyID=&rdn=&uid=&email=&fbID=&pf=1.
McDowell, L. (1997) *Capital Culture: Gender at Work in the City*. Oxford: Blackwell.
McDowell, L. and Court, G. (1994) 'Missing subjects: gender, power, and sexuality in merchant banking', *Economic Geography*, 70(3): 229–47.
MAS (1998) *Singapore's Services Sector in Perspective: Trends and Outlook*. Singapore: Monetary Authority of Singapore, Occasional Paper No. 5. Online at http://www.mas.gov.sg, last accessed July 2005.
Ministry of Manpower (2009) *Labour Market 2008*. Singapore: Ministry of Manpower, Research and Statistics Department.
Pereira, A. (2008) 'Whither the developmental state? Explaining Singapore's continued developmentalism', *Third World Quarterly*, 29(6): 1189–203.
Purushotam, N. (1998) 'Disciplining difference: race in Singapore', in Kahn, J. (ed.) *Southeast Asian Identities: Culture and the Politics of Representation in Indonesia, Malaysia, Singapore, and Thailand*. Singapore and London: Institute of Southeast Asian Studies, 51–94.
Rodan, G. (2006) 'Singapore in 2005: "vibrant and cosmopolitan" with political pluralism', *Asian Survey*, 46(1): 180–6.
Rose, G. (1997) 'Situating knowledges: positionality, reflexivities and other tactics', *Progress in Human Geography*, 21(3): 305–20.
Vertovec, S. and Cohen, R. (2003) *Conceiving Cosmopolitanism: Theory, Context and Practice*. Oxford: Oxford University Press.
Wong, K.S. (2008) *Beyond a Talent Hub to a Great Place to Live*. Speech by Mr Wong Kan Seng, Deputy Prime Minister and Minister for Home Affairs at the Launch of the New Contact

Singapore on 28 April 2008. Online at: http://www.edb.gov.sg/content/edb/sg/en_uk/index/news/articles/beyond_a_talent_hub.print.html.

Yeoh, B.S.A. and Chang, T.C. (2001) 'Globalising Singapore: debating transnational flows in the city', *Urban Studies*, 38(7): 1025–44.

Yeoh, B.S.A. (2004) 'Cosmopolitanism and its exclusions in Singapore', *Urban Studies*, 41(12): 2431–45.

Yeoh, B.S.A. (2006) 'Bifurcated labour: the unequal incorporation of transmigrants in Singapore', *Tijdschrift Voor Economische en Sociale Geografie*, 97(1): 26–37.

Young, C., Diep, M. and Drabble, S. (2006) 'Living with difference? The "cosmopolitan city" and urban regeneration in Manchester, UK', *Urban Studies*, 43(10): 1687–714.

# Servicing British Expatriate 'Talent' in Singapore: Exploring Ordinary Transnationalism and the Role of the 'Expatriate' Club

Jonathan V. Beaverstock

*Singapore hosts many different expatriate communities. Whilst the working worlds of expatriates as transnational elites have been examined, little research has studied their ordinary life-experiences. Earlier research has noted that British expatriates were socially and culturally embedded within distinctive transnational social spaces like 'expatriate' clubs. This paper investigates the role of these clubs in serving the ordinary, professional, social and cultural experiences of British expatriates living in Singapore. The findings were derived from interviews with the General Managers of the British, Singapore Cricket, Hollandse, Pines, Swiss and Tanglin Clubs about their function in serving a British clientele; from interviews with 24 members of the British Club on its role in their everyday life; and from various club publications.*

### Introduction

Highly skilled international labour migration is a recognised driver for world cities to remain competitive in a global urban hierarchy, sustained by transnational corporation inter-company transfers and 'expatriation' (Beaverstock 2007; Ewers 2007). Within this corporeal context, expatriation has become an important process for world cities to secure 'talented' human capital from the transnational elite (Beaverstock 2005) or transnational cultural and capitalist classes (Florida 2002; Sklair 2001 respectively), where their agency feeds into debates about cosmopolitanism and transnational urbanism in the city (Ley 2004; Smith 1999, 2001). Recently, however, Ley (2004) and Conradson and Latham (2005a) have called for the investigation of *ordinary*, banal, everyday geographies of transnationalism, because even the 'talented' expatriate has to 'survive' the rigours of everyday life in a foreign place. Accordingly, this paper investigates the *ordinary*, everyday professional, social and cultural life-worlds of British expatriate 'talent' in Singapore, through a detailed study of one important transnational social space: the 'expatriate' club.

Singapore has always been an expatriate society (Yeoh and Khoo 1998). Indeed, since its inception from the mid-1960s, the Singapore government has been progressively more proactive in seeking expatriate 'talent' to help drive economic development, global competitiveness and the city-state's ambition to be a truly 'cosmopolitan' global city (see Ye and Kelly, this issue). But, despite an estimated 17,000 British citizens in Singapore,[1] little work has studied their everyday life experiences. Beaverstock (2002) has noted that British expatriates were socially and culturally embedded within distinctive transnational social spaces, including 'expatriate' clubs, which served their business, cultural and social needs. Singapore has 36 major clubs, with eight labelled as 'expatriate'—The American, British, Hollandse, Singapore Cricket, Country, Pines, Swiss and Tanglin Clubs—and for many foreign talented workers, club membership still remains one element of the relocation package to the city (Chuan 2002; Singapore International Chamber of Commerce 2003).

The remainder of the paper is divided into five major sections. In the following section, I discuss the role of expatriate talent in producing geographies of transnationalism (and cosmopolitanism) in world cities (see also Ho, this issue). I then explain the significance of expatriate 'talent' to Singapore's economy (complementing Ye and Kelly, this issue), and the growth and relevance of the 'expatriate' club in the second and third sections respectively. In the penultimate section I analyse the findings, before discussing, in the final part, the transnational and cosmopolitan traits of these expatriates, and reporting several conclusions debunking the prevailing rhetoric that these clubs are 'expatriate' spaces.

## Transnationalism, Expatriation and the World City

Two important theoretical contributions explore the everyday life experiences and geographies of highly skilled international migrants in the city: as transnational elites in the city's transnational social spaces; and as 'talented' expatriate labour. The concept of cosmopolitanism complements these discussions of transnationalism and migration, but is not discussed in depth here because this has been done by others such as Ley (2004) or Vertovec and Cohen (2003).

### Transnational Elites and Transnational Space

In order to conceptualise the influx, role and spatialities of expatriate talent in the city, one can explore three highly relevant (and connected) bodies of work which have their roots in the transnationalism discourse: transnational elites and the city, ordinary and middling transnationalism, and transnational social space.

World-city literature has long discussed the role of 'transnational elites' (Friedmann and Wolff 1982: 322) or the 'new international professionals' (Sassen 2001: 188) as the major productive entities of the world city through both their occupational and earnings characteristics, and their cultural lifestyle, hyper-mobility, connections and relationships. For Hannerz (1996), the transnational elite is a major actor which gives the world city its 'world' prefix by bringing into it not only economic, social and cultural wealth and distinctiveness, but also strong ties and relationships to other places through global social networks, hyper-mobile careers and geographical mobility. Moreover, as transnational elites 'flow into or through the city, they bring with them well-established cosmopolitan networks, cultural practices and social relations' (Beaverstock 2002: 525).

Conradson and Latham (2005a: 228–9) deepened the transnationalism debate by arguing that it was important to consider 'the *everyday practices* inherent to transnational mobility' and '"middling" forms of transnationalism ... to emphasise the degree to which transnationalism is in fact characteristic of many more people than just the transnational elites and the developing-world migrants'. This call by Conradson and Latham has spawned various studies of 'middling' transnationals (2005b). In the context of transnational elites, what can be drawn from Conradson and Latham (2005a: 228) is that:

> ... even the most hyper-mobile transnational elites are ordinary: they eat; they sleep; they have families who must be raised, educated and taught a set of values. They have friends to keep up with and relatives to honour. While such lives may be stressful and involve significant levels of dislocation, for those in the midst of these patterns of activity, this effort is arguably part of the taken-for-granted texture of daily existence.

Thus, it is imperative to argue that transnational elites do have an *ordinary* experience of transnationalism whilst carrying out the chores of everyday life, as illustrated in Yeoh and Willis' (2005) study of Singaporean and British transmigrants living in China; Beaverstock's (2005) discussion of the everyday life-worlds of British financial workers in New York; and Ho's (this issue) work on 'the everyday identity politics and cultural asymmetries encountered and produced by highly skilled Singaporean transmigrants living in London'.

In Smith's (1999: 120–4) analysis of transnational urbanism, he argues that the agency of transnational migrant networks, practices and social relations produces particular 'transnational social space' or 'translocalit[ies]' in the city. The prevalence of 'expatriate' social space and the territorialisation of social and cultural relations are, of course, not new in the context of the colonial/imperial city (King 1976), but what is different in the 'transnational' discourse is the importance of hyper-flows into and through the city, and the grounding of ephemeral networks and practices in specific places there. The intertwining of everyday transnationalism in the production of transnational space is discussed by Ley (2004: 157), who argues that the 'life-world... of the transnational elite may be highly localised and restricted to particular territories... hopping from one expatriate enclave to another'. Recent evidence from Waters' (2007: 494) study of overseas-educated local professionals in Hong Kong and Vancouver concluded by suggesting that they 'appear to inhabit separate, segregated social spaces'. Thus, an important social and cultural trait of the expatriate is the tendency to be dotted around the city in distinctive separated, transnational spaces.

*Expatriation, Career Paths and the City*

The term 'expatriation' is more often than not associated with the labelling of highly skilled individuals sent by their employers to work outside their home countries in a subsidiary or private entity for a contracted period of time, requiring a specific temporary immigration status and the receipt of an employer relocation package— including enhanced salary, subsidised accommodation, family health care, and school and club fees (Beaverstock 2002). The study of expatriates has taken several forms. First, there has been much written on the corporate process of expatriation (Beaverstock 2007; Ewers 2007). Second, there has been a growing interest in expatriate careers to explain knowledge circulation in the world of hyper-mobility and transnational work (Beaverstock 2005). Third, and of great significance to this study, there has been a corpus of work which has investigated the socio-cultural characteristics of different expatriate 'communities' around the globe. British expatriates have been studied in Dubai (Walsh 2007), New York (Beaverstock 2005), Paris (Scott 2006) and Singapore (Beaverstock 2002) and other-nationality professionals in Hong Kong and Vancouver (Waters 2006). Almost all the different studies of British expatriate communities have identified a number of salient characteristics which sustain an expatriate's *ordinary*, everyday life-experience in the city:

- expatriate global and local knowledge systems as deeply embedded in workplace social networks;
- expatriate social networks as invariably disembedded from the local, composed of close-knit relationships with very-similarly educated persons of the same or other 'Western' nationalities;
- expatriate social spaces, for example places of residence, particular bars, nightclubs, restaurants and sporting/recreational clubs, and public places like beaches, as playing significant roles in managing 'ordinary' transnationalism and the everyday life-experiences of expatriation; and
- expatriate 'sporting events', combined with the characteristics of social networking and patronage of particular expatriate social spaces, as reproducing a sense of identity and community.

Interestingly, these expatriate traits all resonate with an air of 'cosmopolitanism', as discussed by Conradson and Latham (2007), Ley (2004) and Vertovec and Cohen

(2003) for example (see also Ho, and Ye and Kelly, both this issue). Expatriates have the personal wealth, job security, social and cultural capital and, importantly, 'softer' life skills, to be able to *ground* themselves in foreign lands and steer their way through the challenges of making an *ordinary* working, social and family life in a different cultural and national context. Indeed, it could be argued that the 'talented' expatriate not only embodies an air of cosmopolitanism but also, in the course of his or her 'life-world' (Ley 2004) reproduces the practice of cosmopolitanism through time and space, which helps to foster a 'cosmopolitan' sense of place (see also Smith 1999, 2001; Waters 2007).

**Expatriation and 'Foreign Talent' in Singapore**

The presence of foreign, highly skilled 'talent' in Singapore plays a significant role in the city-state's desire and aspirations to become a truly cosmopolitan global city (Yeoh 2004). The government's overt policy of promoting the inward flow of foreign talent into the high-value economy is an important strategy to enhance economic growth and external competitiveness on a Pan-Asian and world stage (Sim *et al.* 2003; Ye and Kelly, this issue). As Yeoh (2006: 31) suggests:

> [G]iven the aspirations of the natural resource-scarce, labour-short city-state to become a major player in a globalised world, Singapore's main economic strategy is premised on the development of a highly-skilled human resource base as the 'key success factor' in confirming a global future... the state has emphasised the strategy of developing Singapore into a 'brains service node', 'an oasis of talent' and ultimately, the 'Talent Capital' of the New Economy.

Yeoh's (2004, 2006) discussion of the lineage of skilled foreign talent in Singapore illustrates that this policy has derived from many high-profile speeches from Singapore's Prime Ministers to date (see Ye and Kelly, this issue). The speeches acknowledge that such immigrants play vital roles in helping to cement Singapore's 'nation-building', global city and world economic status. Hui (1997) notes that several programmes have been put in place by the Ministry of Manpower and the Economic Development Board to assist domestic and foreign companies to recruit foreign highly skilled labour, including a company grants scheme to reduce the costs of recruiting and relocating 'foreign talent', and 'Permanent Residence' schemes for foreign investors and entrepreneurs. Official data are scarce and dated on the numbers of expatriates in Singapore. In 1990, there were 15,000 expatriates, the dominant groups being Japanese, Americans, Britons, Germans and Swiss (Chang 1995: 141). In 2000, Yeoh (2004: 2440) estimated that there were 80,000 expatriates (from a total of 754,524 immigrants) and suggested that the traditional 'expatriate community' comprised Japanese (10,200), British (6,600), American (5,600), Australian (3,300) and French (1,600) elite migrants. Recent figures suggest that there were 'a record 144,500' expatriates in the workforce (Lewis 2008: 64) and that

Singapore is one of the most popular locations for expatriate foreign postings (HSBC 2008).

There remains a dearth of research on different-nationality 'talented' expatriates and their everyday life-experiences in Singapore, but two exceptions are Chang's (1995) study of the (British) 'expatriatisation' of Holland Village and Beaverstock's (2002) analysis of British expatriates in the financial centre. Chang coined the phrase 'expatriatisation' to explain how Holland Village, a neighbourhood in central Singapore, had become a distinctive expatriate space because of its predominant 'Western' clientele, which was reproduced by its historical development (growing up in close proximity to a British military base), retail specialisation, landscape and identity (biased towards Western tastes and fashions), and significant patronage from British and American communities, as well as 'Western' tourists.

Rather than focusing on an expatriate space, Beaverstock (2002) investigated the global–local knowledge networks of British lawyers, accountants and bankers who worked in the financial centre. Three important conclusions were reached. First, these expatriates participated in closely knit, work-related networks comprising British and other nationalities, and 'Western educated'/experienced Singaporeans. Second, at a social level, these expatriates were significantly disembedded from the local setting, as network formation and the spirit of community were forged specifically with other British and 'Western' expatriates. Third, the 'expatriate' social/recreation club was an important place for both work-related and social activities.

## 'Expatriate' Social and Recreational Clubs in Singapore

Throughout Singapore's history, social and recreational clubs have been important places for foreign industrialists, travellers, traders and civil servants to partake in socialising, drinking, leisure and business. From the 1850s, clubs like the Singapore Cricket Club (1852), Verinigung Deutsches Haus (1856), Tanglin Club (1865), Swiss Club (1871), Polo Club (1886) and Hollandse Club (1908) were established primarily for men. At this time, expatriation might have lasted an entire working career (Hollandse Club 1998; Sharp 1993; Walsh 1991). During the 1950s and 1960s, club development was muted as the pre-existing clubs extended their membership, facilities and amenities to the island's growing foreign and elite Singaporean community (Sharp 1993; Walsh 1991). It was not until after independence in the 1970s that Singapore experienced a second spurt of club development with the American Club, various golf and country clubs (e.g. Seletar Country Club) and the British Club later in 1986. The latest phase of club growth has occurred since 1990, with the establishment of many town and country (e.g. the Temasek Pines), sporting (e.g. Raffles Marina) and private business clubs (e.g. the International Researchers).

Clubs in Singapore are no longer restricted to one (or more) predominant nationality as membership eligibility has been expanded to increase potential market share and to adhere to the Registry of Societies Legislation. However, the 'expatriate' label is still used by some third parties, like Singapore Expats,[2] or expatriation manuals (Chuan 2002), to market such clubs to a foreign 'elite'. There are 107 clubs in Singapore: 14 community, 23 country, 16 international association and 54 sports, recreation and special-interest clubs, and a group of 36 extends to 'expatriates' of all nationalities (Chuan 2002; Club Managers Association of Singapore www.cmas.org.sg). Of these 36 clubs, there are three generic types that expatriates frequent in Singapore.

First, *international social clubs* (like the American, British, German, Hollandse and Swiss clubs), that market their membership benefits to families in 'state of the art' complexes offering, for example, swimming pools, tennis courts, team sports (e.g. hockey), gymnasia, bars and restaurants, cinemas, specialist classes (e.g. wine tasting), the celebration of festive activities (e.g. Mothers' Day) and corporate hospitality. For example, the American Club portrays itself as having everything, 'under one roof':

> Located in the heart of the city, The Club...sets the standard for exemplary customer service, facilities, and hospitality. From casual Poolside dining to the spa, state of the art gym, library, kids club, catering services, or dry cleaning, the sky's the limit. The Club is a sanctuary from the hustle and bustle of life (http://www.amclub.org.sg/; last accessed 22 November 2007).

Second, *international town and country recreation clubs* (like Fort Canning Country Club) that cater to those in pursuit of lifestyle, sport and leisure activities. They offer a variety of services and facilities—from premier dining, restaurants and bars to lifestyle and team sports—but, importantly, also have access to more specialised amenities on site or in close proximity to the club (e.g. golf courses, water sports and various team-play pitches). For example, the Raffles Marina Club badges itself as:

> The premier marina, nautical country club and lifestyle centre...[offering]...first class, comprehensive country resort pool,...gymnasium..., aerobics room, ...tennis...And,...a movie-house quality theatrette,...fully furnished guest-rooms, a games room.... we have...settled for nothing but the best (http://www.rafflesmarina.com.sg/; last accessed 25 November 2007).

Third, *prestige private business clubs* that serve Singapore's business elite, both resident and foreign. For example, the Tower Club located in the penthouse suites of the prestigious Raffles Place plaza, with only 1,600 members and fees of S$9,360 *per annum*, markets itself as

> [A]n exclusive club [that] encompasses the best of both worlds; warm and welcoming...while being exceedingly...sophisticated, reflecting the style and efficiency of a Members business. The essence of a private club is its... 'membership by invitation'...It is conducive to the highest order of business and social entertaining, as well as the most demanding of working meetings and conferences (http://www.tower-club.com.sg/; last accessed 25 November 2007).

From this brief foray into the so-called 'expatriate' club scene in Singapore, it is interesting to note that these 'international' or 'prestigious' entities not only reproduce a 'transnational' social space (as discussed by Beaverstock 2002; Smith 1999; Waters 2007) where 'privileged' people of all nationalities can seek social and cultural enjoyment and a sense of acceptance and belonging, but also denote a seemingly 'cosmopolitan' spatial matrix, where the 'talented' are able to embody and practise their social worlds in particular grounded, cosmopolitan places. In the following empirical section, I present original findings on both clubs and expatriates, and tease out how such entities support the *ordinary* life-worlds of British expatriates and reproduce a sense of transnationalism (and cosmopolitanism) in the city.

## The Role of 'Expatriate' Clubs for British Expatriates in Singapore

To investigate the role, importance and relevance of 'expatriate' clubs in the everyday professional, social and cultural life-experiences of British expatriates in Singapore, I triangulated findings from three principal methodologies:

(i) textual analysis of archival and contemporary printed and virtual sources on expatriation and clubs in Singapore, including government statistics, books on individual clubs and clubs' histories;
(ii) semi-structured interviews with the General Managers (GMs) of the British, Singapore Cricket, Hollandse, Pines, Swiss and Tanglin clubs, questioning their role in supporting the everyday life-experiences of their British clientele;[3] and
(iii) interviews with 24 members of the British Club on its role in their everyday lives,[4] collecting data on members' age, gender, length of stay, occupation, membership and reasons for joining the club (structured), and on the rationale for membership and 'surviving' the rigours of being an 'expatriate' in Singapore (semi-structured).

*'The Management View'*

Six club GMs were questioned about the role of 'expatriate' clubs in supporting the everyday life-experiences of British talent in Singapore (Table 1). Five major inter-linked findings stood out.

First, Singapore's lineage as a 'club society' for foreign talent workers can be traced back to its mercantile and colonial history, which saw an unprecedented influx of foreign highly skilled workers, including government officials, entrepreneurs and traders. Clubs were set up by colonialists for fellow colonialists of different nationality groups. However, all GMs agreed that Singapore's 'expatriate' club scene continued and intensified post-independence. This was due to the wave of multinational corporations locating into the city-state, which swelled the demand for clubs as these firms incorporated membership into expatriate 'hardship' relocation packages. As the GM of the Tanglin Club explained:

**Table 1.** 'Expatriate' clubs surveyed

| Club | Founded | Principal members* | No. of nationalities | Nationalities (%) | Reciprocal clubs worldwide | Fees (S$) (2004 prices) | URL |
|---|---|---|---|---|---|---|---|
| British | 1986 | 2,133 | N.A. | British c51 Singaporean 30 | 86 in 62 cities | Transf. corporate: 21,000 Transf. individual: 21,000 Ordinary (non-trans): 8,500 Annual membership: 3,000 | www.britishclub.org.sg |
| Singapore Cricket | 1852 | 3,363 | N.A. | Singaporean c50+ | Selected 1st-class/-grade cricket clubs | Transf. ordinary: 50,000 Transf. corporate: 75,000 Term (non-trans): 3,745 (n.b. 2006/7 prices) | www.scc.org.sg |
| Hollandse | 1908 | 1,488 | 42 | Dutch 31 British 16 Singaporean 15 | 26 in 22 cities | Transf. corporate: 20,600 Ordinary/associate: 5,250 Term: 2,950 | www.hollandseclub.org.sg |
| Pines Town | 2002 | 1,500 | 20 | Singaporean 51+ | 47 in 41 cities | Transf. corporate: 15,000 Ordinary: 12,000 One year: 3,000 (n.b. 2006/7 prices) | www.thepines.com.sg |
| Swiss | 1871 | 1,300 | 44 | German 33 Swiss 24 Singaporean 20 | 29 in 24 cities | Transf. corporate: 20,000 Transf. ordinary: 20,000 Ordinary/associate: 9,600 Ordinary/associate: 4,800 One year: 3,000 | www.swissclub.org.sg |
| Tanglin | 1865 | 5,700 | 70 | Singaporean 51 British 11 | 160 in 26 cities | Ordinary membership: 20,000 Term membership: 4,000 | www.tanglinclub.org.sg |

*Note:* *Excludes spouses and family dependents.
*Source:* Fieldwork and club websites (as listed above).

> What is the point of getting them to leave their comfort zones of... London?... There must be... two carrots—one is the salary and the second one is... something to go with the country. So the 'expat' who came out here got himself a car, a flat, a maid, a chef and a club... In that sense, the club was always something that you would be given if you came out as an 'expat' and you appreciated it and you used it, and it was good for you and it was good for your family. So that really is how the clubs took shape here.

Second, Singapore's clubs are definitely no longer associated with the 'expatriate' label. All the GMs agreed that the 'expatriate' label is now totally redundant from both a social and a business perspective and that their clubs are international social clubs, drawing members from the Singaporean elite, and all nationalities and racial creeds (see Table 1). The 'expatriate' label had also withered because of the dying corporate-membership category reflecting shortened postings, and because Singapore is no longer a 'hardship' posting. As the GM of the Cricket Club suggested:

> I think that looking at the membership of clubs in Singapore is very interesting. Pre-1965, most of the clubs in Singapore were far and away expatriate clubs. The change was very rapid. The latest now is at least 50 per cent members must be local. That has been wonderful for clubs in Singapore. It has revitalised them... a lot of expats that are here now, are here now on local contracts. You tend to stay longer on a local package than 18 months to two years. The expat community is not the majority of this club.

Third, Singapore's clubs are no longer integral to the everyday lives of British expatriates. Singapore is a thriving world city and being a member of a club is no longer a pre-requisite survival strategy for the 'expatriate' household. The GMs all suggested, however, that clubs do perform important roles in providing social and recreational support, and networks for British (and other nationalities), who live with or without condominium facilities. The British, Swiss and Hollandse clubs have all positioned themselves as family-orientated clubs, where speciality and international events are celebrated throughout the year. As the GM of the Swiss Club explained:

> We are now a social club. Fortunately, what we have here is a very nice piece of land, which attracts a lot of people because of the fact that Singapore is a concrete jungle... It's accessible, very easy and I think that is one of the major attractions of the Swiss Club—its location...We provide a lot of activities. We provide sports, restaurants, and we provide for the kids... It is providing facilities that are not that easily found in the condominiums.

In contrast, the Pines Town and Singapore Cricket Clubs focus their marketing strategy on a lifestyle choice and recreational activity. The Pines Club actively promotes their town location as being 'an important part of life... [with] ... finesse and style... it must be exciting, trendy, interesting and... something... part of their lifestyle' (GM). In a similar vein, the Singapore Cricket Club uses the prime city-centre location to promote itself as the premier sports club: '[T]his particular club has and always will be a sports club. It's sports club first and social club a little way behind it'. The Tanglin Club overtly celebrates its tradition and gravitas in Singapore, drawn from an exclusive 'high society' clientele, including both domestic residents and a wide range of other nationalities. For the Tanglin Club, its badge is 'a class act...top of the tree...we are traditional. People join because of the club, its décor, ambience...' (GM).

Fourth, the GMs all stressed that a fundamental aspect of the clubs' business models is to sustain a thriving corporate hospitality function (e.g. banquets, conferences, training seminars etc.) with different fee structures. As the GM of the Swiss Club noted, '[D]uring the week there are not so many families here so we rent out facilities...corporate hospitality is a business to generate revenue'. All clubs actively promoted 'corporate packages' to secure repeat business from companies, training agencies and government.

Fifth, for the individual, membership of the club actually transcends Singapore because all clubs are members of international reciprocal networks, with other clubs located around the world (Table 1). The Tanglin Club boasts the most reciprocal clubs—160 in total, located in 26 cities worldwide. The GMs intimated that many of their members are frequent business travellers within and beyond the Asian region, and that reciprocal clubs are used for social and business purposes.

*The Role of the British Club in Singapore: Views from the British Membership*

The British Club, established in 1986, portrays itself as 'a relaxing and informal retreat where you and your family will always find a home-from-home in Singapore...with well-designed clubhouses...[and] some of the finest sports and recreation facilities for entertaining family, friends and business associates.'[5] The club uses its location in the heart of Singapore's tropical rainforest in Bukit Timah as a marketing device to sell it as a 'haven of peace in bustling Singapore'. It offers a range of bars, pubs and dining facilities spanning the formal (e.g. the Mountbatten Room), informal (e.g. the Windsor Arms—a traditional British public house) and *al fresco* (e.g. the Racquets Bar and Verandah Terrace Café). For the family, the club has invested in a sports centre and aerobics/dance studio, a children's playroom, a video games room, a library, a reading/TV room, a gaming room and an outdoor swimming pool (with trainer pool). The club also offers its membership a range of activities and organised events (e.g. cooking), specialist coaching (e.g. tennis) and competitive games (e.g. golf, with preferential green fees) (www.britishclub.org.sg).

Twenty-four British members (13 men and 11 women) were interviewed at the club, with an equal share of principal members and spouses. Data obtained from the structured interviews indicate that this group of British members had several salient characteristics (Table 2). First, they were all of white British ethnic origin. Second, 22 (92 per cent) were aged between 25 and 44 years. Third, all were married with at least one child, with a high proportion of children attending two international schools—the Tanglin Trust School (50 per cent) and the United World College South East Asia

Table 2. Personal characteristics of British Club members

| R | M/F | Age range | Children | Stay (years) | Residence | Occupation | Occupation spouse | School | Membership | Other Expatriate postings |
|---|---|---|---|---|---|---|---|---|---|---|
| 1 | F | 25–44 | 2 | 5 | Tanjong Katong | Housewife | Pilot | UWCSEA | Trans. indiv. | |
| 2 | F | 25–44 | 3 | 1 | Holland Village | Housewife | Underwriter | Tanglin Trust | Ordinary | |
| 3 | F | 25–44 | 2 | 1 | Holland Village | Housewife | Marketing | Tanglin Trust | Trans. corp. | |
| 4 | F | 25–44 | 2 | 2 | Dover | Housewife | Engineer | Tanglin Trust | Ordinary | |
| 5 | F | 25–44 | 3 | 3 | Bukit Timah | Housewife | Shipbroker | Tanglin Trust | Trans.indiv. | UAE (Dubai) |
| 6 | M | 25–44 | 2 | 2 | Dover | House-husband | CEO | Tanglin Trust | Ordinary | Belgium |
| 7 | M | 25–44 | 3 | 5 | Bukit Timah | Surveyor | Teacher | Australian Int. | Ordinary | Australia |
| 8 | F | 25–44 | 5 | 4 | Holland Village | Housewife | Manager | Tanglin Trust | Ordinary | |
| 9 | F | 25–44 | 3 | 2 | Bukit Timah | Housewife | Manager | Tanglin Trust | Ordinary | |
| 10 | M | 45–65 | 1 | 5+ | Pasir Panjang | Systems manager | Housewife | Overseas family | Trans. indiv. | Africa |
| 11 | M | 45–65 | 2 | 5+ | Orchard | Surveyor | Housewife | UWCSEA | Trans. indiv. | |
| 12 | M | 25–44 | 1 | 3 | Bukit Timah | Banker | Housewife | UWCSEA | Trans. corp. | Zurich |
| 13 | F | 25–44 | 3 | 5+ | Clementi | Teacher | CEO | UWCSEA | Trans. corp. | |
| 14 | M | 25–44 | 2 | 2 | Holland Village | Insurance CEO | Accountant | Tanglin Trust | Ordinary | |
| 15 | M | 25–44 | 1 | 3 | Bukit Timah | Student | Manager | White Lodge | Ordinary | |
| 16 | M | 25–44 | 1 | 1 | Holland Village | Accountant | Housewife | None | Ordinary | |
| 17 | M | 25–44 | 2 | 5 | Holland Village | CEO | Housewife | UWCSEA | Trans. corp. | |
| 18 | M | 25–44 | 2 | 5 | Upper East C'st | CEO | Physiotherapist | UWCSEA | Ordinary | |
| 19 | M | 25–44 | 1 | 1 | Clementi | Diplomat | Diplomat | Dover Court | Annual memb. | |
| 20 | M | 25–44 | 2 | 5 | Bukit Timah | CEO | Housewife | None | Trans. corp. | |
| 21 | F | 25–44 | 2 | 2 | Bukit Timah | Housewife | CEO | Tanglin Trust | Trans. corp. | |
| 22 | F | 25–44 | 2 | 5+ | Bukit Timah | Teacher | CEO | Tanglin Trust | Ordinary | |

**Table 2** (*Continued*)

| R | M/F | Age range | Children | Stay (years) | Residence | Occupation | Occupation spouse | School | Membership | Other Expatriate postings |
|---|---|---|---|---|---|---|---|---|---|---|
| 23 | M | 25–44 | 2 | 4 | Holland Village | House-husband | CEO | Tanglin Trust | Ordinary | |
| 24 | F | 25–44 | 2 | 1 | Bukit Timah | Medical scientist | CEO | Tanglin Trust | Annual memb. | |

*Source:* Fieldwork.

or UWCSEA (25 per cent). Fourth, the economically active were all employed in professional and managerial, scientific and/or public service occupations. Fifth, almost everyone lived in close proximity to the club in Bukit Timah (38 per cent), Holland Village (29 per cent), Dover/Buona Vista (8 per cent) and Clementi (8 per cent). Sixth, the two highest-ranking reasons for joining the club were for the sport and recreational facilities, and to provide activities for spouses and children (Table 3). The striking homophile features of these talented migrants—their ethnicity, age, occupations and place of residence—do suggest a certain embodied and practised form of transnationalism and cosmopolitanism which ties closely to other studies of transnational professions living and working in the city (see, for example, Beaverstock 2002; Ho, this issue; Walsh 2007; Waters 2006).

Club Membership and the British Club

These members joined the British Club for four main reasons. For 24 per cent '[I]t came as part of the package' (Respondent 2, see Table 2). The second reason was access to sporting and recreational activities, especially for those who lived in houses or condominiums with limited facilities: '[W]ell it's a nice place for children to socialise and meet their friends and go swimming in a nice big pool' (R5). Third, to enable them to socialise with established friends and as a place to meet new people of all nationalities: 'I joined mainly to widen my social circle and to meet people' (R3). Fourth, 'because it is close to our house' (R1) and/or 'it was recommended more as a family club than, say, the Tanglin' (R12). Aside from these four main reasons, the issue of them being 'British' was briefly mentioned as a selection criterion by six respondents, but solely in the context of not having a language barrier to contend with which might have been the case with other clubs like the Hollandse. Interestingly, from these very pragmatic factors which accounted for club membership, one can argue that these British members were comfortable with their own transnational existence, both embodied and practised, because they did not make the conscious decision to join to 'remind them of home', and overtly reproduced their own 'Britishness' in the spatiality of the club. The issue of club membership and British national identity is unpacked further below.

**Table 3.** Reasons given by British members for joining the British Club

| Reason | Multiple responses |
| --- | --- |
| For the sport and recreation | 23 |
| To provide activities for my spouse and children | 23 |
| To meet new people and widen my social life in Singapore | 18 |
| For the food and drink | 14 |
| To socialise with other British families | 11 |
| To celebrate British festivals and events to remind me of home | 5 |
| To further my business contacts | 2 |

*Source*: Fieldwork.

## Club Membership and British National Identity

Seventeen respondents (71 per cent) suggested that the British Club played no significant part at all in maintaining their British national identity in Singapore. Respondents' comments ranged from, '[N]o, not at all. It's the facilities and location' (R5) to 'I do not see my national identity as being important here. If another club had better facilities in a better location we may have not joined the British Club' (R15). Those seven respondents who did comment on the role of the club as a space and practice which facilitated 'Britishness' considered it to be 'marginal' (R17), involving banal activities such as '[W]e quite like the Windsor Bar which is a pubby type of atmosphere so it's quite nice to get a pint of Boddingtons now and again' (R11), or taking part in 'British' traditional celebrations like Christmas Day and watching sporting events (e.g. F1 Grand Prix motor racing). Given these non-committal views about membership of the British Club as an experience to reproduce their national identity, again 71 per cent did not consider themselves as 'expatriates' or as living the 'expatriate lifestyle', with representative views suggesting '[N]o ... I'm just living and enjoying life in another country' (R5) or '[N]o ... we just live a normal life' (R20). Of the seven British members who thought of themselves as 'expatriates' (R4, 6, 7, 10, 12, 22 and 23), five of them had experienced living abroad elsewhere (Table 2) and were more aware of 'living in a foreign country' (R7), where integration with the local nationals was difficult.

## British Club Membership as a Social Survival Strategy

For many spouses, membership of the British Club was an important socialisation process for everyday life and a mechanism to entertain children and cultivate a social life outside the home. For this group of members, club membership was 'essential for keeping a routine where children can do their thing and we can do ours' (R3), and such members regularly socialised with other British people, and a mixture of expatriates of other nationalities. The two house-husbands interviewed (R6 and R23) were members of the 'house-husband club' within the British Club, used as a way of socialising with other men working outside the club in downtown Singapore. In contrast, for the majority of other respondents, the club was not a social survival strategy at all in that they used it as 'a nice escape place if we want to get out of the house and garden' (R5) and socialisation was with other British people and expatriates of other nationalities, and local Singaporeans. One respondent (R19) made a very engaging comment about socialisation and the role of the club, noting:

> It [the club] adds to our lives in Singapore because it gives you an extra dimension. It gives you more socialising and an opportunity to meet with people who you wouldn't otherwise meet ... either through sporting events or socially having meals and drinks and everything else.

These interview findings, coupled with those discussed earlier on the rationale for joining the club, showed that this group of British expatriates, in almost all cases, are able to negotiate and navigate a transnational lifestyle above and beyond their 'Britishness'. Quite clearly, these individuals see themselves as transnational 'citizens' (to borrow a term from Sklair 2001) or global cosmopolitans (as discussed by Conradson and Latham 2007; Ley 2004; Ye and Kelly, this issue) who have the life-course experience, social and cultural capital, and sheer 'savvy' (see Ho, this issue) to embrace a diversity of cultures and practice in a foreign city without the 'comfort blanket' of overtly having to reproduce a British identity through embodied experience and practice. Interestingly, the transnational social space of the club also exhibits a spatial matrix of cosmopolitanism, where members can reproduce the logics and attitudes of cooperation, and celebrate diversity and co-existence with a multitude of nationalities and acceptable social and cultural practices—comparable to Ye and Kelly's (this issue) reading of the cosmopolis of the financial workplace.

## Discussion and Conclusions

This study of the role of 'expatriate' clubs in serving the everyday needs of their British clientele in Singapore has added significant empirical strength to the debates which consider *ordinary* transnationalism and the making of transnational social space in the city (Conradson and Latham 2005b; Ley 2004; Waters 2007). Equally, in doing so, this empirical analysis has embellished the view that 'expatriation' and 'expatriatisation' (Chang 1995) are significant processes and practices in the making and reproduction of the condition of 'cosmopolitism' in the world city. It is no wonder, therefore, that Singapore has a strategic immigration policy to attract foreign talent in order to enhance economic development and its credentials as a cosmopolitan world city (Ye and Kelly, this issue; Yeoh 2004).

### *Expatriation and 'Ordinary' Transnationalism*

Conradson and Latham's (2005a) analysis of 'ordinary' transnationalism has great resonance for the role of clubs as conduits for everyday expatriate life-experiences in Singapore. The interviews with the GMs and British expatriates who had patronage with the British Club teased out the 'ordinariness' of the functionality of being a member of an 'expatriate' club. On the one hand, the GMs observed that their clubs were no longer associated with being a 'perk' to ease the 'hardship' of being an 'expatriate', but were now associated with providing an international and *local* clientele with 'family-orientated' social and recreational facilities in the cosmopolitan world city of Singapore. On the other hand, the case study of the British expatriates who frequented the British Club clearly emphasised the 'ordinariness' of its role in their transnational lives. Whilst some had joined the British Club because it was a part of their corporate package to Singapore, for others, their rationale was because the club had all the facilities they wanted for their family, or they already had friends there, and it was in close proximity to their place of residence. They did not join the club specifically to overtly celebrate or re-invigorate their national identity. For this group of British people, the club was a point of socialisation, participation in sporting and social events and family entertainment. The club was not necessarily an exceptional place to 'survive' the social and cultural rigours of life in a foreign city, but was simply another dimension to their life in Singapore where the traits of ordinary life—like socialising, eating, drinking, playing sports, swimming and participating in everyday and special events—could be performed in a very welcoming, friendly, hospitable and convivial place. Importantly, for this group of expatriates the desire to embrace cultural diversity and not seek the comfort of an overtly 'British' lifestyle enhanced their credentials as transnational and/or cosmopolitan 'citizens' of the world.

*'Expatriate' Transnational Social Space*

Much has been written about the existence of transnational social spaces in the city, and this study provides an example of just such a *place*. These 'expatriate' social and recreational clubs are cacophonies of different nationalities (Table 1) who go about their everyday life in the sanctuary of the club world. The 'transnationality' of the club was being continuously fed by the global–local, micro-networks of individual members, their social and cultural practices, cosmopolitanism and engagement with the worlds of economic activity and the workplace. The GMs interviewed stressed that these clubs were international in scope and reach, and exclusive to all members and cultural sensitivities. They were nodes in a wider space of flows, where the notion of a transnational space was being constantly transmogrified by the incessant turnover of departing and new members, as talented migrants continuously left and came into the city (Beaverstock 2002; Ho, this issue; Smith 2001; Ye and Kelly, this issue). Equally, the dynamism of these clubs as transnational social spaces was constantly being reproduced by the through-flow of business travellers into the city. Finally, it must be noted that the clubs' drive to generate revenue streams through corporate hospitality and attracting businesses from downtown to 'rent' club facilities for private social events also contributed to the production of these places as transnational social spaces. In essence, the clubs became an extension of downtown commerce when it was frequented by the global corporate networks of business men and women, and the performance of their transnational working practices and actions.

*Final Remarks: Expatriatisation' and the City*

In researching the role of 'expatriate' clubs in servicing the needs of talented, expatriate Britons in Singapore, it is important to note that even transnational elites have *ordinary* transnational life-worlds to contend with, and that such life-worlds are enacted in the transnational social spaces of the city. My study has shown that, moving beyond the spaces of the club, it can be strongly argued that the making of the cosmopolitan world city is intertwined with the agency of the expatriate worker, and the entirety of the process of 'expatriatisation'. Chang's (1995) work on Holland Village, Singapore, has explicitly drawn our attention to the 'expatriatisation' of a particular place. In drawing this study to a conclusion, it is important to argue that 'expatriatisation' is a vibrant urban process which transcends time and space, and is reproduced throughout the world system of cities by a homophile 'class' of people— in Sklair's (2001) or Florida's (2002) reading of 'class'—who possess certain traits of economic, cultural, social and network capital, cosmopolitanism and a particular, malleable global sense of place.

## Acknowledgements

This project was funded by The British Academy (project SG-36613). My deepest gratitude is also extended to the Department of Geography, National University of Singapore, which hosted my visits during 2004.

## Notes

[1] Speech by the British High Commissioner, Paul Madden, 'The role of the British High Commission in Singapore' (18 August 2009), NUS Guild House, National University of Singapore. Online at: http://www.ukinsingapore.fco.gov.uk/en/newsroom/?view = Speech&id = 20763456, last accessed 19 October 2009.
[2] www.singaporeexpats.com, last accessed 22 November 2006.
[3] Twelve General Managers were approached for interview, identified from Expat Singapore's definitive list of main 'Expatriate' Clubs (http://www.expatsingapore.com.sg/once/clubs.htm, last accessed 6 April 2004). A 50 per cent response rate was achieved in April 2004. All but one interview was taped and all lasted approximately one hour.
[4] Access for interviewing was granted by the GM of the British Club, which was visited consecutively for a seven-day period, from early morning to mid-evening and including a weekend, in June 2004. Interviewees were selected randomly by snowballing, were confidential and lasted one hour.
[5] Quoted in the marketing brochure for new membership authored by Celeste Seah, Director of Sales and Marketing.

## References

Beaverstock, J.V. (2002) 'Transnational elites in global cities: British expatriates in Singapore's financial district', *Geoforum*, *33*(4): 525–38.
Beaverstock, J.V. (2005) 'Transnational elites in the city: British highly skilled inter-company transferees in New York City's financial district', *Journal of Ethnic and Migration Studies*, *31*(2): 245–68.
Beaverstock, J.V. (2007) 'World city networks from below: international mobility and inter-city relations in the global investment banking industry', in Taylor, P.J., Derudder, B., Saey, P. and Witlox, F. (eds) *Cities in Globalization: Practices, Policies, Theories*. London: Routledge, 52–71.

Chang, T.C. (1995) 'The "expatriatisation" of Holland Village', in Yeoh, B.S.A. and Kong, L. (eds) *Portraits of Places: History, Community and Identity in Singapore*. Singapore: Times Editions, 140–57.

Chuan, G.K. (2002) *Handbook for Expatriates. Working and Living in Singapore*. Singapore: Rank Books.

Conradson, D. and Latham, A. (2005a) 'Transnational urbanism: attending to everyday practices and mobilities', *Journal of Ethnic and Migration Studies*, 31(2): 227–33.

Conradson, D. and Latham, A. (eds) (2005b) 'Ordinary and middling transnationalism', Special Issue, *Journal of Ethnic and Migration Studies*, 31(2): 227–431.

Conradson, D. and Latham, A. (2007) 'The affective possibilities of London: Antipodean transnationals and the overseas experience', *Mobilities*, 2(2): 231–54.

Ewers, M.C. (2007) 'Migrants, markets and multinationals: competition among world cities for the highly skilled', *GeoJournal*, 68(2–3): 119–30.

Florida, R. (2002) *The Rise of the Creative Class*. New York: Basic Books.

Friedmann, J. and Wolff, J. (1982) 'World city formation: an agenda for research and action', *International Journal of Urban and Regional Research*, 3(3): 309–44.

Hannerz, U. (1996) *Transnational Connections: Culture, People, Places*. London: Routledge.

Hollandse Club (1998) *Celebrating 90 Years. Hollandse Club 1908–1998*. Singapore: Hollandse Club.

HSBC (2008) *HSBC Bank International Expatriate Explorer Survey 2008* (Online at: http://www.offshore.hsbc.com/1/PA_1_4_S5/content/international/section_content/expat_explorer/Expat Explorer.pdf0, last accessed on 19 October 2009).

Hui, W.T. (1997) 'Regionalization, economic restructuring and labour migration in Singapore', *International Migration*, 35(1): 109–29.

King, A. (1976) *Colonial Urban Development*. London: Routledge and Kegan Paul.

Lewis, L. (2008) 'The "little red dot" intent on becoming the hub that Asia cannot live without', *The Times*, 11 October, 64–5.

Ley, D. (2004) 'Transnational spaces and everyday life', *Transactions of the Institute of British Geographers*, 29(2): 151–64.

Sassen, S. (2001) 'Cracked cases: notes towards an analytics for studying transnational processes', in Pries, L. (ed.) *New Transnational Social Spaces*. London: Routledge, 187–207.

Scott, S. (2006) 'The social morphology of skilled migrants: the case of the British middle-class in Paris', *Journal of Ethnic and Migration Studies*, 32(7): 1105–29.

Sharpe, I. (1993) *Singapore Cricket Club 150th Anniversary (1852–2002)*. Singapore: Singapore Cricket Club.

Sim, L.L., Ong, S.E., Agarwal, A., Parsa, A. and Keivani, R. (2003) 'Singapore's competitiveness as a global city: developing strategy, institutions and business environment', *Cities*, 20(2): 115–27.

Singapore International Chamber of Commerce (2003) *Expatriate Living Costs in Singapore 2003/04 Edition*. Singapore: Continental Press.

Sklair, L. (2001) *The Transnational Capitalist Class*. Oxford: Blackwell.

Smith, M.P. (1999) 'Transnationalism and the city', in Beauregard, R. and Body-Gendrot, S. (eds) *The Urban Movement*. London: Sage, 119–39.

Smith, M.P. (2001) *Transnational Urbanism: Locating Globalization*. Oxford: Blackwell.

Vertovec, S. and Cohen, R. (2003) *Conceiving Cosmopolitanism: Theory, Context and Practice*. Oxford: Oxford University Press.

Walsh, B.A. (1991) *Forty Good Men: The Story of the Tanglin Club in the Island of Singapore 1865–1990*. Singapore: Tanglin Club.

Walsh, K. (2007) '"It got very debauched, very Dubai!" Heterosexual intimacy amongst single British expatriates', *Social and Cultural Geography*, 8(4): 507–33.

Waters, J.L. (2006) 'Geographies of cultural capital: education, international migration and family strategies between Hong Kong and Canada', *Transactions of the Institute of British Geographers*, 31(2): 179–92.

Waters, J.L. (2007) '"Roundabout routes and sanctuary schools": the role of situated educational practices and habitus in the creation of transnational professionals', *Global Networks*, 7(4): 477–97.

Yeoh, B.S.A. (2004) 'Cosmopolitanism and its exclusions in Singapore', *Urban Studies*, 41(12): 2431–45.

Yeoh, B.S.A. (2006) 'Bifurcated labour: the unequal incorporation of transmigrants in Singapore', *Tijdschrift voor Economische en Sociale Geografie*, 97(1): 26–37.

Yeoh, B.S.A. and Khoo, L. (1998) 'Home, work and community: skilled international migration and expatriate women in Singapore', *International Migration*, 36(2): 159–86.

Yeoh, B.S.A. and Willis, K. (2005) 'Singaporean and British transmigrants in China and the cultural politics of contact zones', *Journal of Ethnic and Migration Studies*, 31(2): 269–85.

# Identity Politics and Cultural Asymmetries: Singaporean Transmigrants 'Fashioning' Cosmopolitanism

Elaine Lynn-Ee Ho

*The politics of identity and difference are often intensely experienced and negotiated in everyday encounters. By examining the experiences of highly skilled Singaporean transmigrants in London and their projects of cosmopolitan self-fashioning, this paper highlights the way in which 'race' and nationality trouble claims to cosmopolitanism. In the analysis I consider the mixing of cultures and selective 'local' norms picked up by this group of migrants. I focus on the oscillating cultural framings that they navigate in their professional and social interactions, particularly in terms of phenotype, cultural discourse and bodily presentations. In so doing, I argue for a more critical view towards popular notions of cosmopolitanism currently in circulation and instead invoke an alternative cosmopolitan urbanism.*

### Introduction

It is often in the domain of everyday encounters that the politics of difference are the most intensely experienced and negotiated by transnational migrants (transmigrants).[1] Research on internationalised flows of talent has gathered pace in recent years, shifting the focus from institutional mechanisms to the individual experience of migration. These studies draw attention to the manner in which migration flows and experiences are embodied in social and cultural ways (Beaverstock 2002; Mitchell 1997; Nagel 2005; Yeoh and Willis 2005), and take place in geographical and historically mediated contexts. In this scholarship on transnational mobility, there has been an accompanying interest in the way abstract macro-scale regulatory structures and phenomena are (re)produced or contested through seemingly nondescript norms, values and routines (Conradson and Latham 2005a; Dyck 2005; Smith 2005). It is with respect to this interest that I situate my study, focusing on the everyday identity politics and cultural asymmetries encountered and produced by highly skilled Singaporean transmigrants living in London, a global city characterised by a blend of 'local' and migrant cultures. I examine the oscillating positionings of ethnicity (or 'race') that they partially premise on phenotype, and situate this in narratives of globalisation, cosmopolitanism and postcolonial nationhood. My discussion also advances some critical views of cosmopolitanism discourse currently in circulation: first, the construing of cultural sophistication as 'cosmopolitanism'; second, the host/migrant-as-stranger binary framing; and third, the limits of invoking 'race' in a cosmopolitanism project.

## 'Racialised' Cosmopolitan Cultures

Highly skilled migration is an increasingly important phenomenon in countries capitalising upon migration to meet labour and population needs. In the international 'talent-for-competition race' (Shachar 2006: 164), the belief that human capital is premium has prompted national governments to institute policies aimed at attracting highly skilled individuals to service their domestic industries and multinational companies. Unlike low-waged refugee and asylum migration, the presence of highly skilled migrants is usually not deemed a problem for the social fabric of the host society, because they are seen to possess the cosmopolitan cultural capital and savvy that would enable them to fit in anywhere in the world. In its philosophical usage, the embodiment of cosmopolitan culture is premised on a sense of belonging to humanity that 'transcends the particularistic and blindly given ties of kinship and country' (Cheah 2006: 487). However, in its popular usage the term 'cosmopolitan' is more often associated with images of Sklair's (2001) transnational capitalist class, depicting individuals with power and privilege who consider themselves citizens of the world.

Recent studies on highly skilled migration have started to expand the optic of globalising people flows beyond the narrow focus on the transnational capitalist class. Instead, these studies bring to the forefront forms of 'middling' transnationalism (Conradson and Latham 2005a), such as the self-initiated mobile professionals who migrate to take up relatively insecure jobs in a host country (Conradson and Latham 2005b; Kennedy 2004). These writings tend to portray cosmopolitanism as a project of 'self-fashioning', or 'self-conscious cosmopolitanisation' (Conradson and Latham 2007) wherein individuals deliberately cultivate a global sensibility by embracing cultural diversity in their friendship and professional networks, developing tastes for foreign music and food, and participating in lifestyle choices (e.g. environmentalism and organic diets) characteristic of a cosmopolitan society. This approach, however, like Nava's (2007: 86) interpretation of historical modernity as cosmopolitanism, only situates cultural difference and the foreign as a 'source of interest, pleasure and counter-identification'. Such readings are anchored on an imaginary celebration of difference and do not actively engage with the uneven social realities of purported cosmopolitanism as an empirical condition (Ho 2006; Yeoh 2006).

Research drawing on ethnographic and interview material shows that highly skilled migrants occupy social spaces of inclusion and exclusion that are mediated by intersecting axes of identity such as class, ethnicity/'race', nationality and gender (Ley 2004; Nagel 2005; Purkayastha 2005; Yeoh and Willis 2005). These spaces of inclusion and exclusion (or boundary-making) are arguably premised upon essentialising ideals of place and constructed, as Massey (1993: 64) posits, out of an inward-looking perspective of the past and static notions of 'local' culture. Local culture is taken to refer to the culture of individuals who live in a bounded space and engage in taken-for-granted, habitual and repetitive acts (Featherstone 1993: 175). This depiction of culture often mobilises racial and ethnic categories to justify sameness and difference (Nagel 2001, 2005).

The apparent 'naturalness' or immutability of 'race' has been critically interrogated by scholars arguing that notions of 'race' are the products of specific historical and geographical forces rather than pre-given categorisations (Jackson and Penrose 1993: 1). This view challenges the material inequalities previously assumed to be an inevitable outcome of unalterable racial divisions. Yet more recent writings on 'race' also critique the social constructionist approach for reifying 'race' by treating it as the basis for finding solutions to address inequalities even as it simultaneously seeks to discredit the idea of 'race'. Thus one counter-view advocates a 'post-race' perspective (Gilroy 2000; Ware and Back 2002) but this approach has been criticised for its universalising premises and depoliticising effects (Nayak 2006). Another counter-view foregrounds the material corporeality of 'race' rather than a discursive deconstruction of race. This view argues that phenotype is a dynamic and mutable biological state but it is the basis through which bodies forge relations with things and places in the social world (Saldanha 2006).

In this regard, the work of McDowell (2008) is also helpful for understanding the way that the migrant labour market is segregated and segmented through the production of 'appropriate' bodies. She argues that discourses about 'different national work ethics, differently sexualised bodies, about different roles in the family and household all affect options in the labour market'. McDowell (2008: 499) adds that bodily presentation of 'accent, dress, self-presentation, behaviour, skin colour, hair jewellery and height' are used to position migrant bodies as appropriate or inappropriate in the workplace. She thus advocates an approach that is cognisant of the need to deconstruct intersecting master categories of race, class and gender, while being simultaneously mindful of the need to address existing social inequalities.

One may ask how theories of performativity, drawing heavily on signification rather than anatomy or phenotype, can be used alongside theories criticising discourse. For Nayak (2006: 423), such an approach has highly productive tensions in that the ontological status of 'race' is disrupted by revealing the way the racialised body is repetitively enacted as a slippery surface of 'race truths'. This view complements

Saldanha's (2006) argument that the material reality of bodies needs to be engaged even as it is recognised that phenotype can morph and connect with other culturally embedded bodies, things and places in infinite ways. For Saldanha, allowing for the proliferation of 'race' as a material reality and understanding the geographical differentiations between bodies is where cosmopolitanism starts. Though Saldanha's argument is persuasive, it inevitably privileges the materiality of 'race' as a dominant organising social category. Instead, intersecting axes of social difference (McDowell 2008), including 'race', class, gender and nationality, should be mobilised for a cosmopolitan project.

By examining the experiences of Singaporean transmigrants and their projects of cosmopolitan self-fashioning (through international mobility and acquiring cultural sophistication), this paper will highlight the way 'race' and nationality trouble claims to cosmopolitanism and instead invoke an alternative cosmopolitan urbanism. My analysis is conscious of the material embodiment of 'race' through phenotype, yet it is also cognisant of the multiple and splintered ways in which cultural meanings are inscribed onto racialised bodies through discourse, representation and linguistics. I focus on the oscillating cultural framings drawing on phenotype, discourse and bodily presentations, which Singaporean transmigrants navigate during their everyday professional and social interactions in London. Instead of dichotomous understandings of racialised inclusion and exclusion, premised on treating 'race' as a reified category, my analysis considers the mixing of cultures and the selective imitative norms that migrants pick up in their destination contexts arising from their ideas about what is or is not 'local'. I also underscore the ways in which the politics of nationality become apparent in the multiple refractions of 'race' amongst Singaporean transmigrants in London. This approach emphasises the fluidity of racial identities and the processes through which racialisation takes place (Wimmer 2007) both discursively and through the material embodiment of 'race'.

This discussion draws on fieldwork conducted in London during 2004–05. I interviewed 43 Singaporeans living and working in London with the purpose of understanding their migration motivations, experiences of living in London and intentions for return. In terming these individuals 'Singaporean transmigrants', I am referring to persons who hold either Singaporean citizenship (38) or Singaporean permanent residency (3), or who identify themselves as 'Singaporean' even after relinquishing their formal affiliation with the state for personal reasons (2). My respondents[2] had all lived in London for at least a year and planned on settling for a longer period of time. The majority were of Chinese ethnicity (31 out of 43), which parallels both the ethnic composition of the Singaporeans found in London and the broader population profile in Singapore. The remainder belonged to the Malay, Indian and Eurasian racial groups officially categorised by the Singaporean state. All had tertiary-level qualifications or extensive professional experience, and about half had been educated in the UK. Three-quarters of the study sample were in their mid-20s–30s and an equivalent proportion held employer-sponsored work permits allowing them to remain in London.

In the remainder of the paper I first discuss some working and socialising norms which Singaporean transmigrants feel they have to acquire to be accepted as 'appropriate' bodies in a foreign workplace. These cultural traits contribute to a purported form of cosmopolitan savvy that helps them navigate a foreign work environment. Second, I examine the way this cosmopolitanism is in fact premised upon essentialising racial constructs that are framed around phenotype and assumed cultural 'sameness' or 'difference'. Third, I highlight the distinctions made between persons of the same ethnicity but different national backgrounds, thus complicating simplistic assumptions of cultural 'sameness' or 'difference' amongst persons of the same phenotype. In so doing, I suggest that cosmopolitanism as an empirical condition should be a project that is premised on a respectful acceptance of intersecting social differences.

## 'Cosmopolitans' Inside/Outside the International Workplace

Recent literature studying intra- and inter-company personnel transfers has argued that transnational elites move at the behest of the parent company, partly for the transfer of skills, knowledge and expertise internationally, but also to further their own career (Beaverstock 2005). The majority of the Singaporean transmigrants I studied had moved to London of their own initiative rather than through company transfers. Like Conradson and Latham's (2005b) study of New Zealanders in London, most of my respondents did not migrate merely for economic incentive such as higher salaries. Many said that their salaries command a lower standard of living in London compared to Singapore. Instead, their migration motivations were interlinked with a desire for self-development and exploration. Nonetheless, they are aware that migration benefits their career advancement in that they are 'build[ing] career competencies and labour market value through transfer across boundaries' (Thomas *et al.* 2005: 341). Oftentimes, these individuals are depicted as engaging in a process of self-fashioning (Conradson and Latham 2007: 249) to become part of an 'emergent cosmopolitan society'. They are acquiring a form of cosmopolitan capital that enables them to navigate the foreign cultures encountered in their internationally mobile work lives. However, this view of cosmopolitanism should not neglect the discursive and embodied power relations in which migrants become embedded when they move to a foreign work environment.

The international workplace represents a new professional and cultural territory that Singaporean transmigrants learn to negotiate as they inhabit it. For instance, Ian (Chinese, male, 30s), who had moved to London to pursue a business postgraduate degree with the intention of working in the city, describes the initial culture shock that he encountered:

> I think there may have been a little getting used to on the cultural side: sometimes people crack jokes that you don't understand; they watch sitcoms that you don't watch; they talk about football or rugby and [you] don't follow it. That kind of

stuff... But when it comes to working I feel that I get the respect. I have been able to hit the ground running and people recognise [my] contribution.

As indicated by Ian's anecdote, Singaporean transmigrants find that there are particular working and socialising norms that they have to acquire to fit into their new work environments. Although the workplace in London is likely to encompass a diversity of migrant cultures, the way my respondents described their work environments usually referred to 'British'[3]—or more specifically, what is still often unquestioningly regarded as 'English'—codes of behaviour.[4]

In terms of work etiquette, Irene (Chinese, female, 20s) who works as a brand consultant, compares her experience of working in Singapore and in London:

> I think [in terms of] the work styles, people are a lot more gracious [in London]... Here people, for instance, would pick up the phone and before they ask you for anything, even if you are an absolute stranger, [they] would say, 'How are you?' and ask how your day was. Then you chat for at least one minute, be polite and move on to what you wanted. When I first arrived at my workplace I [would walk] up to the secretaries and say, 'Could you do this, please?' They looked at me in a particularly crass way, but after a while they figured out [that she] just says exactly what she thinks... I think that is quite an Asian thing. So they have gotten used to me and me to them.

Irene's description depicts a story commonly told by my respondents about the misunderstandings that happen as a result of the different work etiquette they encounter in London. McDowell's concept of 'appropriateness' (2008: 497) comes in useful here for understanding the social negotiations taking place in these interactions. The relatively forthright Singaporean (interpreted by Irene as 'Asian') manner of speaking is contrasted with the less-brusque social rules of English speech. Irene highlights the way she was chastened by 'crass' looks from her colleagues and the appropriate bodily comportment which she learnt in order to be considered an 'acceptable' worker, thus attesting to her successful acquisition of cosmopolitan capital ('They have gotten used to me and me to them'). In considering the experiences of financial professionals in the (predominantly Chinese) Singaporean workplace, Ye and Kelly (this issue) similarly highlight the significance of bodily presentation and comportment for 'fitting' into purportedly international and cosmopolitan work environments. In my study, differences in work and social etiquettes are—as Irene's anecdote shows—attributed to representations of being 'Asian' or 'Western' ('that is quite an Asian thing'), distinctions that are inscribed in the everyday consciousness of the respondents.

Being 'Asian' or 'Western' is also inextricably associated with phenotypical difference, or the materialist basis through which racialisation takes place. This is exemplified in Oscar's account of the British after-work drinks ritual, another work-related norm often brought up by other respondents. Oscar (Chinese, male, 30s), who has worked and lived in both Singapore and London, describes the difference between after-work socialising in Singapore and in London:

> [On] weekdays I normally hang out with my colleagues, mostly the *angmohs* [Caucasians]. Go down to the pub to drink.. [Amusedly] I can stand and drink at the pub for six, seven hours now quite easily...That is something I picked up here. In Singapore you wouldn't stand to drink. [Emphasises] Nobody stands to drink in Singapore. They would think, 'You mad ah?' The other thing is, in Singapore you eat first then you drink. Here you drink and drink and you go back to eat....

The phrase '*angmoh*'[5] is used in Singaporean society to describe persons of Caucasian origin (or the 'white' English in this instance). The expression is variously used in a derogatory or tongue-in-cheek manner by Singaporeans to attribute and explain cultural differences through phenotype. Thus Oscar ascribes the habit of socialising over drinks to *angmoh* culture and as a norm he has picked up from living in London. Although he does not disapprove of the after-work drinks ritual, he describes in a mocking tone the way that his *angmoh* colleagues 'stand and drink at the pub' for a stretch of several hours, a practice that he expects would be looked upon with bemusement in Singapore ('You mad ah?'). Nonetheless, he has cultivated the habit in order to cement social bonds with his colleagues.

The differences described by Oscar may appear banal but the after-work drinks ritual affects the extent to which Singaporean transmigrants feel that they bond with their colleagues at and outside work. Seemingly trivial differences in working and cultural norms can create alienation for those less adept at adapting to their new environment. Dorothy (Chinese, female, 40s), who works at management level in her company, explained her predicament when her Singaporean employer sent her to London:

> I found working here very tough, even tougher than in China... I guess it is because we are a Singaporean-owned hotel and we are the owner's [representative] though the management here is all *white* [emphasis mine]. So it was difficult for them to accept that we are Chinese and coming here to tell them what to do... When we came, we have to implement our policies here and run things the way the management did in Singapore and there was some objection. The way [they] run the hotel is different... It is mainly their attitude towards work. In Singapore if you have a deadline, 'die-die' you have to do but here it is only a report.

Dorothy, who has worked in several international locations including China, regards the management changes that she had to implement in the London office as the most difficult. On the one hand, she associates this with the racial prejudices and vestiges of colonial superiority that her 'white' subordinates might have against her, an ethnic Chinese from a former British colony. On the other hand, she professes that the different management style and what she interprets as the nonchalant work attitudes of her colleagues (professional degeneracy relative to Singaporean work attitudes) could have led to the disagreements too. Such dialectical identity representations between the 'host' and the migrant communities are, as Ehrkamp (2006) points out, integral to the way migrants see, or fashion, themselves.

Dorothy adds that she does not usually socialise with her 'white' colleagues and prefers to spend her social time with Singaporean friends instead:

> Even my colleagues, I find that they are very different from us. If it is after work they wouldn't say 'Let's go for dinner'. I don't know why. I have been here for so long and a lot of my colleagues have been here for a long time. The most is on Fridays; they would have a set timing to go to the pub for a drink.... The problem is when they start drinking they [will] talk nonsense. You really see their true colours and they smoke so when you come out your clothes stink. If I want to go out I want to get to know them better. I would rather go for a nice dinner and talk. It is very strange. All my colleagues don't know each other well... Like for us [during] Chinese New Year we would invite friends to our house but not for them, [even at] Christmas they don't invite. It's kind of like a family thing. I don't go home for Christmas but they don't invite me to their house. It is always the Singaporeans here who group together and cook and go to each other's place to talk.

Dorothy's narrative contrasts the Singaporean preference for after-work socialising over meals with what she associates as the British preference for socialising over alcohol. Her difficulty with the latter arises from what she considers to be the misdemeanours that manifest amongst her colleagues after a few rounds of alcohol, which she believes prevents her from getting to 'know them better'. In Dorothy's case, she equates the drinking and smoking habits of her colleagues with moral degeneracy. Dorothy's narrative, however, also reveals a longing for hospitality from the host society ('I don't go home for Christmas but they don't invite me to their house'). Hospitality is a sensibility that, as Dikec (2002) argues, can advance a cosmopolitan project if it is built on an engagement that facilitates mutual acceptance between the host and the migrant-as-stranger.

The above examples reveal the ways that acquiring 'local' work and social norms are integral to becoming an 'appropriate' body in the British workplace. The meaning of 'local' in London is usually associated with Britishness, even though 95 per cent of those who have moved to London since 1995 were born outside the UK (Tate Modern 2007). Britishness is also often conflated with 'white' English culture, despite the presence of other British-born ethnicities such as the South Asian and Chinese communities. Nonetheless, being accepted in the British workplace necessitates a performance of what is popularly perceived as 'Britishness'. In so doing, Singaporean transmigrants aim to acquire the cultural sophistication that can be converted into cosmopolitan capital. As Dorothy's example makes clear, those unwilling/unable to do so are likely to face social exclusion. Nonetheless, the cosmopolitan savvy of those better at acquiring these cultural competencies should not be taken at face value. These 'cosmopolitan' Singaporeans often struggle to acquire the cultural traits that would facilitate their acceptance in the host society. They are also apt to simultaneously negotiate the multiple subjectivities and cultural politics of defining 'self' and 'Other' that arise from being in London, a global city populated not only by the 'local' British but also by a diversity of other nationalities and ethnicities.

## Embodying and Negotiating Racialised Subjectivities

In this section, I focus on the positive and negative oscillations of identity articulated in my study. On one level, 'cosmopolitan' Singaporeans appear able to accept different cultural work norms and to capitalise on their cosmopolitan savvy to gain acceptance in their new workplace. Yet, on another level, what seems to be cosmopolitan capital on the surface is usually premised on essentialising constructs of 'race', largely framed around phenotypical difference. This is illustrated in the following anecdote by Patricia (Chinese, female, 30s), a lawyer who has worked in both Singapore and London:

> From what I can see and what I experience, the culture is different. It is more professional [in London] in terms of interaction with your colleagues. You don't feel that everything is personally driven. You can have an argument with your boss and after the argument is over it doesn't carry on into your personal life, whereas in Singapore I felt that everything rolls into one. You are you, your work [and] your social life. Work takes your whole life and you are not able to have that professional interaction with your colleagues... In a way, I am being very critical, but I think that Singaporeans have not evolved in their work in terms of professionalism, like work is work and life is life. They are not sophisticated enough to make that distinction. It is also Chinese, taking things to heart that Western people, I think, have less of.

In Patricia's narrative, she associates the lack of 'professionalism' amongst Singaporean workers as a national attribute and presumes that 'Western people' are less likely than the Chinese to take things to heart. Such attitudes reflect a larger malaise in Singaporean society wherein stereotypes conflating whiteness with 'Western' superiority[6] *vis-à-vis* 'Chinese' inferiority (the latter tends to be conflated with 'Singaporean' or 'Asian') are uncritically circulated and reproduced. Significantly, Patricia (like Irene) attributes the differences in working norms to seemingly inherent civilisation distinctions as well. However, her point of view can be usefully contrasted with that of Dorothy, who believed that her 'white' colleagues have less-professional work attitudes than Singaporeans. The same phenotype and signifiers ('white'/Western) are thus mobilised in different ways to explain behaviour.

Despite acquiring the cultural traits that enable them to gain acceptance from their local colleagues, these 'cosmopolitan' Singaporeans unanimously express the belief that they are still regarded as outsiders in their workplace. Steven (Chinese, male, 20s), who was preparing to move to China after having studied and worked in Britain for approximately five years, explained his rationale for doing so:

> I always tell my friends that, no matter what you do in this place, you being Chinese and not European you will always be the 'away' team. You have the 10 per cent of fans supporting you but you can never win over the whole stadium... I am Singaporean and Chinese. If I work really hard I can break through all those things but there will be a lot of setbacks. It is just the way things are around here. You can

> stay for a couple of years but to make it really big, you have to become a total European, which I am not. I can be Westernised but I am not hardcore, *jiak gan tan*⁷ that kind of stuff. I am a more *cheena* [or Chinese] person, which is why I think China or a more Asian environment would be more suitable for me because I get along better with Asians.

The signifier of difference spelled out in Steven's anecdote is not Britishness or Englishness; rather it is more broadly construed in terms of being non-European. His anecdote underscores the widely held belief amongst the Singaporean transmigrants in my study that there is a limit to their career progression in a European-dominated society. Even Ian, who had extolled the meritocracy of his workplace in London compared to the 'foreign talent'⁸ policy in Singapore, admitted that he might encounter a racialised 'glass ceiling' in London later in his career because of his embodied Chinese identity. As such, returning to work in Asia at a later stage is an attractive option for Singaporean transmigrants who believe that, on the one hand, they have a career advantage from the international exposure they had gained in London. On the other hand, they also expect that phenotypical and cultural similarities would make it easier for them to fit in and climb the career ladder in Asian countries.

The perceived similarity between 'Asian' cultures and norms further influences the social networks of these Singaporean transmigrants in London. Even if they have mastered their performance of 'Britishness', their closest social circles still mainly consist of other Asians living there. Steven explains:

> The kind of things [the Europeans] do is just different. They go out to drink and smoke. It is not that I don't want to do this kind of stuff but it is not me. I have tried it and I felt that it is not what I want to do.... Let's put it this way. If we have a housewarming party for a British guy, I would not feel as at home as if it is a housewarming party for a Hong Konger or Malaysian... It is very subtle, really. It boils down to the kind of person you are. I told you that I am more *cheena*. I wish I could be more *gan tan* [Westernised], if you want to use that word. [After] four years in university I have a few good *angmoh* [Caucasian] friends but I hang out more with Asians.

Although Steven has been able to socialise with the European colleagues and friends he has made in London, he feels most at ease with friends from other parts of Asia because of his embodied identity as 'Chinese'. For Steven, going out to 'drink and smoke' is a form of self-conscious cultural mimicry ('I wish I could') that he did in order to fit in with the European clique, whereas he construes his natural inclination ('the kind of person you are') as different. He describes his other group of friends generally as 'Asians', but I later found out that they are Chinese from Hong Kong and Malaysia. His anecdote depicts the 'viscosity' (Saldanha 2006: 10) of bodies wherein the physical characteristics of racialised bodies and associated cultural habits invoke stickiness during social interactions ('I would not feel as at home'), thus producing aggregations of racial clustering in social settings ('I hang out more with Asians').

In fact, living in London tends to reinforce the Chinese identity of the Chinese-Singaporean transmigrants. For instance, Patricia had praised the professionalism in her London workplace and decried the narrow-minded attitudes in her Singaporean one, yet she qualifies that:

> On the other hand, there are a lot of things I would never give up—some of the Chinese values that we have. Like loyalty, respect and filial piety, which I think are on the decline in [Britain]. To a certain extent I think those values are superior to the kind of family relationships they have in [Britain]. So there are good and bad sides but, because I am Chinese and I identify with my upbringing, I see that as my roots.

Patricia's narrative aptly illustrates the oscillating 'Western' and 'Asian' identifications subjectively taken up by Singaporean transmigrants. As I argued earlier, by comparing the narratives of Patricia and Dorothy, selective mobilisations of ethnic identity are used to justify preferred values and behaviours. Patricia's invocation, 'I am Chinese'—referring to phenotype—alongside the reference to 'upbringing', demonstrates the perceived inseparability of these two dimensions in constructions of identity and relationality.

However, references to the distinction between *angmoh*/'Western' and Chinese/ 'Asian' cultures assume the cultural homogeneity and norms of the respective ethnic groups and broader civilisation identity. This is in spite of the diverse representations of cultures and nationalities encountered by Singaporean transmigrants in London and the distinct cultural differences between Chinese communities in different parts of the world. 'Asian values'—a term often used by my respondents as an explanation for social identification and belonging/non-belonging—can be read as a boundary-making process for inclusion and exclusion. The politics of 'Asian values'[9] are discounted in these accounts of cultural interactions and differences. Even the non-Chinese Singaporeans I interviewed in London used the term 'Asian values' to rationalise perceived cultural similarities and difference in an unproblematised manner. This is despite debates in Singapore arguing that the purported shared 'Asian' values popularised by the Chinese-dominated Singaporean government have Confucian origins. Nonetheless, 'Asian values' and cultural familiarity are reasons often cited by Singaporean transmigrants to explain their intentions to eventually return to Singapore or Asia for the sake of their career and family (Ho 2008).

*Splintering 'Race' through Nationality Dynamics*

The viscosity of phenotype and the invocation of shared ethnic/civilisational values as a way of understanding racialised social relations is, however, complicated by the axis of nationality. For Chinese-Singaporeans, it is perhaps the cultural context of their destination country that makes their Chinese ethnic identity more salient amongst a predominantly non-Chinese population in London. Nevertheless, this does not take away the significance of their 'Singaporean identity'. Despite phenotypical 'sameness', Singaporean transmigrants are prone to differentiate their nationality from the other Chinese they meet in London. Like the Chinese-Singaporeans in the studies conducted by Kong (1999) and Yeoh and Willis (2005) in China, Singaporean identity comes to the fore when the Chinese-Singaporean transmigrants in my study interacted with Chinese from other parts of the world. This points to an interpellation of cultural identities that is performed situationally by Singaporean transmigrants, as demonstrated in the following conversation that I had with Michelle (Chinese, female, 20s):

> Being Chinese, I like to say that I am from Singapore. To me that is important. It defines where I am coming from, like whether I am from Taiwan, China or Hong Kong, it is different. Maybe it is because we know Chinese from other places, it is just different. When you say Singaporean it doesn't make you different from Indian-Singaporean... If you [meet] a Singaporean [who is] Indian, being a Chinese-Singaporean you know where that person is coming from whereas [for] an Asian here in London, you know that they don't share similar experiences as you do. If I met an Indian from England, it is different from what you are familiar with. With Indians from Singapore you click. Not that I don't click with the Indians here but we speak *Singlish*, or you use certain slang and you know where each other is coming from. That is how I feel about Singapore.
>
> *What about if you meet a Chinese person from Taiwan and at the same time you meet an Indian from Singapore, who would you identify with more?*
>
> In terms of language, unless you want to be selfish and speak Chinese, then of course you identify with the Chinese more. But if you say where you are coming from then definitely the Indian.

Although the Chinese identity of Singaporean transmigrants in London may become salient in their interactions with a predominantly non-Chinese society, their Singaporean identity becomes dominant during interactions with the Chinese from other parts of the world. English is the *lingua franca* in Singapore but the different ethnic groups learn their respective mother tongues[10] as a second language in schools (except the Eurasians who can choose their second language). The Singaporean political elite reason that this two-pronged strategy is necessary so as to build a cohesive national community out of disparate migrant cultures that converged in Singapore during its trading days under British colonial rule. In addition to that, Singaporeans speak a form of pidgin English known as *Singlish* (Singaporean English) that includes phrases from the different languages and dialects spoken by Singaporeans. Hence Michelle claims that, even though speaking Mandarin (the primary Chinese language used in Singapore) would enable her to communicate well with other Mandarin speakers, her shared nationality with an Indian-Singaporean who speaks *Singlish* means that she would identify better with the latter person.

Similarly Dina, who is an Indian-Singaporean (female, 30s), differentiates herself from other South Asians whom she has met in London and claims a closer affinity to fellow Singaporeans. Commenting on the British use of the term 'Asian', she argues that:

> When they say 'Asian' here it means the Indians. [The Indians] are very conservative here. [They] somehow feel that they are better than [those] in India or Singapore... It is like 10, 15 years ago... They still believe in arranged marriages. The funny thing is, it is not about arranged marriages between two people living in the same city, like someone in London who is doing well or who would be able to take care of their kid. They would educate the child up till university and when it is time to get married, they would look for a husband from India and the guy probably doesn't speak English. So she ends up looking after him. He won't be able to find a proper job [whereas] she is educated. To me that is very backward ... If you think about it, [in Singapore] we have integrated the culture so much so that [...] sometimes if I go to a wedding I [give] an *angpow*[11]... You go to [a food centre] and order *mee goreng* [an Indian noodle dish]. You don't even think that it is Indian. You just think of it as *mee goreng* and Singaporean. We have a better idea of different cultures. I know why you give oranges during Chinese New Year and you know something about Indian culture.... We have a good understanding, maybe not completely but at least enough to know why you do certain things. Over here they can be quite naïve.

Dina's anecdote underlines the intersecting politics of ethnicity and nationality. Here, Dina claims that she identifies better culturally with other Singaporeans even if they are from another ethnic group, rather than with a non-Singaporean Indian whom she might meet in London. She explains that the cultural practices of the British Indian community have made limited historical progress compared to the Indians who had migrated to Singapore. Significantly, she construes the lingering cultural practice of arranged marriages (with an Indian from India) amongst the Indian community n Britain as 'conservative' and 'backward', likening it to the Indian-Singaporean community in the past. The British Indian community is thus portrayed as an unchanging and closed cultural entity. In contrast, cultural integration in Singapore is portrayed as progressive. Dina's example shows that, despite shared phenotype, difference is constituted through intersecting cultural inscriptions of 'nationalised' bodies in social environments. The configuration of difference in these examples reveals 'the racialised body as a highly dubious zone upon which to anchor difference and a treacherously slippery surface on which to sustain race meaning' (Nayak 2006: 423).

The above examples illustrate that boundary-making is a shifting process that adjusts to the dynamics of social interactions, such as depending on the ethnicity/ 'race' or nationality that one meets. By identifying the outsider, one delineates notions of self and defines national identity as well. These are in fact ways of 'making' the nation even whilst such Singaporean transmigrants are physically absent from the territorial confines of the nation-state. Yet, my study also reveals that we should not assume that shared national identification arising out of a common background amongst Singaporean transmigrants equates to a strong sense of national identity. Rather, as I have argued elsewhere, Singaporean transmigrants in London tend to self-consciously question the idea of a 'Singaporean identity' (Ho 2009). The multiculturalism project in Singapore is also contested; several non-Chinese respondents, including Dina, spoke of instances in which they had experienced or been made aware of racial discrimination in Singapore (also see Ye and Kelly, this issue). Such cleavages in Singaporean society are prone to manifest extraterritorially when racialised divisions emerge more acutely amongst the overseas Singaporean community. What I wish to emphasise here, though, is less the way that my respondents laid claim to particular identifications, but more the dance of identities they perform as they pick their choice of cultural identification according to the occasion.

This discussion also highlights the limitations of framing the barriers to cosmopolitanism only through the host/stranger binary often brought up in debates about relationality and responsibility (Coney 2002; Dikec 2002; Massey 2004). Gradations of 'hosts' and 'strangers' are made through migration flows and processes. The British South Asians were earlier migrants themselves but have become legal bearers of British citizenship now, some even spanning a few generations. To what extent are they 'hosts' in British society or are they still considered 'strangers'? The cultural norms that Singaporean transmigrants stress they have to acquire to be accepted in their workplaces are premised on stereotypes of white-British culture/civilisation as the local/host society. The cultural norms of the naturalised British South Asian community are instead depicted as still foreign, less progressive and thus unacceptable to the 'stranger'. Just as the idea of the 'local' needs to be interrogated (Massey 1993), so do our perceptions of the 'host' society. These considerations open up further questions of whose responsibility it is to extend an attitude of openness towards cultural difference—only the host (if so, which host?) or also the migrant-as-stranger?

## Conclusion

In this discussion, I have teased out the complex ways in which 'difference' is encountered and negotiated through 'co-presence, interaction, interlocking understandings and practices, often within radically asymmetrical relations of power' (Yeoh and Willis 2005: 271). The Singaporean case study is unique in some aspects because of the legacy of colonialism that privileges 'white' cultures and the postcolonial project of building a nation out of migrants from China, India and other parts of the world, together with the indigenous Malays. However, the aim of my discussion is to draw attention to the shifting boundaries of identity-making and the strategic interactions arising from relational situations. I further argue that migrants mix-and-match cultures and imitate cultural norms selectively in order to sometimes fit in and, at other times, to differentiate themselves. At times they may use phenotype and simplified cultural codes presuming historical, cultural and moral similarities amongst diverse cultural groupings and mobilise these codes to explain difference. However, as this paper demonstrates, the meanings behind the labels are slippery and shift according to the context. By constructing sameness and difference, migrants inhabit a 'broad field of racialised meanings' (Nagel 2001: 389) that needs to be unpacked instead of taken for granted.

These politicised meanings of racial difference should merit a deeper reflection of claims to cosmopolitanism. The cosmopolitan capital demonstrated by the Singaporean transmigrants in this study is often premised upon essentialising racial/cultural/civilisational constructs framed around the superiority (or inferiority) of some cultures over others. They may be asserting their difference and negotiating it in a productive and affirmative way *for themselves* (Coney 2002) but what about *for the 'Other'*? These framings of cultural hegemony are antithetical to the ethos of a cosmopolitan project in which difference should be received with mutual acceptance (Dikec 2002) and respect for one another's differences. The onus for this attitude of hospitality should not only be on the receiving society; rather it is also the responsibility of migrants to extend such an attitude towards the multiple 'hosts' represented in the receiving society. The empirical findings presented here on intersecting racial and nationality dynamics further demonstrate the limitations of using 'race' as the primary organising social category to advance cosmopolitanism. Saldanha's (2006) vision of cosmopolitanism starts from the proliferation of 'race' in celebration of racial differences. However, a cosmopolitan project is one that needs to take into account the multiple relationships between intersecting dimensions of identity (McDowell 2008), such as 'race' and nationality—as discussed in this paper—and equally gender, sexuality, class and other social axes.

## Acknowledgements

I am grateful to Katie Willis for reading an earlier version of this paper, and to Shirlena Huang and Brenda Yeoh for their editorial advice.

## Notes

[1] I use the term 'transmigrants' to describe my Singaporean respondents and capture the ways in which their 'identities and practices are configured by hegemonic social categories (such as 'race' and ethnicity) that are deeply embedded in the nation-building processes of two or more nation-states' (Basch *et al.* 1994: 34).

[2] The names of my respondents have been changed to ensure their anonymity.

[3] The Commission for Racial Equality in Britain commissioned a study in 2005 to uncover what is signified as 'Britishness' to British citizens from various ethnic backgrounds. The study found that a portion of the focus-group participants still equated 'Britishness' with an exclusively 'white English' society.

[4]  Some of these norms and habits are explained by the social anthropologist Kate Fox (2004).
[5]  *Angmoh* is an old Chinese-dialect expression that can be literally translated as 'red hair' and was originally used to describe Caucasians, who have a different phenotype from the early Chinese migrants in Singapore. Nonetheless, the term is still used in Singaporean parlance today.
[6]  Such racialised representations are likely to have their roots in Singapore's colonial history and continue to be sustained in popular parlance today despite the existence of 'white' populations beyond the Western hemisphere.
[7]  This Singaporean slang is used to refer to Western-influenced speech, behaviour or mindsets. The phrase literally translates into 'consume potatoes' which, in Singapore, is popularly believed to be the staple diet of Caucasians!
[8]  The 'foreign talent' policy refers to the initiatives taken by the Singaporean government to attract highly skilled non-Singaporeans to move to and work in Singapore in order to fill labour shortfalls and meet population needs. This policy is widely contested by Singaporeans, who argue against the preferential treatment accorded to non-Singaporeans by the government and employers alike (see Ho 2006).
[9]  The immutability of 'Asian' values as the product of a distinct cultural civilisation has been disputed by scholars such as Robison (1996) and Kessler (1999). Instead, they point to the political nature of this ideology, which is utilised by bureaucrats, the political elite and corporate interests to advance statist and economic goals.
[10]  The second-language policy in Singapore has been criticised for merging the diverse vernacular languages spoken by the different dialect groups represented in Singapore under the Mandarin (Chinese), Tamil (Indian) and *Bahasa Melayu* (Malay) languages only.
[11]  It is customary among the Chinese in Singapore to give a red envelope [*ang pow*] with some money inside to signify good wishes during the Chinese New Year and other auspicious occasions such as weddings.

## References

Basch, L., Glick Schiller, N. and Szanton Blanc, C. (1994) *Nations Unbound: Transnational Projects, Postcolonial Predicaments, and Deterritorialised Nation-States*. London and New York: Gordon and Breach.

Beaverstock, J.V. (2002) 'Transnational elites in global cities: British expatriates in Singapore's financial district', *Geoforum*, 33(4): 525–38.

Beaverstock, J.V. (2005) 'Transnational elites in the city: British highly skilled inter-company transferees in New York City's financial district', *Journal of Ethnic and Migration Studies*, 31(2): 245–68.

Cheah, P. (2006) 'Cosmopolitanism', *Theory, Culture and Society*, 23(2–3): 486–96.

Commission for Racial Equality (2005) 'Citizenship and belonging: what is Britishness?'. Online at: http://www.cre.gov.uk/research/britishness.html, last accessed 5 November 2006.

Coney, V.A. (2002) 'Chasmopolis', *Theory, Culture & Society*, 19(1–2): 127–38.

Conradson, D. and Latham, A. (2005a) 'Transnational urbanism: attending to everyday practices and mobilities', *Journal of Ethnic and Migration Studies*, 31(2): 227–33.

Conradson, D. and Latham, A. (2005b) 'Friendship, networks and transnationality in a world city: Antipodean transmigrants in London', *Journal of Ethnic and Migration Studies*, 31(2): 287–305.

Conradson, D. and Latham, A. (2007) 'The affective possibilities of London: Antipodean transnationals and the overseas experience', *Mobilities*, 2(2): 231–54.

Dikec, M. (2002) 'Pera peras poros: longings for spaces of hospitality', *Theory, Culture & Society*, 19(1–2): 227–47.
Dyck, I. (2005) 'Feminist geography, the "everyday", and local–global relations: hidden places of meaning', *The Canadian Geographer*, 49(3): 233–43.
Ehrkamp, P. (2006) '"We Turks are no Germans": assimilation discourses and the dialectical construction of identities in Germany', *Environment and Planning A*, 38(9): 1673–92.
Featherstone, M. (1993) 'Global and local cultures', in Bird, J., Curtis, B., Putnam, T., Robertson, G. and Tickner, L. (eds) *Mapping the Futures*. London and New York: Routledge, 169–87.
Fox, K. (2004) *Watching the English: The Hidden Rules of English Behaviour*. London: Hodder and Stoughton.
Gilroy, P. (2000) *Against Race: Imagining Political Culture Beyond the Colour Line*. Cambridge, MA: Harvard University Press.
Ho, E.L.E. (2006) 'Negotiating belonging and perceptions of citizenship in a transnational world: Singapore, a cosmopolis', *Social and Cultural Geography*, 7(3): 385–401.
Ho, E.L.E. (2008) '"Flexible citizenship" or familial ties that bind? Singaporean transmigrants in London', *International Migration*, 46(4): 146–75.
Ho, E.L.E. (2009) 'Constituting citizenship through the emotions: Singaporean transmigrants in London', *Annals of the Association of American Geographers*, 99(4): 788–804.
Jackson, P. and Penrose, J. (1993) 'Placing "race" and place', in Jackson, P. and Penrose, J. (eds) *Constructions of Race, Place and Nation*. London: UCL Press, 1–26.
Kennedy, P. (2004) 'Making global society: friendship networks among transnational professionals in the building design industry', *Global Networks*, 4(2): 157–79.
Kessler, C.S. (1999) 'The abdication of the intellectuals: sociology, anthropology and the Asian values debate—or, what everybody needed to know about "Asian values" that social scientists failed to point out', *SOJOURN, Journal of Social Issues in Southeast Asia*, 14(2): 295–312.
Kong, L. (1999) 'Globalisation, transmigration and the renegotiation of ethnic identity', in Olds, K., Dickens, P., Kelly, P.F., Kong, L. and Yeung, H.W.C. (eds) *Globalisation and the Asia Pacific: Contested Territories*. London and New York: Routledge, 219–37.
Ley, D. (2004) 'Transnational spaces and everyday lives', *Transactions of the Institute of British Geographers*, 29(2): 151–64.
Massey, D. (1993) 'Power-geometry and progressive sense of place', in Bird, J., Curtis, B., Putnam, T., Robertson, G. and Tickner, L. (eds) *Mapping the Futures*. London and New York: Routledge, 59–67.
Massey, D. (2004) 'Geographies of responsibility', *Geografiska Annaler*, 86(B): 5–18.
Massey, D. (2005) *For Space*. London: Sage.
McDowell, L. (2008) 'Thinking through work: complex inequalities, constructions of difference and transnational migrants', *Progress in Human Geography*, 32(4): 491–507.
Mitchell, K. (1997) 'Transnational subjects: constituting the cultural citizen in the era of Pacific Rim capital', in Ong, A. and Nonini, D. (eds) *Ungrounded Empires: The Cultural Politics of Modern Chinese Transnationalism*. New York and London: Routledge, 228–56.
Nagel, C. (2001) 'Hidden minorities and the politics of "race": the case of British Arab activists in London', *Journal of Ethnic and Migration Studies*, 27(3): 381–400.
Nagel, C. (2005) 'Skilled migration in global cities from "Other" perspectives: British Arabs, identity politics, and local embeddedness', *Geoforum*, 36(2): 197–210.
Nava, M. (2007) *Visceral Cosmopolitanism: Gender, Culture and the Normalisation of Difference*. London: Berg.
Nayak, A. (2006) 'After race: ethnography, race and post-race theory', *Ethnic and Racial Studies*, 29(3): 411–30.
Purkayastha, B. (2005) 'Skilled migration and cumulative disadvantage: the case of highly qualified Asian Indian immigrant women in the US', *Geoforum*, 36(2): 181–96.

Robison, R. (1996) 'The politics of "Asian values"', *Pacific Review*, 9(2): 309–27.
Sachar, A. (2006) *The Race for Talent: Highly Skilled Migrants and Competitive Immigration Regimes*. Toronto: University of Toronto, Legal Studies Research Paper No. 883739. Online at: http://ssrn.com/abstract=883739, last accessed 20 December 2010.
Saldanha, A. (2006) 'Reontologising race: the machinic geography of phenotype', *Environment and Planning D: Society and Space*, 24(1): 9–24.
Sklair, L. (2001) *The Transnational Capitalist Class*. Oxford: Blackwell.
Smith, M.P. (2005) 'Transnational urbanism revisited', *Journal of Ethnic and Migration Studies*, 31(2): 235–44.
Tate Modern (2007) *Global Cities*, 20 June–27 August.
Thomas, D.C., Lazarova, M.B. and Inkson, K. (2005) 'Global careers: new phenomenon or new perspectives?', *Journal of World Business*, 40(4): 340–7.
Ware, V. and Back, L. (2002) *Out of Whiteness: Colour, Politics and Culture*. Chicago: University of Chicago Press.
Wimmer, A. (2007) *How (Not) to Think about Ethnicity in Immigrant Societies: A Boundary-Making Perspective*. Oxford: University of Oxford, COMPAS Working Paper No. 44. Online at: http://www.compas.ox.ac.uk/publications/working_papers.shtml, last accessed 14 August 2007.
Yeoh, B.S.A. (2006) 'Bifurcated labour: the unequal incorporation of transmigrants in Singapore', *Tijdschrift voor Economische en Sociale Geografie*, 97(1): 26–37.
Yeoh, B.S.A. and Willis, K. (2005) 'Singaporean and British transmigrants in China and the cultural politics of "contact zones"', *Journal of Ethnic and Migration Studies*, 31(2): 269–85.

# Singaporean and British Transmigrants in China and the Cultural Politics of 'Contact Zones'

Brenda S. A. Yeoh and Katie Willis

*The international migration of professional workers has increased in scope over the past 20 years as skilled workers are needed when companies' activities cross national borders. While this trend has been recognised from an economic perspective, much less has been researched from a social and cultural angle. Using case studies of British and Singaporean migration to China, this paper employs a comparative frame to examine the effect of cultural differences—both in terms of business culture as well as social norms regarding ethnicity and gender—on the dynamics of the 'contact zones' emerging in various cities in China, including the cosmopolitan cities of Shanghai and Hong Kong, the Chinese capital city of Beijing, as well as the industrial townships of Suzhou, Wuxi and Guangzhou. As sites which invoke the spatial and temporal copresence of subjects previously separated by geographic and historical disjunctures, and whose trajectories now intersect, 'contact zones' (as defined by Mary Pratt in the context of colonial encounters) are frontiers where 'difference' is constantly encountered and negotiated. Given very different ethno-historical linkages traced by Singaporeans and Britons to China and as a result a divergence of cultural imaginings about 'China', it is not unexpected that the two groups of transmigrants enact different ways of encountering life in China. The paper explores the differential politics of the Singaporean and British presences in China around three stereotypical images of the foreigner in China—the culturalist, the colonialist and the imperialist.*

# THE CULTURAL POLITICS OF TALENT MIGRATION IN EAST ASIA

## Introduction

Much is increasingly being written about the global city as a product of a high density of 'new' social and cultural transnational practices, relations, networks and sensibilities. Transnational practices and networks constitute a powerful force reshaping not only the physical but also the social and cultural aspects of cities in these times.[1] Constantly (re)shaped by transnational flows, metropolitan cultures open up (and shut down) different bases for infinitely hybridised forms of identifications and mobilisations. The cosmopolitan urban turf becomes a locality and life-space marked out by the stakes of a variety of radical grassroots movements, social alliances, informal networks, immigrant and ethnic 'others', as well as other culturally inscribed bodies which selectively appropriate both local and global social images and imaginaries in their engagement with identity politics and active struggle over resources (Berner and Korff 1995; Law 1997; Sassen 1996; Schmidt 1998; Smith 1995, 1998).

Within this literature, and in these spatially fluid times, the hyper-mobility of the 'transnational capitalist class' (Sklair 1998)—professional and managerial elites moving from one globalising city to another—constitutes an important strand. Such work (Beaverstock 2002; Beaverstock and Smith 1996; Findlay et al. 1996) details the construction of a single global labour market for high-waged professional and managerial workers in global cities and, in turn, the significance of the agglomeration of skilled international migrants in extending the reach of globalising cities. The emphasis on the hyper-mobility of the transnational subjects constituting this elite circuit—forever on-the-move, forever in transit, forever unmoored, forever part of the 'space of flows' (Castells 1996)—however, has tended to have unintended effects. First, the transnational subjects within these elite circuits tend to be treated as highly mobile individual careerists circulating in an intensely fluid world of inter- and intra-firm transfers and career mobility and not as embodied bearers of culture, ethnicity, class or gender (Yeoh and Willis 1999, 2004). Second, there is a tendency to ignore their 'co-presence', with others, 'in place'. As perpetually 'rootless merchant sojourners' (Cheah 2001), 'cosmopolitans' who are 'basically indifferent to where they live', or 'cosmopolites' who are 'habitants of a vast universe' (Robbins 1998), they transcend processes of 'transculturation' in specific places and play out their politics of identity and belonging on a different stage from that of the individual city in which they are, even if only for the moment, located.[2]

We argue here that transnational elites belong as much to the 'space of place' as to the 'space of flows'. As Harvey (2000: 554, 559) argues in his exploration of the dialectic between 'universal' and 'rooted' cosmopolitanisms, any meaningful cosmopolitanism has to confront, and defeat, the real geography of the place inhabited, for 'cosmopolitanism ... is empty without its cosmos'. Despite their fluidity and transience, the presence of cosmopolitan elites does generate a multiplicity of 'contact zones' within the globalising city; and because of the ephemeral and unconsolidated nature of their 'presence' and the strong sense of connectivities with 'elsewhere', these contact zones are differently inflected compared to the more permanent, stable, often historically rooted, presences forged by longer-term migrants, or even by more recent, lower-skilled migrants who arrive in much larger numbers and therefore constitute a stronger bodily presence.[3] For one, these contact zones seldom occur in the sphere of urban politics. As Sennett (2001) notes, the 'new global elite ... avoids the urban political realm. It wants to operate in the city but not rule it; it composes a regime of power without responsibility'. While this may be so, we suggest that the embodied presence of cosmopolitan elites is both catalyst and medium of cultural politics of the everyday sort.

We draw on Mary Louise Pratt's (1992: 7) definition of a 'contact zone' (situated in the context of colonial encounters in her work) as 'an attempt to invoke the spatial and temporal copresence of subjects previously separated by geographic and historical disjunctures, and whose trajectories now intersect'. A 'contact' perspective 'emphasises how subjects are constituted in and by their relations to each other. ... not in terms of separateness or apartheid, but in terms of copresence, interaction, interlocking understandings and practices, often within radically asymmetrical relations of power'. We take 'contact zones' to denote both a sense of embodied presence within geographical space as well as a social and cultural metaphor. The concept insists on analysis of everyday encounters and everyday experiences of sameness and difference and provides a 'grounded epistemic optic' (Smith 2001: 98) to view globalisation and transnationalism, one which is particularly useful in allowing us to adjust the focal length to zoom in on relations and transactions across boundaries.

In this paper, we are interested in exploring the contact zones Singaporean and British skilled transmigrants construct in engaging China. Given very different ethno-historical linkages traced by Singaporeans and Britons in China, and as a result a divergence of cultural imaginings about 'China', it is not unexpected that the two groups of transmigrants enact different ways of encountering life in China and negotiating the frontiers of difference.

## Singaporean and British Transmigrants

The movement of Singaporean transmigrants to China gathered momentum only in recent years, gaining visibility with the Singapore government's Regionalisation 2000 programme, a reconfiguring of Singapore as a major engine of foreign direct investments into the rest of Asia.[4] Singaporeans are encouraged to develop an entrepreneurial spirit and 'go regional'; to regard, in the Prime Minister's words, 'all countries and cities ... within 7 hours of flying time from Singapore as our hinterland' (Goh 2001). Both China and India fall within this hinterland.

In many ways, Singaporean migration to China is a form of 'return migration' with an ironic sense of historical resonance when read in the context of Singapore's history as the product of overlapping diasporas. In the nineteenth and early twentieth centuries, male Chinese migrants (known as *huaqiao*) migrated to the *nanyang* ('south seas'), setting up businesses in Singapore.[5] 'Returning' to China to work or do business sometimes draws on these historical connections and diasporic 'ethnic' ties, as well as invokes practical advantages in the form of the ability to speak Mandarin. Currently, there are more than 5,000 Singaporeans living and working throughout China (excluding Hong Kong where there are another 10,000 Singaporeans). The largest numbers are in Shanghai, followed by Beijing. There are 14 Singapore Clubs dotted around the Chinese cities, largely where there is a critical mass of Singaporeans, set up as part of the state's programme to 'stay connected with Singaporeans abroad by supporting activities which help create a sense of the Singapore identity as well as foster a strong sense of kinship between overseas Singaporeans and Singapore'.[6] Most Singaporeans in China work in the diplomatic service, the manufacturing or real-estate sectors, producer and financial services and government-related infrastructural projects. Singaporean Chinese form the overwhelming majority of Singaporeans in China (all our interviewees were ethnically Chinese).

The British presence in China is coloured by their long-held position as colonial masters of Hong Kong,[7] a position only relinquished in the 1997 'handover'. In our five study areas (Beijing, Guangzhou, Hong Kong, Shanghai and Suzhou/Wuxi), we estimate that there are over 26,000 Britons, including about 16,000 in Hong Kong. Most work in the diplomatic service, the manufacturing sector, and producer and financial services. The bulk of British nationals in China are white, although our interviews did include a very small sample of British-born Chinese.

The paper is based primarily on in-depth interviews with 120 Britons and 160 Singaporeans, the bulk of whom are economic migrants or accompanying spouses, in the five study areas in China (about 12 per cent of the sample are non-migrants or stay-behind spouses). The bulk of the interviewees were highly educated and either held professional or managerial jobs, or were business entrepreneurs. In this sense, our interviewees belonged to the 'elite' strata of society, with two sorts of exceptions. First, while most Singaporean 'accompanying wives' had formerly worked as professionals in Singapore, a small number were housewives, clerical and sales workers who were in China because they were following husbands who had elite jobs. Second, some of the British interviewees first came to China for voluntary work, job attachments or travel before taking on professional or managerial jobs in China. Information about the daily lives of British and Singaporean expatriates was also garnered through participation in social functions such as the Guangzhou 'Hash',[8] Singapore Club and British Chamber social events, as well as informal occasions such as shopping trips and eating out.

## Constructing the 'Contact Zone'

In explaining the different ways expatriates could interact with and experience Chinese society, Nicholas[9] (a British engineer in his 50s) drew on his experiences of 11 international assignments in different parts of the world throughout his 30-year career. He came up with a typology of 'three broad ranges of expatriates', whom he termed the 'culturalists', the 'colonialists' and the 'imperialists'.

> Nicholas: If you are a culturalist it can be a very, very nice thing to do [integrating into Chinese society]. If you are an imperialist, you beware. If you are a colonialist, you go away not having felt the difference!
>
> Katie: So what would you say were the differences between the imperialists and the colonialists?
>
> Nicholas: Well, the imperialists are the ones that want to impose their will on all of us, and have an arrogant style, ... it's the one thing that you must avoid at all costs. To patiently listen, to learn and to understand is probably the first step in integration in China, of course not only from a personal point of view, but also from a professional point of view, it's much appreciated. So imperialists find that pretty difficult to do, because they keep bouncing against a brick wall. Um, I think, it's, if I take a general cross-section of people, if you're young you're adaptable, and you have that tendency to listen, and you probably wouldn't fit into this category. If you're older ... and slightly arrogant, you fit into the imperialist category, especially when you get to my age, over 50, that age you're pretty difficult, and of course it depends on whether you've had any expatriate postings or not, so you know, these are all things to be aware of when you're sending people abroad on expatriate assignments. If you're a colonialist you come in and out without having felt a difference because you tend to build a colonial barrier around yourself.

While other British interviewees also draw in varying degrees from the 'culturalist-colonialist-imperialist' terminology (some matter-of-factly and others with a sense of self-consciousness) in referring to themselves or their compatriots in China, Singaporean interviewees almost never use these terms, preferring to define their relationship with China primarily in terms of career, business and economic motivations, or secondarily in terms of heritage and a 'return to roots'. The language of the contact zone, as will be subsequently clarified, is largely shaped by the larger frames of the colonial past as well as the post-colonial present, and, in the case of Singaporeans, by the ideology of entrepreneurship propelled by the state. In the following discussion, we have chosen to use our interviewees' terms to frame the arguments because these terms not only connect with the wider scholarly literature on 'culture-contact' (King 1976), 'transculturation' (Pratt 1992) and 'Eurocentric diffusionism' (Blaut 1993) but, more importantly, provide us with vocabulary discerned directly from the field to help us make sense of nuances in the way China is perceived.

*Transnational Elites as Culturalists?*

Among British expatriates, the initial encounter with China was often portrayed as a distinctly new experience in a foreign territory. Views range from those who found the 'cultural' challenge fascinating and therefore appealing (Nicholas) to those who saw China as a foreign place to get away from all that was familiar (Adele):

> I'd been in Indonesia already for a total of eight years, and I really liked working in the East, and I decided that China was just that extra bit challenging, that's why I decided to come.... My first visit to China was in 1996, and I was fascinated by the place, and I decided, I would volunteer, rather than be asked.... China is a difficult place to settle down, from a cultural point of view [but] ... China has that challenge which appeals to me (Nicholas).
>
> I came to China the first time in 1990 with a charity organisation which sends people before university out to different countries to do charity work.... I was in China for six months, and the person that I was with, she had parents in India, and so at the end of our term in China, I went to India for a month and I really liked India as well, but when I got back to China, I definitely wanted to study Chinese, I'm not sure what it was but I think that India was so, the links were much closer, and China was much further away, that most people you meet here were running away from something, or really odd, so I guess myself included! (Adele, human resource manager in her late 20s living with her Chinese boyfriend with whom she has a six-month-old son).

Whether as a cultural 'challenge' which is intrinsically attractive (as in Nicholas' case), or as a social 'refuge' to get away from negative experiences at home (Adele was essentially running away from the familiar), this sense of China being a 'different cultural experience' was absent from Singaporean constructions of encountering China. This is partly reflected in the different routes taken by the two nationality groups in gaining expatriate status in China. Among the Britons, while many were on company postings to China, a significant number also arrived in one of the Chinese cities having travelled, often after university, and had stayed on. While they had worked in 'informal' occupations for a while, they had made the most of being 'on the doorstep' and had found jobs in a range of professional settings. Among Singaporeans, no interviewee had found their current jobs through arriving in China and working in bars or staying in China having found their way there while backpacking. This is not surprising given that 'aimless wandering' is discouraged in Singapore's goal-oriented society.

Among Singaporean Chinese, the notion of encountering China as a cultural, 'return-to-roots' experience was for some an appealing one which coloured their motivation to accept a China posting. At the start, many came to China for the first time with an idealised image of the country being the fount of Chinese culture, a view of China as an ancestral homeland and with subliminal ties. Venturing into China even if it is mainly for business and work purposes is couched in terms of the privilege of 'return', a journey 'home', a re-connection to 'motherland', a means of rejuvenating 'lost' or 'suppressed' Chineseness, and a re-discovery of roots. Many framed their move to China in the language of 'return', even though the basic motivation of relocating in China had little to do with such rhetoric:

> I went to China with three objectives in mind. One, to share my expertise, so called, with the people there. Second is to see China. China was not a place I have toured before. And third, to learn to be more independent.... See how well I can survive. ... I've heard so much about China, the people, the culture, the language, they are my roots and I was curious (Priscilla, administrator in a multi-national corporation in Beijing who is single and in her early 30s).

> It has been my interest all this while to come over to China and work here and experience what life in China is all about. ... It's family background. We have always been very traditional in a way. Since young, I have been inculcated with the love for motherland. I mean not so much that I wanted to be a communist, but it's the love for Chinese history, Chinese culture and all its practices. I was thinking that maybe one day I'll go back and do something great for my so-called motherland. Of course it is not really my motherland, as I am Singaporean. But there is always this subliminal thinking all this while (Kian Min, in his mid-30s, runs his own business as a property developer in Suzhou).

However, the vision of China being the 'motherland' or 'heartland' of Chinese culture and values was very quickly discarded on encountering the reality of China today.

> I read lots of Chinese history—5,000 years of history, and came prepared to learn ... but it was totally the other way round. You come here to be disappointed. Things happen the other way round. They are rich in culture, but the behaviour of the people [leaves much to be desired] (Arnold, in his mid-30s and works for a Singapore government-linked company in Suzhou).

The rhetoric of return and the rediscovery of Chineseness soon give way to the politics of difference as the Singaporean identity is distanced from 'PRC Chineseness'. Instead, PRC-Chinese is seen as leached of cultural and moral values. It is the insanitary and degenerate 'other' which helps to define 'self' by positing and mirroring what could have been:

> The Singaporean Chinese is very different from the Chinese Chinese. We keep telling ourselves not to be deceived by skin colour (Hui Boon, in her late 20s, former teacher in Singapore who gave up her job to accompany her husband to Beijing).

> Lucky that our ancestors left the place, or we'd be one of them! (Ellen, in her 30s, former researcher presently accompanying her husband Arnold in Suzhou).

Here, constructing the identity of 'self' and 'other' is operating at a scale where the distance between cultures is narrowed by many similarities of origin and history.

*Transnational Elites as Colonialists?*

While the sun has definitely set on the British Empire, albeit only recently in the case of Hong Kong, certain old colonial practices such as the Hash and the exclusivity of social life centred on clubs and pubs have a continued, if modified, presence for

British expatriates in China. And while it may be said that Singaporean expatriates are free of such historical baggage (and in fact are themselves post-colonial subjects, having experienced, and then detached themselves from, British colonial rule, a period which constituted close to 150 years of Singapore history), social exclusivity is also present, if not more pronounced in some ways.

Among British interviewees, even pre-handover Hong Kong was not perceived as much of a British colonial city; instead, a constant refrain is its 'Chineseness':

> There's so few colonial buildings left or elements of colonialism here, I think. And even less so in the four years I've been here. I think it's very, very Chinese. You walk around any area of town and you're surrounded by Chinese people, Chinese architecture, Chinese shops, language (Eleanor, single, in her 20s).

While there are instances of socialising across the Chinese–Western divide under certain circumstances,[10] this was generally limited:

> The Chinese and Western groups keep very separate. I don't think it's a deliberate, 'I don't want to socialise with them.' But it's a very, very different way of behaving ... and way of socialising. I mean, going out to bars, well, we go out to bars, party and get very drunk. The Chinese will go out and sing karaoke and have one beer. ... I have Chinese friends here but, and I invite them out on various occasions but they don't come. They're either intimidated by *guilos* [literally 'white devils'] or it's just not their thing. I personally think the Brits are very separate, lifestyles as well as culture. Which is a shame in a way, there's probably a hell of a lot to learn from them (Eleanor).

While there are fewer barriers in the form of language and, superficially, 'culture', Singaporeans in China also maintain generally separate social lives beyond the workplace. For both groups of expatriates, especially those working for multinational corporations, embassies or government-linked institutions, residences are concentrated in particular areas, either because of Chinese regulations regarding housing for foreigners (in mainland China), or because of residential preferences (in Hong Kong). Among full-time housewives in both nationality groups, contact with the local Chinese was particularly limited as their social worlds hardly went beyond the expatriate condominium in which they lived, and the international schools to which their children went. Forays into the city itself were traversed in the comfort and isolation of their husbands' chauffeur-driven cars, while social 'conversations' were transacted over transnational space, through phone calls and emails to family and friends back 'home'. Iris (Singaporean, former air stewardess with Singapore Airlines), who had married a Hong Konger involved in the hotel business, represented one extreme of the socially-stranded trailing spouse: all her time was spent in her room watching DVDs while waiting for her husband to come home to have meals with her (cf. Waters 2002). With time, most of these 'expatriate wives' who were not engaged in paid employment developed social ties with other non-local women, either through more formal networks such as the Guangzhou Women's International Committee, Brits Abroad in Shanghai, or the Singapore Club, or more informally through their children's schools or contacting friends from 'home' also living in the same city. While the networks of British women tended to be more international (in a 'Western' sense) in scope, Singaporean women's social circles tended to be more exclusively confined to their 'own kind'.

Among Singaporeans, the negotiation of difference between 'self' and the 'other' (the local Chinese) was played out using a much finer mesh, hence requiring subtle navigation across the space of difference. Social practices in the stream of everyday life became the very means by which self–other identities are refined in the absence of visible and supposedly immutable signs of difference such as 'race' or 'skin colour'.[11] Petty issues from unacceptable social and personal habits to the lack of 'modern' civilities were elevated to the position of cultural and moral markers to bring the difference between the PRC-Chinese and the Singaporean-Chinese into sharp focus:

> And the culture shock at first was quite (tremendous) for we thought we were all Chinese, but their attitude towards life, their attitude towards hygiene, their mannerisms are all totally different from us as Chinese. I quote one example. I brought my son out for shopping in a complex somewhere they call their 'Orchard Road' (the name of Singapore's elite shopping thoroughfare). I was pregnant, so my son held the door open for me. Instead of me easing my way out, the Chinese—young, old, middle-aged—they all just rushed out through the door and squeezed pass me. They just carried on as if he (her son) wasn't there. And they didn't even look back or say thank you. My son told me, 'Mummy, I hate the Chinese'. I said, 'Don't say that, you are Chinese'. He said, 'No, I'm Singaporean. I can't stand them' (Pat, 40s, who gave up catering business in Singapore to accompany her husband to Beijing).

Few see this cultural and moral 'degeneracy' as endemic or innate (impossible, since the Singaporean Chinese also came from the same 'stock', but grafted on a different tree). Hence, unlike colonial discourses of dominance which drew on transhistorical, essentialised notions of difference between coloniser and the colonised, the genealogy of difference is traced back to the Cultural Revolution as the watershed distinguishing the two kinds of Chinese:

> The Cultural Revolution has done much harm to the country [China]. You can actually see it. Basically the country has lost its own character, lost its own culture, it doesn't have a soul. Many customs we keep so steadfastly in Southeast Asia are not practised here. Religion, folklore, for example. Over here, it's a society without a backbone.... For example, the sense of shame and the sense of loyalty formulated in Confucian thinking is not strongly rooted here. Everyone is very selfish. For example, *Qu Yuan* [a Chinese hero] who we read about, seldom do you see people acting [in his mould]. You sense it more in Singapore—people have that sense of shame, you do something bad you lose face for the whole family clan. Over here, they get away with murder. Die, die, they don't care about face. ... I feel it very strongly here because we observe [these traditions] so strictly in Singapore (Kian Min).

Primarily because there was no need to engage in the finely-tuned politics of difference which seemed to trouble Singaporean Chinese who had to stress difference despite shared ancestry, British expatriates tended to find the terrain of difference less difficult to negotiate. Difference itself served to amplify both self-identity and a sense of community among British expatriates:

> I'm very British, your sense of Britishness, or Englishness, goes up remarkably as soon as you're away, suddenly you're very patriotic. What a bunch of hypocrites, what a bunch of hypocrites! I think ... it is because suddenly you're a minority, I'm an ethnic minority, and I'm white, ... therefore your identity becomes that much more important, because you're surrounded by 1.3 billion Chinese, suddenly you stand out a little bit, and suddenly who you are and what you are becomes a little bit more important to you as a person, ... expatriates are just so much closer I find, very strong community spirit (Adrian, mid-30s, working in the hotel industry in Beijing).

While there were similar complaints about the lack of civility among local Chinese on the streets, they were generally accepted as part and parcel of living in a foreign place where 'they do things differently'. 'Difference' was to be expected, and remained an immutable barrier, and in fact offered new opportunities for learning something new, without obfuscating the line between 'self' and 'other'. For example, a number of British expatriates were attempting to 'pick up' Mandarin as a means of learning more about Chinese culture and its people, and appeared not uncomfortable with the lack of mastery of this difficult language:

> Eleanor: I speak a bit of Chinese as well though. ... It's something I picked up, I never made a concerted effort to learn. I should do. But again that comes back to the fact that I never planned to stay here.
>
> Katie: Yeah, and people are quite happy if you're sort of like sitting there trying to talk Chinese, people are quite willing to listen?
>
> Eleanor: They are but they answer back in English and they laugh at me. The Chinese find it hilarious me speaking the language. They think it's absolutely bizarre. But they love it at the same time. They love it, they laugh at you and you know, goad you along, ask you different and new things. And that was a real breakdown of a barrier for me. When I first got here I found it incredibly hard. If I was asking directions from somewhere to a local Chinese person, they would just wave you away, 'cos they thought they couldn't understand you. Whereas if you ask for directions for something in English and you add a Chinese question at the end, they'll help you out, incredible difference!

In contradistinction, for Singaporean Chinese, the facility with Mandarin both narrowed the gap between 'us' and 'them', and at the same time became an important part of the contested terrain of identity politics. For those Singaporeans who were expected to speak Mandarin but spoke it poorly, Mandarin became a sign of racial and national shame.[12]

### Transnational Elites as Imperialists?

Whether born of post-imperial sensibilities, post-colonial guilt or a more cosmopolitan outlook, most British expatriates who had arrived in China in more recent times avoid using imperial lenses to view the place. This is in contrast to some of the long-term British residents in Hong Kong who, despite the 1997 handover, continued to think of Hong Kong as 'British':

> Hong Kong is a place that grows on you, ... but I still of course think of myself as British. When I hear on the radio, the Prime Minister, I think of Tony Blair, whereas the radio is talking about Zhu Rongji. And our president, we don't have a president, we have a queen, you know.

> Um, and I found it very difficult and very emotional on the night of the 30th of June '97 ... there was a sunset farewell parade, and Prince Charles, and the Royal [Yacht] Britannia was here. ... And it rained so much, I've never seen so much rain in the whole of my life, and even in spite of the umbrellas we were all given, [we're] absolutely saturated. And then we went on to the convention centre for a reception and the air conditioning was freezing and steam was rising practically everywhere. And because it was indoors, the flagpoles that had been erected had a little windpipe going up the centre, so the wind would blow ... which I thought was very funny. But one needed something like that to sort of, fight away the, er, the, er, the tears. And so in the earlier farewell parade I think everyone was glad of the rain because you know, it did sort of wash away the tears.

> So I felt very sad, and I still, wrongly I know, I still think of Hong Kong as being British. And I still, I suppose, might use the term 'colonial' to describe myself. Although I don't live a colonial lifestyle, I only live in a little flat that I own. The colonial lifestyle, you live in big flats that you didn't own.

> I have to accept that Hong Kong is part of China, of course. That's the legal position, but I don't actually feel that it is ... of course I never could be Chinese, um, I am British and still think of myself as British, and still think of Hong Kong as being British (laugh) (James, who first came out to Hong Kong in January 1969 with the British army with the specific purpose of learning Chinese).

For more recent arrivals, however, there was little evidence of hankering after an imperial past, or a need to (re)claim colonial associations with Hong Kong or China as a whole. As Eleanor, who arrived in Hong Kong in the mid-1990s prior to handover had put it, while she was aware that Hong Kong was 'colonial', it bore few marks of a colonial presence and was in her mind an overwhelmingly Chinese city. There was also little sense among British individuals interviewed of wishing to reform or improve the locals, in contradistinction to the 'pastoral gaze' intent on 'salvation' (Foucault 1982: 213) characteristic of British colonial rule. As we have noted elsewhere (Willis and Yeoh 2002), while there was a strong sense of national identity among the British transnational elite,[13] there was also a reluctance among some interviewees to 'perform Britishness' (a series of acts which seemed to involve mainly 'drinking an awful lot', 'people throwing parties and you get invited and you meet more people', 'the odd sort of barbecue, but mostly bars').

In the last decade, Singaporean forays into China have been to one extent or another encouraged, if not orchestrated by the state. In the early 1990s, the Singapore state encouraged Singapore firms and Singaporeans to 'go regional' as a means of expanding Singapore's economic space beyond the nation's limited geographical boundaries.[14] It was argued that Singapore had a comparative advantage in encountering China: as part of 'Dragon's diaspora' (that is, overseas Chinese), Singaporeans can draw on their ethnic and cultural identity to effect 'knowledge arbitrage' (that is, 'extracting from one [civilisation] in a way which allows [one] to assimilate the other') and thereby 'add[ing] value as a trader' (George Yeo, quoted in Crovitz 1993: 18). To quote George Yeo further,

> Those who have knowledge of the culture and cultural nuances are able to lower business risks [for foreigners who find the risks unacceptable]. The Chinese overseas understand Chinese culture because they are ethnically Chinese themselves, but they also understand the world outside. . . . They are like modems. They modulate and demodulate and add value in the process.

The state also construed the 'Singapore brand name' as a means to exploit Singapore's national reputation for efficient, non-corrupt administration and a clean, secure and ordered physical environment. The 'Singapore business [and physical] environment' is seen as a national commodity which can be exported across international boundaries, resulting in the creation of industrial spaces and townships such as the Singapore-Suzhou Township modelled after Singapore's Jurong Industrial Estate and planned by Singapore government agencies. The state had also expected to export 'software' to manage the property according to Singapore administrative practices. If by 'imperial' we mean 'the belief that it is good to make or enlarge the empire of one's nation', the strategies of the Singapore state contain at least the seeds of imperialism.

More recently, however, Singaporeans in China are beginning to find that ideas such as 'Singaporeans being "natural allies" by dint of ethnicity', 'Singapore being a favoured "brand name"', and 'Singapore being a "superior country" in a position to "aid" China' somewhat unsustainable. Ho Kee Tong (quoted in *The Straits Times*, 15 August 2001), a 50-year-old Singaporean design consultant who had worked for over eight years in China, who spoke Mandarin 'like a native' and was well-versed with 'Chinese history and Maoist doctrine', explained:

> I'm Chinese-educated. I thought Chinese was in my bones. But even today, they call me *lao-wai* (foreigner)!

Further observing that China was coming of age, particularly with the new-found confidence exuding from having won the Olympic bid, he cautioned Singaporeans wishing to work in China to 'lose their air of superiority':

> For a long time, the Chinese felt bullied by foreigners. But the Chinese consider winning the bid as a sign of coming of age. They realise they are no longer the underdogs.... [For those who are heeding the Singapore government's call to seize business openings in China].... Leave at home notions of Singapore having the best airport and a top port.... What they don't realise is that the Chinese don't have to care about us. I mean, why should they? We need them more than they need us.

Another Singaporean (T.K. Niam, general manager of Volex, Suzhou, quoted in *The Straits Times*, 15 September 2001) reflected similar sentiments in expressing his fear that 'if his children grow up and work in China, they will have to work on local terms', while yet another (identified only as Mr Low in the same article) was worried that 'Singaporeans may some day have to work for the Chinese'.[15] Such anxieties that China is a force to be seriously reckoned with have even made their way into the Prime Minister Goh Chok Tong's annual National Day Rally speech (Goh 2001):

> I have been to China many times, the first in 1971. I have seen China's transformation at close quarters. It is scary. You go to Beijing, Shanghai, Shenzhen, Dalian, Qingdao and scores of other cities, and you will be astonished by how quickly they have learnt and caught up. They write software for Microsoft. They are into life sciences and bio-medical engineering. They have even succeeded in making their toilets at tourist attractions shinier and cleaner than ours.

It would appear then that the tables are turning: if the Singapore government had once harboured imperial-tinted dreams about carving out a niche for the nation-state in China or lending China a hand to pull up its socks through software transfer of Singaporean know-how, the anxiety now is whether Singapore has sufficient time to re-engineer a relationship with China which would allow the nation-state to 'hitch a ride on the China wagon before it is too late' (*The Straits Times*, 15 September 2001).

## Conclusion

> Cosmopolitanism bereft of geographical specificity remains abstracted and alienated reason, liable, when it comes to earth, to reproduce all manner of unintended and sometimes explosively evil consequences. Geography uninspired by any cosmopolitan vision is either mere heterotopic description or a passive tool of power for dominating the weak (Harvey 2000: 557–8).

In examining the cultural politics at play in the construction of contact zones as British and Singaporean transnational elites 'come to earth' and make their sojourn in the cities of China, what is clearly obvious is the multiplicity and complexity of cultural and social transactions with local Chinese. We have attempted to clarify the diversity by contrasting two elite groups distinguished by nationality, each with their own peculiar history of association with China. In doing this, we strengthen the case to view this elite circuit of transnational subjects as embodied beings, bearers of nationality, culture, ethnicity, gender and class.

What we have also made clear is the uneven nature of the power relations on which these contact zones are predicated. The nature of contact zones—their breadth and depth, and degree of transience and permanence—as they develop in the urban landscape is strongly conditioned by the intentions, plans and desires of transnational elites who, by dint of superior economic resources as well as geographical mobility, are in a strong position to construct spatial, temporal and psychological 'limits'[16] to manage these contact zones.

For transnational elites, 'cultural experience'—whether as an encounter with a new world or as a discovery of 'roots'—may be sampled or rejected. 'Culture shock' is an issue that can be managed, sometimes by building psychological and physical barricades, or by maintaining 'distance' in ways reminiscent of colonial cultural strategies. However, the uneven terrain of these contact zones is perhaps also transient. As China pulls itself up by the very lifelines that transnational elites are supposed to provide, these unequal relationships which privilege transnational elites as 'culturalists', 'colonialists' or 'imperialists' in their approach to encountering China are constantly being reworked. Perhaps, in time, this may nudge the cultural politics which inhabit the global city to approach a more cosmopolitan variety. Inasmuch as geography and mobility create a non-homogeneous landscape of multiple contact zones and unequal power relations, it is hoped that would-be cosmopolitans and their local counterparts would develop the 'cultural competence' (Hannerz 1996) to navigate with a sense of their own humanity, and that of others.

## Notes

[1] Smith (2001: 5) terms this 'transnational urbanism' as 'a marker of the criss-crossing transnational circuits of communication and cross-cutting local, translocal, and transnational social practices that "come together" in particular places at particular times and enter into the contested politics of place-making, the social construction of power differentials, and the making of individual, group, national, and transnational identities, and their corresponding fields of difference'.

[2] Discussions of 'cosmopolitanism' tend to centre on transnational political dynamics, including 'the development of a kind of global civil society, the search for potential institutions of global governance, new modes of coordinating social and political movements around the world, and people's increased desire to voice multiple allegiances to causes, places and traditions beyond the resident nation-state' (Report on a conference on 'Conceiving Cosmopolitanism', *Transcomm News*, Issue 4, 2000: 7).

[3] This raises the fraught question as to whether expatriate workers constitute a transnational 'community'. Our view is that the concept of community involves shared identities, often developed in response to 'outsiders'. Among Singaporeans and Britons in China, there is a sense of the on-going politics of difference drawing situational boundaries among people, often on the basis of nationality, but also using other markers, and on different scales. In this sense, these are communities in the making, always fluid but maintained by everyday practices often associated with domestic routines or leisure activities. This sense of community is reinforced by the ideologies and policies of the nation-state. It has also been suggested that transnational elites belong to a 'world of fellows' (Appiah 2001), where the rootless identify with other rootless sojourners, creating a certain sort of rootless,

cosmopolitan identity for themselves. We did not find convincing evidence of this among our interviewees; instead, the lines of nationality, ethnicity, class and gender still featured prominently. By focusing on 'contact zones', our aim is to focus on the construction of the boundary lines between the 'expatriate community' and 'China'.

[4] While Singapore companies have always been involved to some degree in foreign investment, it was since the late 1980s and early 1990s that a regionalisation policy has been heavily promoted. 'Going regional' involves investment in South and East Asia and is an example of how the processes of globalisation have led to an increasingly complex web of international economic flows, and a fragmenting of the previous core-periphery divisions. Singapore has become the node of a regional economy, acting as a conduit for non-Asian funds coming into the region, as well as Singapore firms investing directly in regional economies (see Yeoh and Willis 1997; Willis and Yeoh 1998 for further details). China is currently Singapore's sixth largest trading partner as well as the top destination for Singapore investments overseas in cumulative terms since 1997. Conversely, Singapore is currently the fourth largest foreign investor in China with contractual investment in China worth more than US$33 billion.

[5] Another historical continuity to note is the fact that, among the new wave of skilled migrants coming out of China, Singapore is a significant destination, or stepping-stone before heading for the ultimate choice destination, the United States. PRC nationals constitute one of the largest groups of skilled 'foreign talent' in Singapore, working mainly as engineers, scientific researchers and IT professionals in the city-state.

[6] In China, the clubs are found in Shanghai, Shenyang, Sichuan, Wuhan, Beijing, Fujian, Guangzhou, Qingdao, Tianjin, Hainan, Nanjing, Suzhou, Wuxi and Shangdong (as well as Hong Kong). The quote is from the Singapore International Foundation website: http://www.sif.org.sg/os/osc.html

[7] Under the Treaty of Nanjing (1842), China ceded the island of Hong Kong to the British. The 'unequal treaty' also opened five ports to British residence and foreign trade and granted British nationals 'extraterritoriality' (exemption from Chinese laws).

[8] The 'Hash House Harriers', to give it its full title, is a running and social club, sometimes better known as 'a beer-drinking club with a running problem' (www.gthhh.com). It originated among British civil servants in Kuala Lumpur in 1938. Apparently, the fraternity received its name from the Selangor Club Chambers, which was commonly referred to as the 'Hash House' due to its lack-lustre food. There are approximately 1,500 branches throughout the world.

[9] Pseudonyms are used throughout this paper in order to preserve anonymity.

[10] Many British interviewees in Guangzhou had local Chinese friends. This was probably a reflection of the relatively small British expatriate community in Guangzhou. Beyond the issue of the size of the expatriate community, it should be noted that the contact zone between male Britons and female Chinese is also sometimes crossed by sexual liaisons, or indeed, marriage (Willis and Yeoh 2002).

[11] Apart from everyday social practices of the individual and the group, transnational identity formation is also influenced by state discourses, policy contexts, institutional settings, organisational developments and cultural flows (see Vertovec 2001; Yeoh et al. 2003).

[12] Part of the pressure stems from the fact that Singapore's bilingual education policy binds 'language' to racial identity. While the main curriculum is taught in English, all students learn their 'Mother Tongue' as a second language throughout primary, secondary and junior college education. What constitutes one's Mother Tongue is also prescribed by one's 'race': all citizens classified as 'Chinese' must learn Mandarin as the language of their 'race'.

[13] Most interviewees said that they felt their sense of British identity sharpened away from 'home' and continued to sustain certain nostalgic images of Britain.

[14] The regionalisation strategy was accompanied by state-engineered investments in large-scale infrastructural development projects such as the Wuxi-Singapore Industrial Park and the Suzhou-Singapore Industrial Park.

[15] Within Singapore, this sense of 'awe (at China's rapid rise) coupled with a deep ambivalence' as to whether Singapore would be able to 'ride on' China's growth or be undermined by it is reflected in the flurry of newspaper articles with titles such as 'A wake-up call from China' (*The Sunday Times*, 22 July 2001) and 'Will the Dragon hollow out the Lion City?' (*The Straits Times*, 15 September 2001).

[16] Selmer (2001a, 2001b) recommends a suite of socio-cultural and psychological adjustment strategies for Western business expatriates working in China. One strategy he highlights is learning the language, making the point that 'it is not necessary to master the foreign language to perfection, as demonstrating even very basic skills (survival language), as well as elementary speaking practices, may connote the message to the locals that the expatriate really cares to make an effort to understand the host culture' (Selmer 2001b: 16). Other strategies include interacting with locals beyond the workplace and avoiding living in 'virtual expatriate ghettoes' to minimise social isolation from the host culture; as well as 'cultural empathy to be open to the different norms of the host culture' (Selmer 2001b: 17).

## References

Appiah, A.K. (2001) 'Cosmopolitan reading', in Dharwadker, V. (ed.) *Cosmopolitan Geographies: New Locations in Literature and Culture*. London: Routledge, 197–227.

Beaverstock, J.V. (2002) 'Transnational elites in global cities: British expatriates in Singapore's financial district', *Geoforum*, 33(4): 525–38.

Beaverstock, J.V. and Smith, J. (1996) 'Lending jobs to global cities: skilled international labour migration, investment banking and the city of London', *Urban Studies*, 33(8): 1377–94.

Berner, E. and Korff, R. (1995) 'Globalization and local resistance: the creation of localities in Manila and Bangkok', *International Journal of Urban and Regional Research*, 19(2): 208–22.

Blaut, J.M. (1993) *The Colonizer's Model of the World*. New York: Guildford Press.

Castells, M. (1996) 'The reconstruction of social meaning in the space of flows' (originally published 1989), in LeGates, R.T. and Stout, F. (eds) *The City Reader*. London: Routledge, 493–8.

Cheah, P. (2001) 'Chinese cosmopolitanism in two senses and postcolonial national memory', in Dharwadker, V. (ed.) *Cosmopolitan Geographies: New Locations in Literature and Culture*. London: Routledge, 133–70.

Crovitz, L.G. 'Dragon diaspora: cultural links should bolster economic growth (interview with George Yeo)', *Far Eastern Economic Review*, 156, 2 December 1993: 18.

Findlay, A.M., Li, F.L.N., Jowett, A.J. and Skeldon, R. (1996) 'Skilled international migration and the global city: a study of expatriates in Hong Kong', *Transactions of the Institute of British Geographers*, 21(1): 49–61.

Foucault, M. (1982) 'The subject and power', in Dreyfus, H.L. and Rabinow, P. (eds) *Michel Foucault: Beyond Structuralism and Hermeneutics*. Brighton: Harvester Press, 206–26.

Goh, C.T. (2001) *Prime Minister's National Day Rally Speech, 2001: New Singapore*. Singapore: Ministry of Information and the Arts.

Hannerz, U. (1996) *Transnational Connections: Culture, People, Places*. London and New York: Routledge.

Harvey, D. (2000) 'Cosmopolitanism and the banality of geographic evils', *Public Culture*, 12(2): 529–64.

King, A.D. (1976) *Colonial Urban Development*. London: Routledge and Kegan Paul.

Law, L. (1997) 'Cebu and Ceboom: the political place of globalization in a Philippine city', in Rimmer, P.J. (ed.) *Pacific Rim Development: Integration and Globalization in the Asia-Pacific Economy*. Sydney: Allen and Unwin, 240–66.

Pratt, M.L. (1992) *Imperial Eyes: Travel Writing and Transculturation*. London: Routledge.

Robbins, B. (1998) 'Introduction part I: actually existing cosmopolitanism', in Cheah, P. and Robbins, B. (eds) *Cosmopolitics: Thinking and Feeling Beyond the Nation*. Minneapolis: University of Minnesota Press, 1–19.

Sassen, S. (1996) 'Identity in the global city: economic and cultural encasements', in Yaeger, P. (ed.) *The Geography of Identity*. Ann Arbor: University of Michigan Press, 131–51.

Schmidt, J.D. (1998) 'Globalisation and inequality in urban South-East Asia', *Third World Planning Review*, 20(2): 127–45.

Selmer, J. (2001a) 'Psychological barriers to adjustment and how they affect coping strategies: Western business expatriates in China', *International Journal of Human Resource Management*, 12(2): 151–65.

Selmer, J. (2001b) 'Adjustment of Western European vs North American expatriate managers in China', *Personnel Review*, 30(1): 6–21.

Sennett, R. (2001) 'New capitalism, new isolation: a flexible city of strangers', posted on CRIT-GEOG-FORUM, 16 February 2001.

Sklair, L. (1998) *Transnational Practices and the Analysis of the Global System*. Oxford: University of Oxford, Transnational Communities Working Paper Series No. 98–04, Transnational Communities: An ESRC Research Programme.

Smith, M.P. (1995) 'The disappearance of world cities and the globalization of local politics', in Knox, P.L. and Taylor, P.J. (eds) *World Cities in a World System*. Cambridge: Cambridge University Press, 249–66.

Smith, M.P. (1998) 'The global city—whose city is it anyway?', *Urban Affairs Review*, 33(4): 482–8.

Smith, M.P. (2001) *Transnational Urbanism: Locating Globalization*. Malden, MA: Blackwell.

Vertovec, S. (2001) 'Transnationalism and identity', *Journal of Ethnic and Migration Studies*, 27(4): 573–82.

Waters, J.L. (2002) 'Flexible families? "Astronaut" households and the experiences of lone mothers in Vancouver, British Columbia', *Social and Cultural Geography*, 3(2): 117–34.

Willis, K. and Yeoh, B.S.A. (1998) 'The social sustainability of Singapore's regionalisation drive', *Third World Planning Review*, 20(2): 203–21.

Willis, K. and Yeoh, B.S.A. (2002) 'Gendering transnational communities: a comparison of Singaporean and British migrants in China', *Geoforum*, 33(4): 553–65.

Yeoh, B.S.A. and Willis, K. (1997) 'The global–local nexus: Singapore's regionalisation drive', *Geography*, 82(2): 183–6.

Yeoh, B.S.A and Willis, K. (1999) '"Heart" and "wing", "nation" and "diaspora": gendered discourses in Singapore's regionalisation process', *Gender, Place and Culture*, 6(4): 355–72.

Yeoh, B.S.A. and Willis, K. (2004) 'Constructing masculinities in transnational space: Singapore men on the "regional beat"', in Jackson, P., Crang, P. and Dwyer, C. (eds) *Transnational Spaces*. London: Routledge, 147–63.

Yeoh, B.S.A., Willis, K. and Fakhri, S.M.A.K. (2003) 'Introduction: transnationalism and its edges', *Ethnic and Racial Studies*, 26(2): 207–17.

# Global Nightscapes in Shanghai as Ethnosexual Contact Zones

James Farrer

*Beginning in the 1980s, bars and dance clubs re-emerged as important zones of intercultural interaction within Shanghai, particularly for expatriates with otherwise little casual social contact with Chinese citizens. Based on interviews with bar- and club-owners and customers, and on field-notes from participant observation over the last 15 years, this historical ethnography describes the changing organisation of the ethnosexual contact zone of the nightlife. Nightlife is a context in which casual interactions among foreign travellers, sojourners and settlers and the increasingly mobile People's Republic of China (PRC) citizens are common and relatively spontaneous. Despite the complexities of these interactions, the ethnographic evidence here points to the continued relevance of postcolonial racial categories in which a struggle for gendered status within the nightscape is described as a competition between a dominant but declining Global Whiteness and a rising Global Chinese racial identity. This mapping of a fractious global nightscape challenges the idea of a seamless transnational capitalist class, and instead points to racial and gendered sexual competition as an important feature of the leisure culture of transnational mobile elites.*

## Global Nightscapes

With waves of foreign skilled migration beginning in the 1980s, Shanghai has emerged as one of the major 'contact zones' of global capitalism (Pratt 1992: 4; Yeoh and Willis 2005), with Western and Asian expatriates and mobile PRC nationals competing and interacting in the same transnational labour markets and the same social spaces. Although the notion of contact zone is evocative of spaces of face-to-face interaction, little ethnographic research has been conducted on how elite skilled migrants from various national and ethnic backgrounds interact in the face-to-face contact zones of emerging global cities, including workplaces (but see Ho; and Ye and Kelly, this issue) and leisure venues (Walsh 2007). It has become increasingly obvious to researchers that global cities cannot be studied as abstract nodes in transnational networks of capital and demographic flows. We also have to consider the local topographies of these transnational flows (Burawoy 2001; Sassen 2007), including how categories such as race, nationality, gender and sexuality interact in local urban geographies of globalisation. This paper maps the social geography of intercultural contact in one global city by looking at the practices of transnational migrants in one category of social space—the international nightlife zones of Shanghai. These *global nightscapes* are shown to be spaces of racial and sexual stratification and an important site for the production of racialised and gendered identities for skilled migrants.

This mapping of the social topography of Shanghai's *global nightscapes* takes the perspectives of elite transnational migrants—North Americans, Europeans, overseas Chinese, and socially and geographically mobile PRC nationals—who also participate in these spaces. The term *nightscape* refers to socially constructed geographies of commercial nightlife activities (Chatterton and Hollands 2003). Nightscapes can be organised into *nightlife genres*—bars, dance clubs, KTV (karioke) clubs, saunas and brothels (see Farrer 2008)—physically contiguous *nightlife zones* (nightlife districts or bar streets), and *nightlife circuits* of individuals moving through these genres and zones (sometimes idiosyncratic but often standardised routines). This paper focuses on the nightlife genres and zones the most commonly featured in the nightlife circuits of transnational migrants.

The idea of a *global* nightscape refers to the ways in which these local urban nightscapes are sites of transnational flows (Appadurai 1990) and also constructed through globalising cultural and corporate processes that homogenise and stratify nightlife experiences (Chatterton and Hollands 2003). Pragmatically, nightlife globalisation means that anyone familiar with nightlife in other global cities could pick his or her way through Shanghai's global nightscapes with relative ease upon landing in the city, using the categories of spaces learned already in similar settings, such as bars in London or Chicago, international dance clubs in Singapore (Ye and Kelly, this issue) or expatriate nightlife circuits in Dubai (Walsh 2007). This does not mean that global nightscapes are constructed identically across global cities. While Shanghai's British pubs described below resemble those described by Walsh in Dubai, religious restrictions in Dubai produce more ethnically segregated clubbing spaces in that city (Walsh 2007). Globalised nightlife spaces are thus differentiated and heterogeneous sites of sexual and racial stratification. Even in the early manifestations of global nightlife culture in the twentieth century, dance halls were sites of both racial conflict and interracial intimacy (Cressey 1932). To use a term from Nagel (2003), global nightscapes are 'ethnosexual contact zones' in which individuals find solidarity with co-ethnics, but also seek contact across ethnic boundaries, with one major form of cross-ethnic contact being sexual interaction (Tanaka 2007). At the same time, these patterns of stratification, avoidance and mingling are shaped by local policing and more subtle forms of urban governance (Chatterton and Hollands 2003).

The growing population of foreigners living in and visiting Shanghai has fuelled the development of Shanghai's global nightscapes. According to Chinese government sources, 130,000 foreign nationals were residing legally in Shanghai in 2008 (Lu 2008: 273), but unofficial estimates were higher. Consular and chamber of commerce officials I interviewed estimated that 70,000 to 100,000 Japanese, 20,000 to 30,000 Americans, and 12,000 to 20,000 Germans were living in Shanghai on various types of visas (personal communications 2006). With the exception of Willis and Yeoh's original research (Willis and Yeoh 2002; Yeoh and Willis 2005), this group has also been studied very little by social scientists, with no ethnographic studies. Increasingly expatriates find themselves in the same labour and housing markets and consumer spaces as a fast-growing Chinese population of 'returnees' (*haigui*) with foreign degrees, and upwardly mobile Chinese from Shanghai and other provinces, competing to join and define what Sklair (2001) has called the 'transnational capitalist class' but which, in this study, is shown to be a racially and sexually heterogeneous mix. Although expatriates are only a portion of this geographically and socially mobile population, they are a highly visible portion, especially in the cosmopolitan nightlife scenes which are the subject of this paper. Expatriates— especially European and American and overseas Chinese—have long been visible consumer market leaders in Shanghai, and even important 'attractions' in Shanghai's nightlife scenes (see Farrer 2002; Field 2008).

*Global nightscapes* are also important in the political and commercial promotions of cities, or city branding. Increasingly, nightlife is used to promote global cities as destinations for tourism and investment. Nightlife developments in Singapore, such as the 'Three Quays', have been used to promote Singapore as a cosmopolitan (rather than simply an Asian business) city (see Ye and Kelly, this issue), just as the redevelopment of a 'cleaner' Times Square has been used to promote New York as a safe city for tourism and living. Now, nightlife zones are also being used to promote Shanghai as a new cosmopolitan metropolis, especially the developments of Xintiandi and Shanghai's historic Bund that have become showcases of the city's modernity and openness to foreign culture (Hibbard 2007; Ren 2008). Even before these recent developments, Shanghainese long-associated nightlife with the image of the city (Cheng 1989).

Global nightscapes are also sociologically important because they are among the most open and loosely governed 'contact zones' for mobile populations. In comparison with the often covert or unstated racial and ethnic stratification of professional workplaces (see Ho; and Ye and Kelly, in this issue), the nightlife zones of global cities allow for more-overt expression of racial, ethnic and gendered discourses, but also more chances for subverting ethnic hierarchies and crossing boundaries through sexual intimacy. Nightscapes are spaces in which people seek out intercultural, interracial and cross-gender sociability for a variety of reasons, including the actualisation of fantasies of mobility, status and boundary-crossing sociability (Liu-Farrer 2004). Global nightscapes are, in this view, zones of movement, productivity and contradiction within the racialised and gendered fractions of the transnational capitalist class.

Nightlife may be particularly important for understanding the cultural and social lives of mobile expatriates. Similar to Walsh's study of British expatriates in Dubai, many of my informants said that night clubs, going out and consuming alcohol were more central to their lives in Shanghai than in their own homelands. Many informants were young and single and thus more prone to nightlife activities. However, even among older and (more-or-less) attached people, nightlife in Shanghai was described as having a pull that was unequalled in their home countries. Many were attracted by the permissive sexual atmosphere associated with a 'holiday' or 'vacation' mentality (see Walsh 2007). Social isolation and removal from long-term social networks attracted foreigners to nightlife. The same factors also influenced Chinese informants. A young Western expatriate in a first job and a young Chinese office worker from outside Shanghai were equally in need of social contacts, and many such people found one another in the nightlife. A factor particular to non-Chinese-speaking foreigners, however, was their relative inability to enjoy many other cultural activities in a city where few had an adequate knowledge of the Chinese language and Chinese culture. Many sought comfort with their own co-ethnics in ethnically marked nightlife spaces. For some of the same people, however, nightlife was seen as one of the very few options for integrating or participating in a larger Chinese society outside work. From the perspective of expatriates, nightscapes consist of a patchwork of *enclaves*, or escapes from Chinese society, such as German or Irish pubs, and *contact zones*, or spaces in which socialising with Chinese people was possible, such as bigger bars, dance clubs and bar streets.

Because of limits on length, this paper focuses mostly on the latter—the contact zones—and on the expression of masculinities and femininities in these still racially mixed but class-stratified spaces. It is organised in three parts: a general introduction to the development of Shanghai's global nightscapes, a section on transnational masculinities, and one on transnational femininities. I outline the boundaries and hierarchies that characterise Shanghai's global nightscapes, while also elucidating the tactics of contestation and competition of various participants.

## Data and Methodology

This paper represents an overlap of two qualitative ethnographic studies. The first is a series of studies of nightlife interactions in Shanghai conducted over the past 15 years, including interviews with owners and workers in the types of establishment discussed below, and hundreds of nights of ethnographic observations and interviews conducted from 1993 to 2009. The second is an interview-based study of long-term expatriates or settlers in the city, involving over 200 interviews with expatriates and their Chinese partners, friends and co-workers conducted from 2002 to 2009, with some ethnographic involvements lasting much longer. The author is a white

North American male and frequent visitor to this scene, which may colour some of the findings and interpretations. However, this paper is not an auto-ethnography, and is constructed from interviews with foreigners and Chinese alike, and men and women of all social classes. Although ethnographic, the aim is not a micro-level account of the interactions in one particular space, but rather to map out the zones of ethnosexual interaction. It does not attempt a full typology of Shanghai's nightscapes, which has been partly addressed elsewhere (Farrer 2002, 2008). Nor does it deal with the large and important populations of Japanese, Taiwanese or Koreans in the city. Methodologically and theoretically, however, it attempts to address questions that would apply to similarly mobile populations in other global cities.

## The Re-Emergence of Shanghai's Global Nightscapes as Ethnosexual Contact Zones

Shanghai's international nightlife scenes can be divided into at least four major genres of establishment, all of which are products of global flows of people, capital and culture over several decades—discos and dance clubs, bars, karaoke clubs and saunas and barber shops, often brothels (Farrer 2008). I only deal here with bars and dance clubs, because they are the sites in which transnational mobile elites compete and interact with one another in relatively open spaces. Many of these spaces have predecessors in the pre-1949 era of foreign settlement in the city, and were closed down in the 1950s. Here I focus on their redevelopment since the opening and reform measures of 1978.

*Dance clubs* are the most prominent of Shanghai's nightlife venues. Although commercial social (ballroom) dance venues opened in Shanghai in the early 1980s (Liu 1989), Shanghai's international dance scene dates back to the opening of the disco in the Jinjiang Hotel in the late 1980s. At first, hotel discos were restricted to foreigners in a deliberate policy of limiting social contacts between local Shanghainese and foreigners. Massive 'disco plazas' began opening in Shanghai in the early 1990s, attracting both foreigners and Shanghai youth, and opening up unprecedented interethnic contact zones in the heart of the city (Farrer 1999, 2002). By the late 1990s, an international-style clubbing scene emerged in which Shanghai was reintegrated into global circuits of dance and music culture, including overseas investment capital, foreign (often 'overseas Chinese') managers, international DJs and international fashion styles (Field 2008). Over the past 20 years, Shanghai clubs have become more clearly stratified by age, ethnicity and music style. By 2008, many hip-hop clubs (such as 'Guandi' or 'Bonbon') catered to a young group that included Shanghainese youth and high-school students from the international schools in Shanghai. Some clubs (such as 'Babyface' on Huaihai Road) were known among expatriates as 'local' (i.e. Chinese) clubs. In contrast, a few dance clubs on Shanghai's newly redeveloped Bund catered to an older, heavily European crowd, partly because of the higher prices associated with the scenic and touristic location. Although 'Babyface' was rumoured to restrict the entrance of single 'foreign' (white) men, most clubs were open to anyone with cash. Doorway selection based on looks and connections, common in London and New York, was rare in Shanghai. Despite informal ethnic segregation and occasional discrimination, racial and age segregation in Shanghai clubs was very relaxed in comparison to many larger cities in Europe, Japan or the US, and seldom would a visitor feel unwelcome or afraid on these grounds. Some regular clubbers described nightlife circuits of wandering between these venues precisely to enjoy the novelty of differently marked spaces.

*Bars* are another important genre of space in Shanghai's global nightscapes. Small privately owned bars sprang up near the big international hotels that opened in central Shanghai in the late 1980s (Farrer 2008). The style of service was more Japanese than Western and, indeed, some were opened by Shanghainese who went to Japan to work in the 1980s. Although modest by contemporary standards, Shanghai's bars in the 1980s were associated with the glamour of the new 'high society' of the market economy, and with 'gold-digging' local women who looked for husbands or simply easy money among the private entrepreneurs and foreigners who frequented them (Ah Yan 1988). By the late 1990s, a scattering of international-style British, American and Irish pubs began serving the growing expatriate population. Some served as ethnic enclaves in which few local Chinese regular customers could be seen, while other bars attracted a more mixed clientele.

A major turning point in the development of Shanghai's global nightscapes was the advent of lively 'bar streets' on Hengshan, Maoming and Julu Roads during the late 1990s. Until this period, ethnosexual contacts in Shanghai's international nightlife had been mostly limited to young clubbers and the relatively small and marginal bar scenes near hotels. On Maoming Road, in contrast, local and foreign entrepreneurs opened dozens of venues, in an unplanned development that included restaurants, dance clubs, live-music pubs, 'hostess' bars and numerous street vendors. Maoming clubs and bars did not charge entrance fees, and prices were reasonable even to students and young Chinese office workers. In the summer of 2000, on weekend nights, literally thousands of customers clogged the narrow street, making it impassable to car traffic. Live and recorded music blared out from open terraces. The vast economic gulf between Shanghai's rising middle classes and the migrant poor was a veritable street performance every Friday night. This nocturnal panorama included the fashionable and sexily dressed bar customers, prostitutes accosting middle-aged foreign visitors, rural children aggressively selling flowers, and beggars mobbing taxis arriving at the bars. Exasperated policemen stopped fights, tried to control street prostitution and urged on traffic.

Maoming Road in the summers from 1999 to 2003 was a space of rampant social intercourse among foreign visitors, local Shanghainese and Chinese from other provinces on a scale not seen before in Shanghai. It was known as a place where foreign men could meet local Shanghainese women for romance, or a Chinese prostitute from the provinces. There were seemingly fewer relationships being formed between Chinese men and foreign women, and the racially skewed sexual marketplace was a source of the interethnic tensions on the street. Although seldom reported in the state-run Chinese media, some of these fights became urban legends among the foreign community, including the following story posted on a popular English website:

> Three weeks ago at the end of Mao Ming Road I got beat up by about 20 Chinese guys. They broke two bottles on my head and beat me with a wooden stick screaming 'Go back to your country!' I ended up in the hospital with ripped clothes and full of blood. Luckily the only damage was a broken nose and three big scars on my face... I'm an American living in Shanghai for a bit. I don't usually have conflicts and haven't hit a person since I was 14. That's 16 years ago. I was walking down the street of Mao Ming and a little Chinese guy kept wanting to fight me. He wouldn't stop. I was laughing at him thinking, 'Why would this skinny little 20-year-old want to fight me?' It became a stupid argument and I finally just punched the punk in the face. I hit him one time. That's all. Not a smart move. Soon about 20 guys came and beat the crap out of me, almost killing me. Warning to all foreigners: DON'T GET IN A CONFLICT WITH ONE CHINESE GUY HERE BECAUSE THEY WILL ALL JUMP YOU REAL BAD! You are a foreigner and don't forget it. When it comes down to [it], it is them against us. They will all team up against you... (posted on '*Shanghai Expat*', 23 May 2004).

This unverifiable story was widely discussed among Westerners in Shanghai. There was also a popular version in which a foreign man was beaten to death on the street (although this is almost certainly not true). The Chinese, in turn, also had their negative perceptions of the foreigners on these streets. One taxi driver told a Chinese female informant riding in his taxi, 'Of course foreigners love it here. They can just do whatever they want. There is "no law and no heaven" (*wufawutian*). They could never get away with this in their own countries'.

This eclectic and sometimes explosive scene ended abruptly in the summer of 2003 when many Maoming bars were closed for noise violations. Rumours abounded of the hidden hands of high officials living in the vicinity, but informants who experienced the crackdown described traffic problems, public fighting and drunkenness, open-air music, and aggressive solicitation by prostitutes on the streets as reasons for the street being closed down. Shanghai's Public Security officials, while extraordinarily tolerant of such behaviour in private establishments, drew a line at such open public display. Noise violations were easily prosecuted, because they could be blamed squarely on the bar-owners. This was the second time in three years that the street had been closed down by the police, and it never recovered.

With the suppression of Maoming Road, Shanghai's bar streets did not disappear, but they were increasingly stratified by class. A related turning point in Shanghai's nightlife geography was the now-world-famous development of 'Xintiandi' in the 1990s, which transformed a swathe of vintage housing into an upper-class shopping, restaurant and nightlife space. In contrast to Maoming Road, a public street, Xintiandi was a thoroughly privatised form of 'public space' controlled by a Hong Kong real-estate company, eliminating begging, street-vending and other unauthorised uses of its deceptively open courtyards and greenways. After Xintiandi, nightlife was no longer considered a politically or morally suspect feature of urban geography. Instead, Xintiandi presented a relatively sanitised and heavily policed pedestrian mall in which disorderly behaviour was rarely observed or tolerated. Street-walking prostitution (which became common in Xintiandi for a time) was suppressed by a security force that exclusively worked there. Foreign and domestic tourists and young white-collar Shanghainese eager to experience global nightlife for the first time flocked to the area.

A similarly gentrified nightlife development emerged on Shanghai's postcard waterfront, known as 'The Bund'. Starting with the opening of the exclusive restaurant and bar venues at 'Bund Three' in 2003, a series of exclusive nightlife venues in renovated buildings on Shanghai's colonial-era riverfront also began attracting the wealthiest of tourists and nightlife sophisticates of both sexes. Expatriates were a major presence in most bars on the Bund, partly because of the association with historical foreign Shanghai, but Chinese white-collar workers, artists and entrepreneurs were also important customers. Bars on the Bund could be described as an urban 'stage' for the transnational elite of all races and nationalities. Unlike Maoming Road or Xintiandi, there was no street-level socialising on the Bund, and the elite clientele were separated by a busy highway from the domestic tourists who strolled along the embankment of the Huangpu River. Some Bund bars also established a reputation for cutting-edge design and style.

Bar Rouge—opened by two already successful French nightclub entrepreneurs on the seventh floor of the stylishly renovated former British Chartered Bank building—was known in 2005 as Shanghai's hottest bar, and as a hangout for expense-account expats, fashion industry insiders, models and English-speaking Chinese prostitutes. Many of the customers were foreign businessmen and women, 'overseas Chinese' and 'returnee Chinese' working in international business. English was the common language. An anonymous on-line review from an (ostensibly) Asian female customer describes why she enjoyed the bar:

> I spent several Friday nights at Bar Rouge and it was very fun. Everybody rolled up in smooth cars such as BMW's Z, Mercedes M class, and plenty of convertibles. Pros: *definitely a place to see and be seen *well-dressed men and women *getting attention from guys was not hard—show a little skin, a little smile, and a sexy little walk (all that isn't a problem if you're an Asian girl! yeah ladies!) .... *everybody knows how to dance and friendly grinding is welcomed and returned *plenty of seats to sit on—or a lap *bathrooms very clean most of the night—and very far from the men's so you always feel safe *always a watchman during after hours to get a taxi and chase away the derelicts (Posted on 'Smart Shanghai', 22 August 2005).

Many other anonymous reviewers on the same English-language site found the Bar Rouge to be pretentious, expensive, and full of wealthy posers and prostitutes. These critical comments focusing on price and snobbishness also point to the increasing class stratification of Shanghai nightlife, and the sense that even many foreign internet reviewers—to say nothing of lower-class 'derelicts' turned away on the street—no longer felt at ease in Shanghai's choicest establishment.

In sum, Shanghai nightlife has become increasingly stratified and segregated, especially by class, age and musical taste, and to a lesser extent by nationality or race. Zones of contact and friction remain but, as Chatterton and Hollands (2003) write of Europe, regulation and policing have furthered the process of gentrification and stratification of nightlife districts in Shanghai, as less-governable spaces are closed down and replaced with more-easily governable middle-class tourist zones. In Shanghai, the governance of nightlife in the city underwent a transformation from a focus on the suppression of vice through campaigns such as those seen on Maoming Road in 2000 and 2003, to a promotional approach focused on developing sanitised and classy nightlife districts worthy of a global city. Expatriates and the transnationally mobile Shanghainese tended towards these more expensive and approved venues in the prestigious development zones, though they also could make use of the remaining underground scenes for clubbing and cruising.

## Competing Racialised Masculinities in Shanghai's Global Nightscapes

Expatriate men—especially white European and North Americans who fit the image of *laowai* ('foreigners')—have enjoyed an elevated status since the beginning of Shanghai's international clubbing scene. Indeed the first discos in hotels catered exclusively to foreign guests. Popular discos in the early 1990s allowed foreigners in for free, or encouraged foreigners to attend by distributing VIP passes to obviously foreign-looking guests (Farrer 1999). White men were seen as big spenders who attracted young Chinese female customers hoping to meet foreign men. Such policies annoyed Chinese regulars and especially foreigners with Asian faces who were not always accorded VIP treatment.

As foreigners became less rare and the spending power of the Chinese increased, free passes for foreigners or foreign students became a thing of the past. Still, interactions inside clubs remain marked by widely recognised racial and gendered categories. White and Asian, Chinese and foreign, men and women—all experienced nightlife spaces very differently. From the point of view of white or Asian foreign men, Shanghai clubs were an easy place to meet Chinese women, and many foreign men described Shanghai's clubbing scene as a 'sexual paradise'. One young blond American told me that he could take home a different woman every other night that he visited the popular Park 97 during the late 1990s and early 2000s. Eric, a handsome 28-year-old Chinese-American man in the fashion industry, described his luck meeting women at Shanghai clubs:

> Everything gets so easy to you—it's handed to you on a silver platter. So you are back in the States and you think you can get only a [lower] quality of woman, but here, they look as beautiful—for example, I go through model after model, actress after actress! And they are beautiful and stunning...

Men realised that they were trading on their economic and national status in these seductions. Foreignness still meant glamour and sex appeal. Eric described it simply as a 'difference'. Whereas white men relied on their exotic looks to signal difference, Chinese American and Japanese men relied more on their 'foreign' cultural backgrounds and the prestige accorded their nationality.

Some informants described a racial hierarchy in which white men and Chinese-American men competed for attention from Chinese women, some of whom preferred white men, and others preferred Asian-looking men with bicultural backgrounds. African and South Asian men were seldom mentioned, but it was clear that they were positioned closer to the bottom of the hierarchy. Nationality mattered as much as race, with US citizenship generally conferring high sexual status.

Women's racialised sexual preferences for men could be read as personal preferences or as politically significant prejudice and 'arrogance'. Asian men sometimes complained that foreign men had an easy time in the clubbing scene, and resented their sense of sexual entitlement. They also challenged these racial hierarchies. Chinese-American Eric's transnational cultural capital as a fashion-industry insider was probably his most important clubbing resource, but he also spoke at length about the importance of specifically Chinese cultural capital:

> You have the pure ABCs [American-born Chinese] and then the people like us—people who are multicultural—we all speak English perfectly, and Chinese and then you have the white crowd. ABCs and us get along a lot better—the white crowd always have this extra-superiority complex—we have all noticed it out here. They somehow get themselves into a lot of fights for no reason. You know in Asia, if you're ABC or local or whatever, there is a concept of face. You give each other face. So if you see a table in a club and there are women there, and they are with a group of guys, and you pretend to maybe know one of the guys and he introduces you to the girls, and that's OK, but you don't just walk up and hit on their girls—it just causes trouble, especially with the locals. And even for us or ABCs, it's the same thing. But I realise for white guys, they always go in there and get themselves into trouble and they always wonder why... haha... like if you are going to hit on this girl who is sitting there with 20 guys, come on man. I don't care how drunk you are, it's just logic. But they are like, 'What happened?' That's why you have a black eye there and stitches there... They have that complex where they feel they can do more and just get away with it.

Tension between white and ethnically Chinese men related to their different approaches to the space of the club. Chinese men—including 'overseas Chinese' men with more connections to the local culture—were more likely to book tables and invite a group of friends to share the space. Booking a table was also a way of indicating social and economic status, and claiming ownership of social space through agreeing to pay a high minimum charge (usually RMB 2,000–5,000 or US$300–750). White expatriates tended to come in pairs and cluster at the bar, meeting women on the dance floor and in the public areas of the club. Some ethnic Chinese men interpreted such foreign behaviour as 'cheap' and predatory. One

Shanghainese-American entrepreneur, who had lived in the US and worked in the Shanghai nightlife industry for many years, said to me while talking near the dance floor of Park 97:

> Now the city is just filling up with this white trash. These guys, they come in here and you can see them. They are all full of themselves, but they don't have any money. They are beer warmers. You go out to the bar and you see them holding a beer for an hour. They will come in and dance with a girl, and if she won't agree to go home with them right then and there, they won't even buy her a drink. You ask these guys what they do and they say, 'Oh, English teacher'. That means what? That means they are doing nothing here, nothing!

Behind this comment was a general sense that Chinese men would not show up in such an elite club unless they had the money to reserve a table and purchase bottles of liquor, while some Western men simply tried to rely upon their racial capital, despite their low-paid job in the city. Or, as white informants said of themselves, they simply preferred standing up at the bar where they could meet more women and talk with passers-by of both sexes.

In sum, transnational migrant men—including Asian Americans—experienced an enhanced sense of gendered sexual status in the clubbing scene. Social prestige among men was predicated upon sexual competition for women's attention, and this was often construed as a kind of racial competition between the dominant Global White and a rising Global Chinese. Despite the more extreme views expressed in these quotes, sexual competition was not so strong as to lead to voluntary racial segregation or a generally hostile atmosphere. Individual white men were often seen sitting in mostly Asian groups, and there was little resentment or surprise over racially mixed couples in clubs, although there was more over what was seen as predatory or aggressive behaviour by lone men. Significantly, this rhetoric of racial competition seemed stronger *within* the transnational population than among the local Shanghainese men, who were generally more welcoming and tolerant of foreigners, perhaps because they felt themselves to be less a part of the international scene.

## Competing Racialised Femininities in Shanghai's Global Nightscapes

The women who frequented Shanghai's clubs included Chinese women from Shanghai, other provinces and overseas, as well as foreign women. Chinese women included many university students and office workers from a wide range of backgrounds and income levels. In particular, it was not unusual to meet white-collar women from other Chinese provinces, living and working in the city alone. Such 'New Shanghainese' were an increasingly important mainstay in Shanghai's global nightscapes and, unlike men with a similar background, they did not need to spend much money in such clubs, because men would often buy them drinks or invite them to their tables.

Eve, a successful white-collar professional who grew up in Qingdao and had never lived abroad, explained why she hung out in the international nightlife, dating foreign men who were also living alone in the city with few friends, similar to her situation:

> Yeah well I think there isn't so much an expat by definition, by skin color, whatever; it is basically a lifestyle decided by the fact that you are alone in this city—like whether you come from a different country or city is the same thing—your family is not here, your friends are not here...you are alone in this place, you rent a place and this is your world. So you are alone—you have two options—one is to go out and one is to go home and watch a DVD and most of us choose to not go home and watch a DVD...If you don't have a boyfriend or husband here, your parents here, then you go out...and you go out and because the expats here are the same...they don't have their family and friends here, so they go out...and number two, probably those people who have a very stressful job, they work hard and play hard. And I am the same way—half of my office is foreigners so it's not because I am Chinese that I can take more stress or I don't feel the stress so it's the same way...and I enjoy a few good drinks, and good music, and also you have to be able to financially afford it so that's another thing...and I am lucky enough to have a reasonably good job and can keep up with it...

Eve said that she went out *nearly every night* of the week to a bar or club. She had dated a Dutch man for four years, and now was very much hoping to meet another foreign boyfriend. She was not attracted to Chinese men because they did not share her interests and lifestyle.

Some women in this scene more explicitly preferred Asian-looking men. Olive, a 22-year-old Shanghainese night-club promoter, said she preferred meeting 'cute ABCs'. She described how her female Shanghainese friends judged men they meet at Babyface, one of their favourite venues.

> My girlfriends are all different. Some pay attention to looks. Other friends pay more attention to material things. Of course they all want to have both of these things, but they will have different priorities. I think the type of people who go to Babyface care more about money. They will look at how many bottles of liquor a man will open on a table. The size of the table will tell them the minimum charge he had to pay, and that may tell you if he is has money. A girl will notice these things, because she may be just looking for a rich guy to buy her something, or maybe she will think that with a rich guy she can have more fun. After all this is just a way of measuring the quality of a guy...Others are looking to meet some good-looking guys. Everyone pursues beauty, looks at appearances, right! But no one goes to a club look looking for 'a good person' or someone with 'character'; there's no way you would go to a club looking for that!

Olive personally preferred alternative rock cafés, but would occasionally go out with her friends to Babyface, wearing her sexiest 'bling bling' clothes, to meet men on the dance floor. After sitting and drinking with the guys at their 'VIP' tables, the men might take them out for a 'night snack' afterwards, occasionally leading to more private sexual encounters. 'Girls now are very open', she said, dismissing the idea that casual sex was a moral issue. For her and her friends, men's sex appeal included components of money, race, nationality, good looks and originality in their approach to women, all forms of 'sexual capital' that could be displayed or indicated in interactions with women in the club (Farrer 2010).

In comparison with white foreign men—who generally sensed a racial advantage over Asian men—many white foreign women saw themselves as sexually disadvantaged in the clubbing scene. They complained that they were ignored by foreign men, although they themselves seldom paid much attention to the Asian men they encountered in these spaces. Japanese women and Asian American women did not have the same complaints of being desexualised or ignored—though many did complain that foreign men were spoiled by the Shanghai women who 'threw themselves' at foreign men. This sense of gendered disadvantage was thus marked by class and nationality as well as race.

The greatest social and sexual barrier in Shanghai's nightlife scenes appeared between white women and Asian men. Although increasing numbers of young Western women were working in Shanghai, they were less often seen dancing and flirting with Asian men. The racial barrier between white women and Asian men was attributed to a lack of interest on both sides. Nina, an Asian American woman, said that, despite her Asian appearance, the local Chinese were turned off by her independent personality:

> I know that even by American standards I'm a bit of a freak in that I'm very independent, I travel on my own all the time. I don't need a guy. So it takes a strong American guy to accept that—much more so relative to Asian guys. What are they going to do with someone like me? If I'm at a bar, they see that by the way I carry myself and the way I am interacting in a group. It comes across. I don't try to hide that. And actually, I've had Chinese women tell me that. They might ask the same question which is 'Oh, have you dated any of the local guys and what are they like?' [And I say] 'Oh they don't come to me'. And I had one woman say 'Oh, well yeah, because you're not the type'. And I said 'Oh!' I knew what she was going to say but I just asked the question for the hell of it. I said 'Oh, what do you mean by that?' [She said] 'Because you're not the sweet, innocent type'. I said 'You're right! You're right!'

Some foreign women said simply that they were not attracted to Chinese men, because they were too short or lacked the requisite cultural skills and shared interests. As this quote shows, ethnically 'Asian' women varied in their orientations to this dating scene, depending on their backgrounds and previous dating experiences.

In comparison to their general silence about Chinese men, many foreign women complained about the obsession of foreign men with local women. Frances, a white British woman who worked in a popular, high-end bar on the Bund, described her ambivalence at watching the flourishing dating scene between white men and Chinese women in her bar:

> Four years ago, going to Park 97 after work, when I used to see a whole floor of Western men and Chinese women... the whole lounge was full of Western men and Chinese women trying to pick up each other.... I can't tell if I am being sensitive to it because as a Western girl it's a hard thing to see, so often, guys who only go out with Chinese girls. It can be a bit confronting, not annoying but I don't know, I guess it's disappointing. Not that I would suggest that they shouldn't see Chinese people, but that it's the only person they want to see—that they would choose a person by race rather than by meeting them, or by personality.

As reported by Walsh in Dubai (2007), expatriate women described a 'holiday' or 'vacation' mentality among the foreigners in Shanghai. In the clubbing scene this takes the form of men expecting women to warm to them very quickly. As Frances put it:

> Especially in bars and nightlife and travelling—when people come to another city it's a ticket to do whatever you want... like when you are at home with your parents and employer, obviously you have to be a bit more well-behaved... people are very badly behaved in Shanghai I think... They go out to bars and get really drunk... or go out and pick up a different person every week. It's a good time for people to explore a little bit and do things they wouldn't do at home...

Younger expatriate women reacted to this scene more positively, accepting the more permissive sexual ethics that seemed to be required of participants in Shanghai's international nightlife. Sophia, a 23-year-old Bulgarian woman, described a sense of sexual liberation after arriving in Shanghai. When I asked her what changed for her in Shanghai, she said with a laugh:

> I learned to fuck around. [*I asked her if that was good or bad for her.*] Yes, it was good. It was something that I couldn't get away with back home. You can't imagine how people back home talk about girls. Like, you would be a slut or a whore if you did that. But here, no one cares. You can do what you want.

In contrast, some single expatriate women in their 30s and 40s described avoiding the clubbing scene altogether, hanging out at expatriate-dominated bars in order to avoid the sight of Western men hunting or being hunted by Chinese women. Few expatriate men I spoke with had the same negative reaction to the interracial dating scene in Shanghai clubs, showing that the nightlife zones are structured by gender as well as by race.

Regardless of age, single expatriate women perceived themselves as competing sexually with local Chinese women. However, because they shared many of the same interests and lifestyles—as well as complaints about men—they often became friends with the 'international' Chinese women, who were English-speakers and interested in Western culture (and Western men), and often worked in professional white-collar jobs in the city. Thus it was not uncommon to see foreign and Chinese women enjoying evenings out together in the clubbing scene. These same-sex friendships, and outings in the nightlife, were both a way for Western women to integrate into 'local' society, and a way for 'local' women to integrate into the 'international' scene that these foreign women and men represented. As Walsh (2007) points out, same-sex friendships were often a more stable element of this transient global nightlife scene than were sexual relationships.

## Discussion: Global Nightscapes as Socially Structured Spaces of Consumption

Global nightscapes are spaces of both consumption and production of the culture of global cities by transnational mobile elites, and for the expression and contesting of racialised masculinities and femininities among young professionals. Global nightscapes can also be seen as sites of ethnosexual competition and contradiction within the elite factions of the transnational capitalist class, now joined by mobile women and men, and by transnational Asians and Westerners. To complicate the analysis of migrant cultures, global nightscapes are also access points to an 'international' lifestyle for local residents of global cities, spaces that facilitate alliances and interactions with people travelling across national borders, blurring distinctions between local and migrant cultures. As complex ethnosexual contact zones, nightlife spaces produce multiple points of contact, alliances and conflicts, with greater freedom from institutional controls than the workplace. Nightlife patrons may avoid or seek contact across class and ethnic lines, flirting, fighting or fleeing depending on their desires or whims.

Despite the complexities of these racial and gendered topographies of contact, the ethnographic evidence here points to the continued relevance of postcolonial racial categories in a gendered competition between a dominant but fading global whiteness and a rising global Chinese racial identity. This mapping of a fractious global nightscape challenges the idea of a seamless transnational capitalist class, and instead describes racial and gendered sexual competition as an important feature of the leisure culture of transnational mobile elites.

Previous research generally points to an elevated sexual status enjoyed by white men and more recently Asian women in such transnational spaces, and the types of cultural resistance that such ethnosexual hierarchies provoke. Looking at Western men's sexual capital from the point of view of mobile Asian women, Karen Kelsky (2001: 148) argues that the whiteness and culture of Western men are 'hegemonic constitutive elements' of the freedom and modernity that mobile Japanese women long for for themselves. Conversely, Susan Koshy (2004) argues that Asian women have gained 'sexual capital' in the West through glamorous accounts of transnational romance produced by Westerners. As Ho and Tsang's (2000) research on interracial gay relationships in Hong Kong shows, these racialised sexual hierarchies can change significantly in a short period of time, depending on larger shifts of economic and cultural power. Similarly, Erwin's (1999) participant observation study of the filming of a transnational romance family drama in Shanghai points to the symbolic claims of a resurgent Chinese masculinity, which had been seen to be in decline or 'crisis' in the first two decades of the reform era (Zhong 2000).

This ethnography of Shanghai's global nightscapes maps these familiar racial and sexual categories onto a changing and contested topography of gendered and racialised nightlife zones that offer possibilities for multiple sexual strategies and idiosyncratic nightlife circuits. Within some specialised zones, many white men still experienced their embodiment of national and racial characteristics as a sexual bonus, as did some transnational Asian women and Asian men (particularly Asian Americans who embodied desirable physical and cultural traits). In this local mapping of national and racial bodies, some white women experienced distressing forms of desexualisation, though some younger white expatriate women described the 'touristic' space of Shanghai's nightscapes as a liberating arena for sexual consumption and exploration. As Moskowitz's (2008) ethnography of a 'foreigner bar' in Taiwan points out, even a single nightclub is a polysemic space in which different types of actor are differently able to mobilise their racialised and gendered attributes.

Although sometimes intensely competitive and even hostile, the interactions in the global nightscape mapped in this paper were largely narrated to me by clubbing insiders in a postmodern discourse of racial/sexual consumption rather than in terms of ethical or political action. For most informants, both the consumption and the embodiment of racial and sexual difference are part of the 'touristic' quality of ethnosexual contact zones. Transnational sexual capital is a good that clubbers try to both embody and consume. Being considered a desirable sexual commodity generally was not judged as insulting or alienating, whereas not being considered one certainly was. The complaints of some white Western women about desexualisation in Shanghai's nightscapes are evidence of the status associated with this embodied sexual capital. Although limited in its focus on nightlife, this study suggests that one of the more important considerations in transnational mobility may be the enjoyment or dismay resulting from rising and falling sexual status in the nightscapes of global cities (Farrer 2010). Indeed this may be one motive for further transnational moves.

Finally, global nightscapes are not simply the outcomes of transnational flows. Spatial nightlife stratification is the product of deliberate urban planning focusing on developing some spaces into profitable nightlife zones and the suppression of more-unruly and unprofitable spaces (Chatterton and Hollands 2003). While previous studies have focused on this politics of nightlife development as neoliberal development and policing strategies, this study points to the less-overt racial and gendered politics of nightlife development. Global nightscapes are produced in a tension between goals of policing and controlling interethnic conflicts (and limiting interethnic intimacies), and those of promoting cities as attractive destinations for transnational elites, opening up and shaping the terrains of these cities as ethnosexual contact zones. The 'play spaces' of global nightscapes thus cannot be divorced from the politics of race and sexuality that shape both their formation and the interactions within them.

## References

Appadurai, A. (1990) 'Disjuncture and difference in the global cultural economy', *Theory, Culture & Society*, 7(2–3): 295–310.
Ah Yan (1988) 'Jiuba, jiuba', *QingNianYiDai*, 6: 2–4.
Burawoy, M. (2001) 'Introduction', in Burawoy, M., Blum, J.A., George, S. and Gille, Z. (eds) *Global Ethnography: Forces, Connections, and Imaginations in a Postmodern World*. Berkeley: University of California Press, 1–40.
Chatterton, P. and Hollands, R. (2003) *Urban Nightscapes: Youth Cultures, Pleasure Spaces and Corporate Power*. New York: Routledge.
Cheng, N. (1989) 'Shanghairen shuo Shanghai yeshenghuo', in Gu, Y. (ed.) *Shanghai Yeshenghuo*. Shanghai: Shanghai Culture Press, 1–3.
Cressey, P.G. (1932) *The Taxi-Dance Hall: A Sociological Study of Commercialised Recreation and City Life*. Chicago: University of Chicago Press.
Erwin, K. (1999) 'White women, male desires: a televisual fantasy of the transnational Chinese family', in Yang, M.M. (ed.) *Spaces of Their Own: Women's Public Sphere in Transnational China*. Minneapolis: University of Minnesota Press, 232–60.
Farrer, J. (1999) 'Disco "super-culture": consuming foreign sex in the Chinese disco', *Sexualities*, 2(2): 147–65.
Farrer, J. (2002) *Opening Up: Youth Sex Culture and Market Reform in Shanghai*. Chicago: University of Chicago Press.
Farrer, J. (2008) 'Play and power in Chinese nightlife spaces', *China: An International Journal*, 6(1): 1–16.
Farrer, J. (2010) 'A foreign adventurer's paradise? Interracial sexuality and alien sexual capital in reform era Shanghai', *Sexualities*, 13(1): 69–95.
Field, A. (2008) 'From DD's to YY to Park 97 to Muse: dance club spaces and the construction of class in Shanghai, 1997–2007', *China: An International Journal*, 6(1): 18–43.
Hibbard, P. (2007) *The Bund: China Faces West*. Hong Kong: Odyssey.
Ho, P.S.Y. and Tsang, A.K.T. (2000) 'Negotiating anal intercourse in inter-racial gay relationships in Hong Kong', *Sexualities*, 3(3): 299–323.
Kelsky, K. (2001) *Women on the Verge: Japanese Women, Western Dreams*. Durham: Duke University Press.
Koshy, S. (2004) *Sexual Naturalization: Asian Americans and Miscegenation*. Stanford: Stanford University Press.
Liu, Y. (1989) 'Daochu kejiande wuting wuhui', in Gu, Y. (ed.) *Shanghai Yeshenghuo*. Shanghai: Shanghai Culture Press, 105–27.
Liu-Farrer, G. (2004) 'The Chinese social dance party in Tokyo: identity and status in an immigrant leisure subculture', *Journal of Contemporary Ethnography*, 33(6): 651–73.
Lu, H. (ed.) (2008) *Zhuanbianzhongde Shanghaishimin*. Shanghai: Shanghai Academy of Social Sciences.
Moskowitz, M.L. (2008) 'Multiple virginity and other contested realities in Taipei's foreign club culture', *Sexualities*, 11(3): 327–51.
Nagel, J. (2003) *Race, Ethnicity and Sexuality: Intimate Intersections, Forbidden Fruits*. New York: Oxford University Press.
Pratt, M.L. (1992) *Imperial Eyes: Studies in Travel Writing and Transculturation*. London: Routledge.
Ren, X. (2008) 'Forward to the past: historical preservation in globalizing Shanghai', *City & Community*, 7(1): 23–43.
Sassen, S. (2007) 'Introduction', in Sassen, S. (ed.) *Deciphering the Global*. Princeton NJ: Princeton University Press, 1–18.
Sklair, L. (2001) *The Transnational Capitalist Class*. Oxford: Blackwell.

Tanaka, M. (2007) 'Kontakuto zon no bunkajinruigaku he: teikoku no manazashi wo yomu', *Contact Zone*, *1*: 31–43.
Walsh, K. (2007) '"It got very debauched, very Dubai!" Heterosexual intimacy amongst single British expatriates', *Social and Cultural Geography*, *8*(4): 507–33.
Willis, K. and Yeoh, B.S.A. (2002) 'Gendering transnational communities: a comparison of Singaporean and British migrants in China', *Geoforum*, *33*(4): 553–65.
Yeoh, B.S.A. and Willis, K. (2005) 'Singaporean and British transmigrants in China and the cultural politics of "contact zone"', *Journal of Ethnic and Migration Studies*, *31*(2): 269–85.
Zhong, X. (2000) *Masculinity Besieged? Issues of Modernity and Male Subjectivity in Chinese Literature of the Late Twentieth Century*. Durham NC: Duke University Press.

# Shanghai Rush: Skilled Migrants in a Fantasy City

Yen-Fen Tseng

*While global cities obviously require a supply of skilled workers, the latter are equally dependent on high-level job markets and lifestyles offered by global cities. Drawing from empirical research on skilled Taiwanese migration to Shanghai, this article argues that, with the exception of those at the top rank, most skilled migrants cannot afford to be rootless, for a number of valid economic, social and cultural reasons. Many benefit from specific types of industrial development in the places they settle. Migrants also value the cultural attractions and lifestyles associated with particular destinations. Shanghai's emergence as the most favoured 'career city' for Taiwanese skilled migrants illustrates the fact that many contemporary metropolises present to both residents and outsiders a distinctive charm produced by combining high-level career opportunities with a theatricalised urban lifestyle. To Taiwanese skilled migrants, Shanghai is a present-day gold-rush destination—a place to fulfil modern economic goals and postcolonial cultural dreams.*

> I think of myself as being global. I see myself participating in global activities: sitting in jets, talking to machines, eating small geometric food, and voting over the phone (Rem Koolhaas, cited in Buruma 2003).

This jet-setting image is said to characterise the 'transnational capitalist class', Sklair's (2001) memorable term for elites working for global corporations who profess allegiance beyond their national identities to a dominant transnational class interest. In reality, Koolhaas—an architect from the Netherlands who has moved constantly between countries along with his projects and has himself become a global brand name—represents only a tiny fraction of the entire population of skilled migrants. The stereotypical image of jet-setting skilled migrants has emerged from an overwhelming emphasis in media coverage, and from research projects focusing on IT specialists and professionals whose skills are considered 'generic' and applicable to related industries worldwide. These workers are more than ready to follow the trails of industrial relocation. On the contrary, other types of worker encounter more barriers in applying their credentials and skills in foreign settings; once they move, they consequently tend to plant their roots in the new destination (Favell 2008; Scott 2006). Indeed, whether most skilled migrants, including the subjects of this article, embrace a global identity, remains an open question.

This article argues that, with the exception of those at the top rank, most skilled migrants *cannot afford* to be rootless, for valid economic and socio-cultural reasons. Skilled migrants are not as hypermobile as imagined. They value the cultural attractions and lifestyles associated with particular destinations, and are inclined to put down roots once they have settled in a new place they call home.

Rather than continuing to view skilled migrants as rootless workers, I draw on empirical research on Taiwanese migration to Shanghai to advance a city-sensitive thesis. Most of my interviewees care about where they *live* at least as much as where they *work*. I argue that, on the one hand, foreign professionals and skilled workers are filling various jobs in different global cities, and these economic opportunities are very much tied to the unique characteristics of industries in each city. On the other hand, as Kipnis (2006: 5) asserts, places can provide workers with psychological rewards, 'incorporating, besides human and social assets, a variety of physical, cultural and social service elements'. This paper understands migration as a process greatly informed by specific characteristics of global cities such as Shanghai.

### The Agency of Globalising Cities in Skilled Migration

Previous studies on what perpetuates the migration of skilled workers across borders suffer from a narrow interest in organisational or institutional channels. For years, the flow of skilled workers had been largely channelled by an internal labour market composed of expatriates within transnational corporations (Beaverstock 1994; Mahroum 2001; Salt and Findlay 1989). Because their overseas assignments are temporary, these workers can be said to 'flow' between places. An increasing number of workers are moving independently, however, due to more host countries providing work permits and residency rights as they compete globally to attract these desirable workers (Bauer 2004; Iredale 1997). As a result of freer movement for skilled workers, the mechanisms facilitating migration have gone considerably beyond the internal labour market of transnational corporations (Salt 1997). In recent years, online sites offering global job information have joined personal networks and headhunters to accelerate international job searches. Despite such emerging patterns, an earlier generation of scholarship on the international movement of skilled workers has tended to concentrate on the development of employers' internal labour markets and governments' institutional frameworks facilitating skilled migration.

I instead examine the increasing number of expatriates who migrate in response to organisational career demands requiring global relocation for promotion within global companies, but later changed their expatriate status to become local workers. This study mainly focuses on these local job 'hoppers' and independent movers. In many cases, the demand-side (organisational requirements) and supply-side (independent path-finding) stories actually converge, providing a more diverse and complex picture of the international movement of skilled workers.

Most studies on skilled migration explain their choice of research sites in terms of career development opportunities in occupations provided by industries common to large cities. The literature on global cities also credits the expansion of producer services in world cities with the convergence of professional workers (Sassen 1991). Such scholarship tends to relegate to the background the importance of destination in skilled migration decisions, the job opportunities available for foreign talent being somewhat generic to all global cities.

Some researchers, however, have pointed out that skilled migration is city-sensitive. The best-known popular theory was outlined by Florida (2002: 223–32), who proposes that certain types of place attract specific kinds of worker. Florida lists several criteria for skilled workers, or what he calls the 'creative class', to evaluate the *quality of place:* 'thick' labour markets, lifestyle, social interaction, and diversity. Other recent studies on the flight and flow of skilled workers have also paid attention to place-specific characteristics beyond economic considerations. Favell's (2008) research on European free movers in major European cities is one such project. He concludes that, beneath the assumed uniformity of global cities, unique cultural, social and political characteristics clearly distinguish major cities. Researchers studying careers in the cultural products industry frequently attend to the diversity that urban places offer workers. For example, Molotch (2002) studied automotive designers to determine how characteristics of places influenced the designers' migration and settlement patterns. He found that, beyond simple job-market considerations, certain types of designer tended to prefer specific cities, due to the lifestyles, subcultures and leisure activities that characterise each place (2002: 666–8).

I agree with Sam Scott's (2006) assertion that, when studying skilled migrants, it is important to recognise the importance of the agency of the world city as both an economic and a cultural centre. As Allen Scott (2004) observed, cities courting skilled workers have actively reorganised the built environment to suit the everyday life and work of urban workers. In the creation of the cultural metropolis, Soja (2000) highlights the official efforts to theatricalise the built environment as a setting for everyday urban work and leisure for city-sensitive people. Hannigan (1998) coined the term 'fantasy city' to describe how the urban environment, the high-level job opportunities, and the world of cultural meanings are tightly bound together in the theatrical setting of global cities. This paper will analyse how Taiwanese at home and in China help to construct Shanghai as a 'fantasy city', making many Taiwanese migrants want to live and work there—and in some cases, *only* there.

## Data

This paper draws on 45 in-depth interviews conducted during 2007 and 2008 with Taiwanese skilled workers. Most of the interview subjects remain in Shanghai today, but some have already returned to Taiwan. In this study, skilled workers are defined as professionals, managers and technical specialists. I relied on snowball sampling via informants in various occupations. The sample was created to document diverse migration channels and occupations. It covered four major types of work: manufacturing, the cultural products industry (design, media etc.), business services (banking, consulting), and international trading. A few interviews conducted with housewives who followed their spouses' relocation focused on their husbands' career-oriented migration choices and family incorporation issues. I also interviewed five repeat migrants who have moved in and out of Shanghai more than once, focusing on their work history, professional life, migration and housing choices and reflections on Shanghai, such as what they liked and disliked the most about, and how they evaluated the prospect of, living and working there, and whether they would move on to other cities or back to Taiwan. Migrants with children were asked questions covering education decisions—whether they chose local or international schools—and their expectations for their children's prospects, particularly whether they expected them to stay in China.

## Taiwanese Migration to China

A great majority of Taiwanese are the descendants of migrants who moved to Taiwan from South China over the past 400 years. The largest recent migration stream from China to Taiwan was composed of more than a million exiles following the defeated Kuomintang regime after World War II, a move accompanied by initial hopes of returning to the homeland soon. Since the early 1990s, when labour-intensive industries started to relocate to industrial zones in South China, there has been a steady wave of capital-linked migration consisting of small-business owners and expatriates working for Taiwanese firms with operations in China (Lee 2001; Leng 2002).

Migration is an especially challenging issue due to the political standoffs between Taiwan and China. In all official legal documents, Taiwanese are Chinese nationals, yet their Taiwan residency status disqualifies them from the rights and obligations of Chinese citizenship. Meanwhile, the policy by which Taiwanese may apply for citizenship is highly restrictive.[1] In recent years, however, China has moved to loosen its immigration policy in an effort to achieve cross-strait unification, and Taiwanese are now given multiple entrance visas and automatically approved for a year of residency once they apply for temporary residency status with a local government agency.

Another significant policy change favouring Taiwanese migration involves work permits. In 2005, the Chinese government announced a new policy granting

Taiwanese the unrestricted right to work in China. Before this change, Taiwanese were treated as other foreigners, who may only be employed after difficulties in filling a job vacancy are proven. According to the new regulations, such requirements are waived when hiring Taiwanese. The incorporation policy also offers education entitlements to the children of Taiwanese migrants. Taiwanese have capitalised on these emerging opportunities by expanding their job searches to mainland China.

As a result, migration from Taiwan to China has picked up speed and volume during the past decade. It is very common now for Taiwanese to have someone close to them working in China. According to the Taiwan Social Change Survey (2007), conducted in 2006 on a random household sample, over half the respondents had family members, relatives, or close friends currently working in China. According to a figure released by the Council of Cross-Strait Affairs in Taiwan,[2] Taiwanese residing and working in China in 2005 have increased to an estimated 750,000 and the number of Taiwanese business associations has grown to 84.[3] Table 1 shows the increasing regional integration across the strait, including visits, telecommunication and trading volume.

The migration stream is primarily composed of skilled workers and professionals, according to a study by Tsai and Chang (2006), and flows from more-developed to the less-developed regions. Taiwanese of the professional, managerial, and technical classes move because they can find comparable or even better wage packages in China. Such possibilities are almost exclusively funded by foreign capital investments that offer internationally comparable wage structures to global talent. Tsai and Chang's study also shows that social connections formed in the Taiwanese diaspora to China help significantly to facilitate the intention of moving to China. Having friends or neighbours working in China positively affects individuals' anticipation and willingness to move to China for jobs.

**Table 1.** Indicators of cross-strait increasing interaction 1991, 2001, 2008

| Activity | 1991 | 2001 | 2008 |
|---|---|---|---|
| Number of visits to China ('000) | 946.6 | 3,442.0 | 4,054.9 |
| Phone calls time (in million minutes) | 53.3 | 831.8 | 2,252.5 |
| Outbound | 27.1 | 509.8 | 1,538.5 |
| Inbound | 26.3 | 322.0 | 714.0 |
| Direct investment* | | | |
| Amount (in millions USD) | 1.7 | 27.8 | 98.4 |
| Per cent of total FDI | 9.5 | 38.8 | 57.1 |
| Trade volume | | | |
| Export | 80.5 | 299.6 | 1,054.0 |
| Amount | 69.3 | 240.6 | 739.8 |
| Per cent of total export | 9.1 | 19.6 | 28.9 |
| Import | | | |
| Amount | 11.3 | 59.0 | 314.2 |
| Per cent of total import | 1.8 | 5.5 | 13.0 |

Note: * Investment projects approved by Taiwan government.
Sources: Ministry of Mainland Affairs, Ministry of Transportation, Ministry of Economic Affairs, Taiwan.

## Shanghai: The Job-Hub City

Among all the destinations in China that receive Taiwanese migration, Shanghai has become the most favoured host city. With the most rapidly growing population and GDP in China, it is already one of the largest cities in the world (Rose and Tang 2002). Shanghai is the principal business centre of the country's most important economic region, the Yangtze River Basin, where one-third of the national population produces more than 50 per cent of the country's industrial and agricultural output (Rose and Tang 2002). Internal investments in Shanghai are characterised by higher-order enterprises, such as headquarters, representative offices and service centres of firms whose manufacturing sites are located outside Shanghai (Wu 2000).

Over the past decade, along with the opening up of China's national economy to foreign firms, the Shanghai metropolis has become a focal point for converging global flows of commodities, capital and talent. According to an investigation comparing the extent of global linkages in Hong Kong, Taipei, Beijing and Shanghai by measuring their connections with top global service firms, Shanghai emerges as a global city, while Taipei is more 'regionalist' (Taylor 2006). Shanghai hosted the 2010 World Exposition—the first to be hosted by a city in a developing country—which has brought many business and job opportunities related to the internationalisation of Shanghai (Wang 2007). During the 1990s, China's central government poured resources into improving the city's infrastructure and, since then, massive redevelopment of the central city has transformed Shanghai's urban landscape into a showcase for China's open policy, designed to attract foreign capital (Wu 2000). Active global networks help to bring in new actors and new ideas, as Sassen (1999: 108) remarked, and such networks have profoundly changed Shanghai's urban and cultural landscape.

Although Beijing continues to be the first stop for most foreign companies planning to set up offices, Shanghai offers more job opportunities to Taiwanese. On the online sites targeting Taiwanese job-seekers—such as 104 Job Bank (www.104.com.tw), the largest online site with global job opportunities in Taiwan—Shanghai lists the most potential jobs of all Chinese cities. On 26 December 2007, for example, there were 862 job opportunities for Taiwanese in Shanghai, but only 60 listed in Beijing. Online job sites have played an increasingly significant role in matching workers from Taiwan with jobs in China. 104 Job Bank has recently launched an operation in China (www.104china.com) whose main mission is to match Taiwanese workers with jobs in major Chinese cities. Among my interviewees, the younger the worker, the more likely they were to have found their first job in Shanghai through such online sites.

An estimated 450,000 Taiwanese are currently residing in the greater Shanghai area, forming the largest Taiwanese diaspora community in the world (Hu 2005). While economic factors are the primary force driving the immigration stream, complex social and cultural aspects of living and working are important considerations that feature in its sustainability. I found that skilled Taiwanese in the Shanghai area display several distinctive characteristics compared to their counterparts in other cities. Most importantly, Shanghai-bound migrants are usually accompanied by their families. The concentration of transnational corporations' regional headquarters has furnished Shanghai with an infrastructure and lifestyle that suit international families, including comfortable apartments, stores stuffed with Western food, and English-speaking schools at all levels. Compared to South China, Shanghai is considered a more suitable place for the whole family to settle (Lee 2001).

Secondly, although the earliest waves of Taiwanese migrants were mostly expatriates sent by Taiwanese companies, many Taiwanese skilled migrants in Shanghai independently seek job opportunities there instead of waiting for overseas assignments. Their migration is mediated through diverse channels. Many came to find jobs or entrepreneurial opportunities on their own, but even those who initially migrated as expatriates tend to find other jobs or become business-owners/self-employed once their expatriate status ends.

Finally, female migrants are very visible in Shanghai, compared to South China cities (Shen 2005). The Taiwanese Professional Women's Society (TPWS) was established in Shanghai in 2002, with current regular membership of around 100 career women, with another 300 registered as associate members. According to its president, the association was founded to facilitate migrant career women's lives and work by offering regular forums and social activities as platforms for exchanging information and ideas (Sina Global News, 16 July 2007). In marked contrast to the male-dominated Taiwanese business associations in most major cities, TPWS remains the only organisation exclusively serving Taiwanese career women in China.[4]

*Regionalisation of Business Structures*

Most of my sources attributed their move to Shanghai to its global job opportunities. As Sassen (1996: 191) has argued, the economies of many peripheral countries are thoroughly internationalised due to 'high concentrations of multinational corporations in all economic sectors and of heavy dependence on world markets for "hard" currency'. Although the headquarters of most transnational corporations are located elsewhere, Shanghai is considered one of the regional centres in the East Asia market (Shi *et al.* 1996), leading to the transfer there of many jobs, including those once located in Taiwan. An interviewee who works for the buying office of a transnational firm offered the following observation:

> When Western firms first establish their operations in China, they all look for key personnel from Hong Kong, Singapore and Taiwan. If they do not want to offer an expatriate package, such as housing costs, they would hire migrants from the above places in the local market.

As transnational corporations have gone local, they have gradually integrated Taiwan and Hong Kong operations into the 'Greater China' scheme under the command of regional headquarters located in major cities in China (Lu 2007). When expanding to overseas operations, most companies seek to fill key positions internally. Many Taiwanese working in Shanghai migrated as expatriates with Taiwanese-owned companies or other transnational corporations. Among my interviewees, there were expatriates working in automotive and computer manufacturing, telecommunications, and business service industries such as advertising, insurance and finance. According to them, expatriate opportunities are on the increase in the Shanghai job market, with large numbers of skilled workers in Taiwan relocating to regional headquarters in Shanghai or Beijing.

*The Talent Gap*

Shanghai has developed into a regional and global hub for many sectors in just a decade. This sudden transformation has created many gaps in the talent supply. Skilled Taiwanese moved their careers to Shanghai mainly to fill these gaps. One area short of talent is the design field. According to Olds (1997), elite non-Chinese design professionals have played a significant role in designing and building the new financial district in Pudong. The shortage is the result of local workers lagging behind in both formal training and tacit knowledge. Given the sudden demand for instant growth in many design sectors, the local education system has proven ill-equipped to supply design professionals in certain fields. An interviewee who earned his professional degree in both Taiwan and the Netherlands and now works for a Japanese-owned transnational company in landscape design describes the shortage of local talent:

> In terms of job security, I think at least for the time being I do not have to worry about being replaced by local Chinese because landscaping is a very new discipline in China. China just established a department of landscaping in the formal education system. It will take quite some time for the local system to train its own talent.

Design professions also involve aspirations for a better quality of life that require experience and tacit knowledge beyond formal training. An interviewee specialising in architectural design interpreted the talent shortage in the architectural design professions this way:

> I think to design something is to improve the quality of life. That often requires you to come from societies that have enjoyed affluence for quite some time, because only in such societies do people care for something more than survival—about the sensibility of living. So I think the barrier to entering this type of job lies not in the formal training, but in the aspiration for a higher quality of life.

Another interviewee who specialises in designing products for international customers adapted from the Chinese craft tradition believes that her skill niche lies in creating bridges between Chinese culture and the outside world. She said:

There are many good aesthetic elements in Chinese craft and art traditions, but if they are to be applied to products, these aesthetics must be connected with modern needs. I think we can do much better than local Chinese in terms of understanding such modern needs.

A further area in short supply is talent for the purchasing offices that provide merchandise to major retailers such as Kmart and Wal-Mart. As China becomes the major 'world factory' for mass merchandise, purchasing offices have relocated to China, impacting on the skilled employees located in Taiwan and Hong Kong. For a while, these purchasing managers flew back and forth between South China and Taiwan, but the cost became so high that many offices decided to close their branches in Taiwan and relocate to China. With more and more manufacturing sites moving from the Pearl River Delta to the Yangtze River Delta, Shanghai has become a command centre linking these world factories with world markets (Wang 2007). This centralisation has created a migration stream to Shanghai of skilled workers with buying functions. An interviewee who used to work for the purchasing office of Home Depot in Taipei moved to China independently and found a job leading an international sales department for a Taiwanese-owned garment manufacturer. Another interviewee, who works for a Hong Kong-owned trading giant that takes and places orders for everything a department store carries, talked about her job security:

> I don't think the Chinese will be capable of doing my job for a long while to come. The person doing my job (in the garment sector) needs to understand some of the implicit thoughts behind each specification. Most of my Chinese colleagues have to study very hard to understand what our customers really want, even though they have formal training in cloth-making. This expertise requires extensive work experience in this field.

Her remarks point to expertise that has more to do with tacit knowledge acquired through experience than with formal education. In similar reflections on her attachment to Shanghai's economic development, a realtor put it this way:

> In the past decade or so, the Taiwanese have been heavily involved in Shanghai's real-estate sector. We brought Taiwanese business models accumulated over 30 years to Shanghai and have demonstrated their great impact in a very short period of time. As a result, this industry is very dependent on migrants like me to tap our experiences in Taiwan.

## 'An Instance of the Global'?

Migrants differ on how central Shanghai is to their mobile career. As Favell points out in his study on free-moving professionals in European cities, engineers, especially in information technology, who tend to pursue more independent careers, exhibit the least rootedness toward place. For these workers, place is an 'instance of the global'

(Favell 2003, 2008). Those whose occupations are enabled by local linkages, however, develop more emotional attachments to their new promised land.

Similarly, those Taiwanese whose prosperity is very much tied to particular characteristics of Shanghai display the highest identification with the city. For example, job markets related to real estate and construction sectors have benefited from the fast growth of building projects in Shanghai. Migrants working in related industries are among the most rooted migrants and do not expect to move elsewhere in the near future, as expressed by an interior designer who has been in Shanghai for five years:

> For an interior designer, the prospect here is better than in Taiwan. Although I haven't earned as much money as I earned back in Taiwan, I have accumulated quite a number of projects to begin to learn the local clients' demands. All these steps require time and effort, so it is not easy to be back and forth. It is really a journey of no return.

Another landscape designer pointed out that the accumulated effect of investing time and effort in certain types of work function associated with local demand makes it increasingly difficult to move elsewhere:

> When I first came to work in Shanghai, I gave myself two years to try it out. Now it has been five years. The more I get used to the size and speed of projects in Shanghai, the harder it is to adjust myself to work in other places, including Taiwan.

These reflections all point to the same fact: that many skilled migrants have to choose a specific locality with career prospects where they can find some economic stability over a mobile career. In a conversation with an American architect—currently settling in Taiwan after four years working in a temporary position—about my study on mobile careers across the strait, he made an interesting comment on this pursuit of roots in an era of globalising careers:

> I don't think people like to move around. People like me who have moved several times across places and countries often feel tired about these changing scenes in your career. I think it is people's nature to settle, even in a globalising era (20 June 2008).

## Shanghai Rush

Shanghai's development into a regional economic giant has been widely covered by mass media and popular writers in Taiwan. According to M.T.Y Huang (2006), the media coverage has painted a rosy picture of Shanghai's development, rendering such migration options even more attractive. Due to current job-market dynamics, to go or not to go to Shanghai is already a hot topic among Taiwanese skilled workers, and this has led to locals referring to such migration as the 'Shanghai rush'—a modern-day gold rush to capitalise on immediate opportunities for wealth creation in Shanghai. Although Taiwanese also migrate to other major cities such as Shenzhen and Beijing, the Taiwan media has never referred to these migration streams in equivalent terms, such as the 'Shenzhen rush' or 'Beijing rush'.

The term 'Shanghai rush' emerged in the late 1990s. In 2001, several public forums discussed the background leading to the intensive promotion of Shanghai as an ideal migration destination for Taiwanese in the mass media. For example, in September 2001, a forum called 'Shanghai Rush' was held, with prominent panellists, including public intellectuals and writers, offering their observations and explanations of the phenomenon (Cultural Studies Monthly 2001). According to a survey conducted that same year, most interviewees who were willing to move to China preferred Shanghai for such a move (Leng 2002: 232). Such discussions remain very popular and visible; in 2007 alone, almost every major business magazine in Taiwan offered at least one special report on the experience of living and working in China. Among these reports, the Taiwanese in Shanghai were more visible and frequently mentioned than those in other Chinese cities. In a recent example, one of the major business magazines in Taiwan, *Global Views Monthly*, had a 2008 special report on 'new' opportunities in China's job market for white-collar workers—and the entire story focused on Taiwanese experiences in Shanghai. Quite consistently, contemporary media observers seem to equate China with Shanghai.

An interviewee reflects here on the media's effect on her decision to migrate to Shanghai:

> In 1999, when my husband was considering an offer to work in a mainland Chinese company, we were heavily influenced by the mass media's favourable tones about China. The media wanted you to think that, if you passed up the opportunity of working in China, you would regret it.

Another interviewee offered the following comments about the image of Shanghai in Taiwan's media:

> Taiwanese mass media tend to report only good news about Shanghai that glosses over the image of Shanghai. You have to come to see it yourself. I would advise Taiwanese not to rely too much on mass media coverage as they seek to understand the city.

Beyond the new economic opportunities, Taiwanese have long been interested in Shanghai's symbolic status in modern Chinese history. Many interviewees expressed their interest in its colonial legacy—Taiwanese affection can be traced back to collective memories formed by representations in literature and films, such as images of old Shanghai represented in many films based on the work of famous writer and Shanghai native Eileen Chang (M.T.Y. Huang 2006).[5] The most recent example is *Lust, Caution*, directed by internationally acclaimed Taiwan-born director Ang Lee.

For Taiwanese exposed to these popular culture representations, old Shanghai denotes a special kind of cultural chic, with the imagined charm of 'East meets West'—the origin of Chinese modernity. Taiwanese writer Pai Hsien-yung, son of a famous general from Shanghai, spent his childhood there. His best-known novel, *Taipei People* (1971), is about a group of displaced Chinese exiles from, and their common nostalgia for, Shanghai. Chinese literary critic Ni (2003) points out that the novel's nostalgia is not about old China, as many previous critics assumed, but about an emerging Chinese modernity wrapped up in images of an internationalised and cosmopolitan Shanghai. Of the emerging 'Shanghai Rush' in Taiwan, Ni satirically noted, 'Shanghai Rush cannot disconnect itself from Shanghai Fantasy' (2003: 15). As it turns out, the guidebooks to China available in Taiwan reveal that Pai's childhood home in Shanghai, a Western-style mansion, has become a favourite sight-seeing spot for Taiwanese visitors.

### Constructing Shanghai as a 'Fantasy' City

While renovating old Shanghai, officials intentionally targeted overseas Chinese collective memories of Shanghai as an exotically modern city open to foreign influences. Its transformation into the new involved a combination of looking both backwards *and* forwards (Tseng 2002). Among the first journalists to profile Shanghai in the post-reform era, James Fallow (1988: 77) observed:

> Shanghai's appeal has little to do with Chinese history or indeed with anything Chinese. But the effect is entrancing, even magical. To visit Shanghai is like being able to walk into the Manhattan or Berlin of fifty years ago.

Shanghai's history as a world city is deeply influenced by the multinational powers that once colonised its territory. The foreign influence in Shanghai was multiple, instead of single, which gives the city a special international flavour. An interesting question about contemporary internationalisation in ex-colonial cities, as Sassen (1996: 190) has remarked, is to what degree such a multinational flavour is an intrinsic part of postcolonial spaces. When recalling their first positive impression of Shanghai, many Taiwanese mention the sublime image of the Bund, the heart of the city's colonial-era foreign settlements. Renovated based on this nostalgia for the international flavour of the cityscape, the Bund in Shanghai is among the most famous 'memory lanes' of the old 'Paris of the East.'

Taiwanese migrants have been actively involved in renovating old Shanghai as a new cultural fantasy. For example, *Emigrate to Shanghai Magazine*—published by early Taiwanese migrants to Shanghai with a circulation in cities where many ethnic Chinese reside such as Taipei, Los Angeles and San Francisco—has long promoted to ethnic Chinese the charm of mixing new and old. Taiwanese in Shanghai have been involved in renovating some landmark buildings and landscapes from old Shanghai. For example, in early 2000, Taiwanese investors rebuilt and reopened the landmark dance hall Shanghai Paramount. Deng Kun-Yan, a famous Taiwanese interior designer, was among the first cultural workers to advocate preservation of the old factories along the Suzhou River. His involvement was widely covered by the media in both China and Taiwan, and his efforts earned him an Asia-Pacific World Heritage award from UNESCO in 2004. The Shanghai local media declared him the pioneer of architectural renovation in Shanghai (*Digital Times* 2007).

Back in Taiwan, cultural events representing the Shanghai fantasy have also played an important role in connecting the emotions of many Taiwanese to a city otherwise very foreign. For instance, the National Taiwan University Student Association organised the 2008 prom around the theme 'Old Shanghai Charm'. Its promotional newsletter had the following to offer:

> This year's annual prom is set against a backdrop of 'Old Shanghai Charm'. The decorations bring us back to the Shanghai Paramount, a famous dance hall in Shanghai during the 20s and 30s. We encourage you to dress in old Shanghai style to suit the stage, which will be decorated to remind people of old Shanghai, where the East meets the West. We hope you will enjoy one night of indulgence in the good old Shanghai days.

In 2008, a musical entitled *A Love Story between Taipei and Shanghai*, produced by the Taipei Philharmonic Foundation, opened in Taipei and appeared in Shanghai in 2009. A contemporary romance between two young people, one living in Taipei and one in Shanghai, it is filled with songs from Shanghai's colonial period and devoted to memories of the old days. This multimedia musical also features numerous old photos of streetscapes and architecture, along with words from novels by Eileen Chang that appeal to Taiwan's nostalgia for old Shanghai.

Such cultural events demonstrate the continuous construction of collective memories of colonial Shanghai, utilising cultural materials and built environments as elements to feed a contemporary fantasy. Even though in reality Shanghai may be remote from most people's everyday lives, these common cultural images allow Taiwanese to take part in the project of building a 'fantasy city'. The currency of these cultural images also helps to ease the transition when some of them eventually depart for Shanghai.

In short, Shanghai has served as both a major global player in today's world economy and a powerful 'fantasy' city that enchants Taiwanese, and reveals itself in some interviewees' sentimental expressions about the city. One interior designer, for example, said that she experienced an instant 'crush' on Shanghai when she visited the French Quarter, which reminded her of stories about old Shanghai. She felt thrilled to be able to take part in restoring the old city to its own glamorous image. An architect acknowledged a similar infatuation:

> It was like love at first sight when I first came to Shanghai by visiting the Bund. The mixture of building styles influenced by worldwide architects at different periods of time really creates a natural charm.

## Settling in a Space of Flows

For most Taiwanese skilled migrants, however, the relationship with Shanghai is primarily career-oriented based on short-term prospects. Most interviewees, when asked about the prospect of living and working in Shanghai, would not predict their whereabouts beyond five years. Such expectations reflect in their physical spatial arrangements while settling. In systematic research comparing the interiors of Taiwanese migrants' houses in Shanghai and in Taiwan, Wang (2002) found that migrants tend to pay much more careful attention to decorating their homes in Taiwan than in Shanghai. Indeed, Wang's migrants treated their homes in Shanghai as containers to hold something still 'floating'. The Taiwanese expatriate community in Shanghai is what Castells (2000) termed a 'space of flows', characterised by both physical infrastructure and cultural elements that mainly serve to facilitate the flow of things, transactions and people.

As Castells (2000) contends, however, the transnational elite who live in such spaces do not want to 'become flows themselves'. Yeoh and Willis (2005: 270) argue that members of this elite class have a sense of belonging to the 'space of place', as well as the 'space of flows', as they discovered when they investigated Chinese metropolises as contact zones for Singaporean and British expatriates working in China. Although most Taiwanese migrants do not have long-term plans for settling in Shanghai, they tend to live in places that afford them some sense of belonging. Most of my interviewees own their homes. The high incidence of home-ownership offers some indication of the migrants' bonds with their local communities. A Taiwanese writer who moved to Shanghai without anticipating long-term settlement wrote:

> I never thought that I would own a small flat in Shanghai, although many writers I admire have lived in Shanghai. Not long after I moved there, I went to an antique shop to buy an old-style clock. I asked the shop owner to give me a more reasonable price. I told him that I am not a tourist but a resident here, and this clock is for my home use. After five minutes, I got it at the price I bargained for. But despite this little antique clock, I still had not come to terms with living in Shanghai (Hu 2001: 4).

Taiwanese in Shanghai have developed two spatial strategies for constructing a 'space of place' in their living environments. The first is a conventional ethnic enclave with concentrations of fellow migrants. The Shanghai metropolis area of Gubei, the city's first Taiwanese settlement, still boasts a large concentration of migrants from Taiwan. Unlike most ethnic enclaves, characterised by exclusive co-ethnic businesses and residents (Light 2006), the Gubei community is more international. The area is also a favourite residential community of Koreans and Japanese, and businesses catering to both groups are very visible in the district (Y. Huang 2006).

A concentration of fellow Taiwanese makes the space of flows feel more like home. According to a two-time migrant who came to Shanghai from Los Angeles, but originally hails from Taiwan, Shanghai's Taiwanese ethnic enclave is more spatially condensed than in Los Angeles:

> I feel more at home in Shanghai than in Los Angeles. Despite the fact that I speak the same language and share same culture with Chinese, I am surrounded by more Taiwanese here than in Los Angeles.

The second strategy is to live in gated communities where other international expatriates reside—very prominent in Zhongjiang High-Tech Park around the newly developed Lujiazui Central Financial District. Taiwanese live in housing whose spatial forms are designed to 'unify the symbolic environment of the elite around the world', as Castells (2000: 447) remarks. These spatial forms are carefully designed to contain residential and leisure functions in segregated spaces, with easy access by subway to cultural life and entertainment in the central city. However, residents in such communities experienced less rootedness. An interviewee described the limited sense of community, since expatriate families constantly move in and out:

> For children from expatriate families, there is a serious lack of stability of friendships. They cannot enjoy the kind of 'growing up together' friendship that most children enjoy back in the homeland. Here, the children are all international visitors. Once they leave the country, it is hard to keep up the friendship. My kids often feel sad about this reality.

## Cosmopolitanism: Old and New

As a native Taiwanese, for a very long time before I had a chance to visit the city, Shanghai stood out for me as a metropolis coined by the term *shili yangchang*—literally, 'ten-mile-long foreign zone'. When Leo Oufan Lee investigated this term while writing *Shanghai Modern*, a book that attempts to remap Shanghai's urban culture in the colonial period, he found a Chinese–English dictionary that defined *shili yangchang* as a 'metropolis infested with foreign adventurers, usually referring to pre-liberation Shanghai' (1999: 345). The term *shili yangchang* expresses very well the deep sense of cosmopolitanism that Shanghai urban culture has embraced. After analysing the cosmopolitan tendencies of Chinese literary productions in pre-liberation Shanghai, Lee concluded that 'the phenomenon of Chinese writers eagerly embracing Western cultures in Shanghai's foreign concessions is a manifestation of Chinese cosmopolitanism, which is *another facet of Chinese modernity*' (1999: 313, italics mine).

In the contemporary, post-reform era, this cosmopolitanism is encapsulated by a journal launched in 1993, *Shanghai Culture*. In its opening statement on bringing back the spirit of old Shanghai: 'It [the journal] reaffirms the deep and solid foundation of the school of Shanghai culture, with its splendid tradition of assimilating outside cultures with an open mind' (cited by Lee 1999: 340). The rapid increase of international or Western architectural languages in new buildings certainly suggests that the spirit of assimilating outside cultures continues unabated (Tran 2007). Through major city-landscape development, government officials have been crafting Shanghai's public image of openness to all kinds of foreign participants.

In Shanghai, city planning and architectural design have been heavily influenced by foreign corporations, a phenomenon unknown and unthinkable in cities such as Beijing (Olds 1997). Shanghai's skyline and cityscape consequently serve as a showcase for such openness.

To many of my interviewees, Shanghai is attractive precisely because of its image of being cosmopolitan which, in their understanding, refers to being open-minded towards outside influences. I found that Shanghai as an open structure linked to the outside world is an asset not only for the economic opportunities, but also for the pursuit of cosmopolitan lifestyles. International influences—the contemporary version of cosmopolitanism—are greatly appreciated by my interviewees. Relocating to Shanghai is perceived by many as a way to pursue the opportunity to become more internationalised—sending children to international schools is one such strategy. Compared to Taipei, Shanghai has a much larger number of international/English-speaking schools.

In the mobile world of Taiwanese migrants, internationalisation means mastering English and Western cultural skills. Therefore, Shanghai's international appeal includes a choice of international schools for younger members, the majority of whose families emphasised the benefits of sending children to schools with curricula transplanted from English-speaking countries. This style of education is considered beneficial not only because the students learn an all-English curriculum that will help them to build up human capital, but also because they have the opportunity to make friends with children of expatriate families from other countries. According to an official figure on the national origins of cross-border migrants living in Shanghai, there were—besides Taiwanese—sizeable migrant populations from Hong Kong, Japan, Korea, the US, Singapore and Australia (Y. Huang 2006: 94). One migrant who relocated from Los Angeles remarked:

> After my kid came to Shanghai and went to international school here, he became more informed of activities and values in other parts of the world besides the US. He has now returned to California to attend university, and he found that his American friends in college are very parochial, very US-centred, while he is much more open to other types of worldview. He is more internationalised than his American counterparts. Without going to school here, it would have been impossible.

Several interviewees even listed the availability of schools with an 'international' (all-English) curriculum as one of the major attractions of moving to Shanghai. An interviewee whose family moved with her husband's job in a large Chinese state-owned company put it this way:

> One of the reasons that my husband decided to quit a very good job in Taiwan and take the offer here was the children's education. We think that if they can be educated in a more international environment, that would be wonderful.

Another clearly saw the advantage of education in an all-English environment:

> My daughter is very fluent in English because she went through the international school system. Even though she ended up graduating from a rather inferior local university, that didn't seem to matter too much when she was looking for jobs in transnational corporations. The transnational corporations are looking for workers with international perspectives. Eventually she did well in many job searches.

Such international perspectives and communication skills can be viewed as cultural capital—as forms of knowledge that confer on a person a higher status in society. Migrants invest in educating the young to become endowed with cross-cultural capital for the purpose of class mobility. As Castles (2002: 1159) pointed out, transnational elites thrive by adopting strategies that 'involve adaptation to multiple social settings as well as cross-cultural competence'. Such cultural capital is the object of dogged pursuit. In some cases, for example, even when the family breadwinner had been transferred back to Taiwan, the rest of the family stayed on so that the children could continue their education in Shanghai's international schools.

## Conclusion

Of all the destinations in China for Taiwanese migrants, Shanghai is the top choice. Shanghai's emergence as the most favoured 'career city' of Taiwanese skilled migrants illustrates what Soja (2000) has argued: that many post-metropolises present to residents and outsiders a distinctive charm produced through the combination of high-level job opportunities and theatricalised urban lifestyle. To Taiwanese skilled migrants, Shanghai is a present-day gold-rush destination—a place to fulfil modern economic goals and postcolonial cultural dreams. Their migration and living and work choices are simultaneously economically logical and fuelled by social and cultural motivations.

The Taiwanese migrants to Shanghai whom I interviewed are hyper-mobile, few having plans for permanent settlement. While most are unsure about their future plans, a few of the more mobile have moved in and out of Shanghai more than once. During their time in Shanghai, they develop ways of settling in spaces of flows, and they manage their settlement with mobility in mind by creating spaces of places. Thus, as Favell (2003: 25) points out, professional and skilled employment in global cities offers new opportunities 'combining mobility with settlement'; yet there are also tensions 'between mobility opportunities and accumulation through settlement'. By examining Taiwanese skilled migration to Shanghai, this article demonstrates how global metropolises offer new 'mobile nests' of opportuniy for these birds of passage. These migrants utilise the city's economic, cultural and spatial resources to develop strategies that ease the tensions of mobility by putting down roots here and now. Contrary to the portrait of the skilled migrant as someone who does not need to be attached to a particular place, I argue that migrants' sense of economic and cultural connection with the city along the migration journey is central to their migration and settlement decisions and outcomes. This resonates with Ho's (this issue) argument that 'cosmopolitanism as an empirical condition should be a project that is premised on a respectful acceptance of intersecting social differences'. The project involves very specific understandings of what cosmopolitanism in each global city offers to the cultural capital baskets of these skilled migrants.

Further research on the work and lives of skilled workers in transnational settings could expand our understanding of how skilled migrants form identities that embrace particular global cities, given their detachment from national identities, as documented by Castles (2002: 1159). While global cities obviously require a supply of skilled personnel, skilled workers are equally dependent on the thick job markets and cosmopolitan lifestyles offered by global cities. More research on the interdependency of global cities and skilled migration will further illustrate how mobile people live their everyday lives in concrete cities and the sense of rootedness they might develop in the here and now.

## Notes

[1] Taiwanese who fulfill at least one of the following two conditions can apply for such citizenship: 1) those who live in Taiwan alone without any family support and have family members (parents or children) in China who have both the willingness and the financial capability to support such applicants, who must be financially independent; 2) those who have been married to Chinese citizens for at least three years.
[2] This is a semi-official agency assisting the Taiwanese government with logistics associated with cross-strait matters.
[3] See http://www.sef.org.tw/html/seftb/seftb1/seftb1.htm
[4] In other Taiwanese concentration areas, there are migrant women's organisations which draw participation from both the wives of expatriates and from career women.
[5] Most of Eileen Chang's novels were written after she was exiled from Shanghai.

## References

Bauer, T. (2004) *The Demand for High-Skilled Workers and Immigration Policy*. Bonn: IZA Discussion Paper No. 999.
Beaverstock, J.V. (1994) 'Re-thinking skilled international labour migration: world cities and banking organizations', *Geoforum*, 25(3): 323–38.
Buruma, I. (2003) 'The sky is the limit', in Patteeuw, V. (ed.) *Considering Rem Koolhaas and the Office for Metropolitan Architecture*. Rotterdam: Nai, 53–72.
Castells, M. (2000) *The Rise of the Network Society*. New Malden: Blackwell.
Castles, S. (2002) 'Migration and community formation under conditions of globalization', *International Migration Review*, 36(4): 1143–68.
*Cultural Studies Monthly* (2001) 'Shanghai, immigrants, gold rush? A critical roundtable'. Online at: http://hermes.hrc.ntu.edu.tw/csa/journal/08/forum_7.htm
*Digital Times* (2007) 'Renovating old factories along Huang-Pu River', 15 February. Online at: http://www.bnext.com.tw/LocalityView_4375
Fallow, J. (1988) 'Shanghai surprise', *Atlantic Monthly*, July: 76–8.

Favell, A. (2003) *Eurostars and Eurocities: Towards a Sociology of Free-Moving Professionals in Western Europe*. San Diego: University of California, Centre for Comparative Immigration Studies, Working Paper 71.

Favell, A. (2008) *Eurostars and Eurocities*. Oxford: Blackwell.

Florida, R. (2002) *The Rise of the Creative Class*. New York: Basic Books.

Hannigan, J. (1998) *Fantasy City: Pleasure and Profit in the Postmodern Metropolis*. London: Routledge.

Hu, C.F. (2001) 'Migrating to Shanghai', *Cultural Studies Monthly*, 8. Online at: http://hermes.hrc.ntu.edu.tw/csa/journal/08/journal_forum_72.htm

Hu, S.Y. (2005) *Taiwanese Migrants and Their Life in Shanghai*. Shanghai Academy of Social Sciences Working Paper (24/05/2005). Online at: http://www.sass.org.cn/ggl.jsp?sortid=1199&artid=2723

Huang, M.T.Y. (2006) 'The cosmopolitan imaginary and flexible identities of global city-regions: articulating new cultural identities in Taipei and Shanghai', *Inter-Asia Cultural Studies*, 7(3): 472–91.

Huang, Y. (2006) *Social Stratification and Residential Segregation in Major Chinese Cities*. Shanghai: Tong-Ji University Press.

Iredale, R. (1997) *Skills Transfer: International Migration and Accreditation Issues*. Wollongong: University of Wollongong Press.

Kipnis, B.A. (2006) *A World City, Psychological Rewards and the Creative Agencies, Globalization and World City Networks*. Loughborough: University of Loughborough. Research Bulletin 207, http://www.lboro.ac.uk/gawc/.

Lee, L.O.F. (1999) *Shanghai Modern: The Flowering of a New Urban Culture in China, 1930–1945*. Cambridge: Harvard University Press.

Lee, T.H. (2001) 'Three hundred thousand Taiwanese migrating to Shanghai: issue on entrepreneurship', *Business Weekly*, 723: 88–106.

Leng, T.K. (2002) 'Economic globalization and IT talent flows across the Taiwan Strait: the Taipei/Shanghai/Silicon Valley triangle', *Asian Survey*, 42(2): 230–50.

Light, I. (2006) *Deflecting Immigration: Networks, Markets, and Regulation in Los Angeles*. New York: Russell Sage Foundation.

Lu, C.F. (2007) 'Taiwan, look forward: new jobs cross Strait', *Cheers*, 1 July: 66–128.

Mahroum, S. (2001) 'Europe and the immigration of skilled labour', *International Migration*, 39(5): 27–43.

Molotch, H. (2002) 'Place in product', *International Journal of Urban and Regional Research*, 26(4): 665–90.

Ni, W.J. (2003) 'Shanghai rush and narratives of Chinese modernity', in *2002 Literature Critics*. Beijing: Springwind.

Olds, K. (1997) 'Globalizing Shanghai: the "global intelligence corps" and the building of Pudong', *Cities*, 14(2): 109–23.

Pai, H.-Y. (1971) *Taipei People*. Taipei: Erya.

Rose, G.F. and Tang, Z.L. (2002) 'Shanghai: reconnecting to the global economy', in Sassen, S. (ed.) *Global Networks, Linked Cities*. New York: Routledge, 273–307.

Salt, J. (1997) *International Movements of the Highly Skilled*. Paris: OECD Occasional Papers 3.

Salt, J. and Findlay, A.M. (1989) 'International migration of skilled manpower: theoretical and developmental issues', in Appleyard, R.T. (ed.) *The Impact of International Migration on Developing Countries*. Paris: OECD, 159–80.

Sassen, S. (1991) *The Global City: New York, London, Tokyo*. Princeton: Princeton University Press.

Sassen, S. (1996) 'Analytic borderlands: race, gender and representation in the new city', in King, A.D. (ed.) *Re-Presenting the City: Ethnicity, Capital, and Culture in the Twenty-First Century Metropolis*. New York: New York University Press, 183–201.

Sassen, S. (1999) 'Hong Kong–Shanghai: networking as global cities', *2G: International Architecture Review*, 10(2): 106–111.

Scott, A. (2004) 'Cultural-products industries and urban economic development: prospect for growth and market contestation in global context', *Urban Affairs Review*, 39(2): 461–90.

Scott, S. (2006) 'The social morphology of skilled migration: the case of the British middle class in Paris', *Journal of Ethnic and Migration Studies*, 32(7): 1105–29.

Shen, H.H. (2005) '"The First Taiwanese Wives" and "The Chinese Mistresses": the international division of labour in familial and intimate relations across the Taiwan Strait', *Global Networks*, 5(4): 419–37.

Shi, P.J.J., Lin, H. and Liang, J.S. (1996) 'Shanghai as a regional hub', in Yeung, Y.M. and Sung, Y.W. (eds) *Shanghai: Transformation and Modernization Under China's Open Policy*. Hong Kong: Hong Kong Chinese University Press, 529–49.

Sina Global News (2007) 'Taiwanese career women active in Shanghai'. Online at: http://news.sina.com/tw/chinapress/101-102-101-105/2007-07-16/11412188838.html.

Sklair, L. (2001) *The Transnational Capitalist Class*. Oxford: Blackwell.

Soja, E. (2000) *Postmetropolis: Critical Studies of Cities and Regions*. Oxford: Blackwell.

Taiwan Social Change Survey (2007) *Taiwan Social Change Survey: Basic Findings*. Taipei: Academia Sinica, Institute of Sociology.

Taylor, P.J. (2006) *Shanghai, Hong Kong, Taipei and Beijing Within the World City Network: Positions, Trends and Prospects*. Loughborough: University of Loughborough, Globalisation and World City Networks Research Bulletin 204. Online at: http://www.lboro.ac.uk/gawc/rb/rb204.html.

Tran, H.A. (2007) 'Globalisation, redevelopment, and social consequences: the Xintiandi Project in Shanghai'. Lund: Lund University, Department of Architecture, unpublished manuscript.

Tsai, M.C. and Chang, C.F. (2006) 'China-bound: labour markets, ethnic politics, networking influences and job seekers from Taiwan'. Paper given to the EASS Taipei Conference, Academia Sinca, 19 June.

Tseng, Y.H. (2002) 'The Grand Shanghai-Land Project: a study on revitalization strategies of an urban historical scene'. Taipei: Tamkang University, Department of Architectures, unpublished MA thesis.

Wang, J.L. (2002) 'Floating home: the family and house identity among spouses of Taiwanese business migrants'. Taipei: National Taiwan University, Institute of Architecture and Urban Planning, unpublished MA thesis.

Wang, R.H. (2007) *Innovation of Changjiang Delta*. Beijing: Social Sciences Academic Press.

Wu, F.L. (2000) 'The global and local dimensions of place-making: remaking Shanghai as a world city', *Urban Studies*, 37(8): 1359–77.

Yeoh, B.S.A. and Willis, K. (2005) 'Singaporean and British transmigrants in China and the cultural politics of "contact zones"', *Journal of Ethnic and Migration Studies*, 31(2): 269–85.

# Making Careers in the Occupational Niche: Chinese Students in Corporate Japan's Transnational Business

Gracia Liu-Farrer

*Expanding international education and economic globalisation have changed both the make-up of international labour migrants and the patterns of immigrant economic adaptation. Chinese student migrants' employment experiences and economic mobility in Japan suggest that an immigrant occupational niche has emerged among Japanese firms characterised by a set of corporate positions that specifically deal with businesses in China. These firms preferentially recruit Chinese student migrants to fill these positions. This paper discusses the mechanisms that shape such an immigrant occupational niche and the opportunities and constraints presented to Chinese students in Japan. It discusses the paradoxical effects the existence of an occupational niche has on Chinese students, and argues that it provides a pathway for immigrants to enter a previously inaccessible labour market. However, the existence of an immigrant occupational niche itself is a product of prevailing institutional, structural and cultural barriers in the host society.*

Lawson, the second-largest convenience-shop chain in Japan, announced a few years ago that, in 2009, it planned to recruit 110 to 130 new university graduates, and a third of them—30 to 50—would be international students mainly from China.[1] Because of its expanding business overseas, Lawson reasoned, it needed to include more foreign employees in its products and services development.

Lawson's personnel decision stirred up a heated discussion on the internet. Most Japanese bloggers were enraged, condemning Lawson's decision and vowing to boycott the chain. However, a minority voiced approval. As one blogger asked the people who were criticising Lawson: 'Don't you think, in order (for Japan) not to become a closed country, Lawson's decision is rather wise? Theirs is a global enterprise after all'.[2]

Lawson's announcement and the bloggers' reactions illustrate what has become a reality: Chinese student migrants are an increasingly important labour force in corporate Japan. In many cases they are sought to develop Japanese firms' overseas businesses, especially in China. Following this observation, I investigate Chinese student migrants' career experiences and outcomes in corporate Japan under conditions of an expanding global economy. I suggest that an occupational niche for Chinese students has emerged in Japanese firms consisting of a set of corporate positions that specifically deal with businesses in China. I discuss the mechanisms that shape such an immigrant occupational niche and the opportunities and constraints they present to Chinese students in Japan—by allowing immigrants access to a previously inaccessible labour market and paving the way for career advancement. At the same time, the niche is limiting, its characteristics reflecting the institutional and cultural barriers facing immigrants in Japan.

This case-study of Chinese student migrants' career experiences in corporate Japan's transnational economy brings new perspectives to immigrant incorporation scholarship. It shows that new patterns of migration and immigrant career practices and different scales of immigrant transnational activities have emerged under conditions of economic globalisation. At the same time, Chinese students' experiences illustrate the complex multiplicity of talent migration beyond the stereotypical depiction of 'talent migrants' as hyper-mobile professionals moving in a 'frictionless space' in the global economy (Yeoh and Huang, this issue). As with the Taiwanese migrants in Shanghai (Tseng, this issue) and the Singaporeans in London (Ho, this issue), Chinese student migrants are 'embodied bearers of culture, ethnicity, class or gender' (Yeoh and Huang, this issue). Though educated and skilled, Chinese migrants are still treated as immigrants from a less-developed country to an advanced economy. Although enjoying increasing opportunities, they are making careers in the host labour market under considerable cultural, social and institutional constraints. Their mobility, or the lack of it, clearly shows the tensions between the market logic of economic globalisation and the racial and gender stratification characterising the local structure.

## The Occupational Niche and Skilled Migration in an Age of Globalisation

The scholarship on immigrants' economic incorporation typically asks how immigrants fare in the host labour market and whether their socio-economic standing in the host society is improving. Studies show that immigrants often gain socio-economic mobility in the host society by engaging in a niche economy, the dominant pattern of which is ethnic entrepreneurship. Chinese laundrymen (Siu 1987), Korean grocers (Kim 1981) and South Asian owners of Dunkin' Donuts (Rangaswamy 2007) are a few such examples. These immigrants' ability to develop entrepreneurial niches has to do with market demand, the strength of ethnic networks and the financial and social resources that come through them, immigrants' willingness to endure hardship, and cheap labour supplied by family members and co-ethnics (Min 1988; Waldinger 1986, 1996). Ethnic entrepreneurship is often seen as an economic strategy which immigrants adopt when they have no access to the primary labour market and see no hope of achieving mobility through employment (Min 1984).

Immigrants also create economic niches by penetrating and dominating certain occupations locally or globally. The Egyptian and Indian civil servants in the New York City government after the 1970s (Waldinger 1994), West Indian immigrant workers in New York's food business (Waters 1999), Mexican immigrants in janitorial jobs in Los Angeles (Cranford 2005), and Filipina domestic workers all over the world are examples of immigrant niche occupations. Immigrants were able to enter these occupations because of the particular labour demand at a historical moment or employers' preferences for flexible and low-wage labour (Waldinger 1994; Waldinger and Lichter 2003). Immigrants' monopoly of these occupations shows, again, the triumph of ethnic networks. Carving out occupational niches is a competitive and often usurping process for immigrants, as they replace native workers who previously occupied these positions (Sanders *et al.* 2002; Waldinger and Lichter 2003).

In recent decades, with increasingly globalised economic production and consumption, the development of communications technology, and the easy availability of air travel, immigrants have both the means and the incentive to maintain strong ties with home societies. Some actively look for transnational economic opportunities. While scholars debate the scope and the prevalence of immigrant transnationalism and whether it has become such a generalised pattern of practices (Waldinger and Fitzgerald 2004), immigrants' transnational economic strategies, particularly their entrepreneurship, are extensively documented: courier services of different scope and levels of formality that serve co-ethnic immigrants' need for transporting material and money to and from their native countries; the trading and marketing of ethnic goods and cultural products catering mostly to the immigrant community but in some instances also to the host market; and investing in businesses in their native lands and supplying hometowns with industrial goods or high-tech commodities from the host society (Kyle 2001; Landolt *et al.* 1999).

However, while studies of immigrants' transnational entrepreneurship flourish, very little research scrutinises changes in immigrants' employment practices and labour market outcomes. By introducing Chinese student migrants' occupational niches in Japan's transnational economy, this study examines the changing immigrant labour market practices under conditions of economic globalisation, focusing primarily on how immigrants' transnational strategies are demonstrated in their employment patterns.

The study also shows the diverse range of skilled labour migrants and the complexity of their career outcomes. Previous research in skilled migration has tended to focus on two (sometimes overlapping) types of skilled migrant: those who possess specific technical skills, especially in the high-tech industries; and those who are corporate, professional and entrepreneurial elites. The former often become subjects of the 'brain drain', 'brain gain' and 'brain circulation' debate (see Hawthorn 2005; McLaughlan and Salt 2002; Saxenian 2002, 2005, 2006; Ziguras and Law 2006). The latter are the subjects of envy—the hyper-mobile globetrotters with privileged positions in the global economy, moving around the world to advance their careers or business interests through institutional channels or professional networks (e.g. Beaverstock 2005; Sklair 2001).

However, this case-study, along with other papers in this special issue of *JEMS*, argues that the population of skilled migrants includes individuals with diverse skill sets and different degrees of privilege in the process of economic globalisation. In particular, it questions often biased notions of the international student body. While people naturally associate international students with graduate students majoring in science and technology, in reality, the majority of them study languages, cultural subjects and social sciences (Liu-Farrer 2009). This paper shows that Chinese student migrants in Japan, typically majoring in humanities and social sciences, use their linguistic and cultural skills to access a specific labour market in corporate Japan, although their career mobility bears no resemblance to that of the transnational elites. The occupational niche where most Chinese students are employed is both an opportunity and a constraint. While providing Chinese students with career channels in Japan's primary labour market and to some extent privileging the immigrants, working in this niche also delimits their career development.

## Data

Both qualitative and quantitative data are used in this paper. The qualitative data include primarily interview transcripts and Chinese media publications. From 2001 to 2004, and again in Autumn 2006 and Summer 2007, I conducted in-depth interviews with 150 Chinese immigrants whom I solicited in various immigrant leisure and religious venues, and through social networks. Among them, 108 lived in Japan at the time of interview and 42 were residing in China. Each interview lasted between one and four hours. There were multiple interviews with key informants. Of the 150 interviewees, 115 entered Japan as students. This study primarily analyses 60 who were working or had worked in Japan as full-time white-collar employees.[3] In addition, I obtained narratives and cases from Chinese immigrant media in Japan. I subscribed to and collected Chinese-language newspapers and regularly visited websites popular among the Chinese in Japan. I referenced publications such as *Writing Histories in Japan (Fu Ji Dong Ying Xie Chun Qiu)* (Duan 1998)—a collection of autobiographies written by 100 Chinese people, the majority of whom had studied in Japan between the late 1980s and mid-1990s.

The quantitative data include a sample survey administered to 218 Chinese immigrants between May and December 2003. Four-fifths of the respondents were randomly recruited at Chinese supermarkets, restaurants, leisure and religious venues, where I conducted participant observation. Twelve questionnaires were gathered in a housing compound in Saitama Prefecture, north of Tokyo, where over 400 Chinese families lived at that time. Another 40 respondents were obtained through personal connections. Although this is a convenience sample, with the exception of Fujian immigrants whom I over-sampled, I tried to achieve as varied a sample of respondents from different sending regions and visa categories as possible. In total, 120 out of 218 of my respondents first arrived in Japan as students. In addition, I used official statistics, including annual immigration statistics by the Japan Immigration Association and Ministry of Justice (MOJ), data on international students' post-school mobility trends from Japanese Students Support Organisation (JASSO), and student enrolment statistics from Ministry of Cultural, Education, Sports and Technology (MEXT). Statistical data are used descriptively, mainly for the purpose of illustrating main trends in the phenomena observed.

## The Emergence of an Occupational Niche

Since the end of 2007, at 606,889, Chinese nationals have become the largest foreign resident population in Japan (Ministry of Justice, Japan 2008). This number does not include the nearly 100,000 Chinese immigrants who have obtained Japanese citizenship over the last two decades. Among all means of contemporary migration from China to Japan, student migration represents one of the dominant patterns (Liu-Farrer 2009)—over 300,000 have entered Japan since the mid-1980s.

Upon completing their education, many Chinese students seek employment in corporate Japan. Although there are no public data available about exactly how many Chinese students stayed in Japan and how many returned home, according to the statistics published by JASSO, among the known 24,961 foreign students who graduated from Japanese tertiary schools in 2004, only 13 per cent returned to their own countries for employment or education and 1 per cent went on to a third country to work or study.[4] Sixty-nine per cent were either employed or continued their education in Japan.[5] This survey included all foreign students who graduated from Japanese tertiary educational institutions. Given that Chinese students represent two-thirds of the foreign students in 2004, the trend is indicative of Chinese students' post-education mobility. In addition, according to JASSO statistics, the least likely to return to their home country were college and junior college graduates, and post-secondary vocational-school students. Chinese students happen to concentrate in these academic categories. They made up 72 per cent of foreign students in four-year colleges and 78 per cent of those in junior colleges in 2003. Only 8 per cent of foreign college graduates and 6 per cent of those from junior colleges returned to their home country for employment.[6]

According to the Ministry of Justice's statistics on visa status changes, since 1991 the majority of employment visas have been granted to Chinese students. In 2009, over 6,300 Chinese students joined the labour force in Japan upon graduation. Since the student migration trend began, the total number of Chinese students who had obtained employment visas reached 58,178 by 2009, a number which has risen particularly fast in recent years (Figure 1).[7]

Chinese students' employment patterns in Japan demonstrate the phenomenon of occupational 'niching'. Legally, they are the most likely to be granted the visa status of 'Specialist in humanities/ International services'—in 2008, this applied to 75 per cent of all Chinese students who received an employment visa. In total, nearly 80 per cent of such visas—intended for foreigners who, according to the Ministry of Justice 'have the particular knowledge and cultural competence of a foreign country'[8]—were granted to Chinese students.[9] Among them, the majority (and 50 per cent of my 60 interviewees) are employed by Japanese companies to work in marketing and sales related to the transnational business with China. A popular title is 'Sales Representative' or 'Overseas Sales Representative' (Table 1).[10]

Receiving an 'Engineer' work visa—usually granted to professionals in IT and other technical fields—does not mean that the immigrants will be working exclusively in a technical position. Their linguistic and cultural backgrounds are also an important factor in their employment. As a female architect who worked for one of the biggest Japanese construction firms told me, she was hired into a 'China team' that consisted exclusively of Chinese architects and engineers. The firm was in the process of launching businesses in China. Although, in the four years she worked for this company the business with China had not been actualised, she was told from the very beginning that she would be handling the firm's business with China.

In high-tech industries with fast-expanding off-shore production, many engineers and software professionals acquire the title of 'Bridge Engineer' or 'Bridge Software Engineer (SE)'. The software engineers I have interviewed defined a 'BSE' as a project

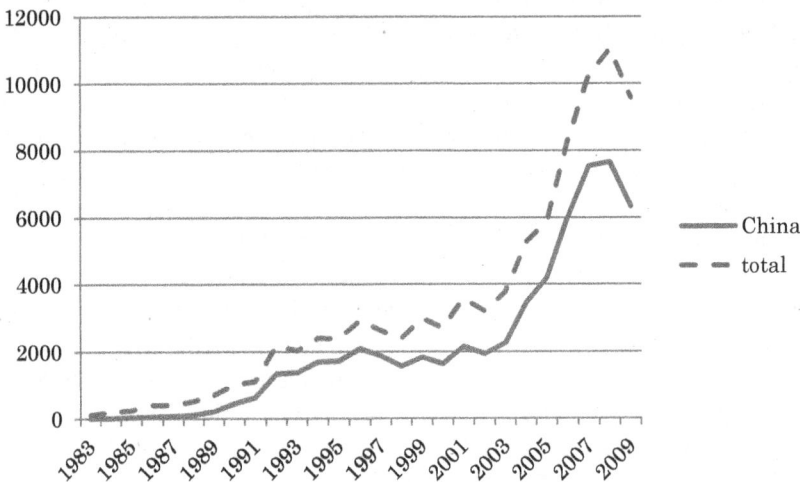

**Figure 1**. Chinese Students Who Obtained Employment Visas in Japan (1983-2009)
Source: The data for this figure is compiled with annual data published by Japan Ministry of Justice. The data from 1984 to 1999 was cited from Wang (2001:385).

**Table 1.** Occupational categories of the 60 interviewees

|  | Men | Women |
|---|---|---|
| Sales representatives | 13 | 17 |
| Engineer/design | 15 | 5 |
| Others* | 5 | 5 |
| Total | 33 | 27 |

*Note*: *includes self-employment (3), college professor (1), editor of Chinese newspaper (1), kindergarten teacher (1), human resources (1), unspecified positions related to managing Chinese workers (2), hired to work in China (1).

manager who could design the programme with Japanese clients and lead the Chinese programming team to complete the project. A qualified 'BSE' typically requires three types of skill—software development, language and communication in both Chinese and Japanese, and management. Therefore, only Chinese employees who have mastered the Japanese language and have been working in Japanese firms for an extended period are able to do the job. As a result, 'Bridge SE' is considered a milestone in technical workers' career paths, a role that is increasing in demand and a vacancy many aspire to fill.

Moreover, as I explain later, many Chinese engineers eventually worked or aspired to work in the sales and marketing positions dealing with China because that is where they saw their careers developing. The statistics about Chinese students' labour market outcomes in Japan clearly indicate that there exists an occupational niche in the labour market for Chinese student migrants—situated in the sphere of transnational production and marketing between Japan and China.

## The Occupational Niche in the Transnational Economy

The making of an occupational niche involves both labour market demand and immigrants' ability to meet the demand (Waldinger 1994). Economic globalisation has restructured the labour market domestically and globally. Skilled Taiwanese professionals rush to Shanghai to look for career opportunities because the regionalisation of business structure has made this global city a job hub with many talent gaps the locals are unable to fill (Tseng, this issue). Similarly, Chinese students' tendency to occupy positions in corporate Japan's transnational business operations has to do with the increasingly close economic relationship between Japan and China over the past two decades. Japan is the largest foreign investor in China and the top importer of Chinese workers. China has surpassed the US to become Japan's largest trade partner. Not only do big conglomerates have most of their production done in China and want to sell a big portion of their products in China, but numerous medium and small Japanese firms are also active, and to some degree desperate, players in the transnational economy between Japan and China. In 2007, Shanghai alone had 4,828 Japanese corporate branches (Sasatani 2007). In such an economic context, Chinese student migrants who have recognisable Japanese higher-educational credentials, speak both Japanese and Chinese fluently and, to some degree, understand both Chinese and Japanese society, are ideal candidates to fill the existing positions or to actualise the firm's plan of entry into China. A few informants found that they were the first foreign employees the companies had ever hired.

On the other hand, the making of an immigrant occupational niche is not merely a result of labour demand. The characteristics of Chinese students in Japan influence their positions in Japan's economy. The first reason why they are predominant in marketing and sales positions is their educational preferences—in 2003, 73 per cent (62,349) of self-financed foreign students in Japan's higher education majored in 'arts—*bunkei*' (includes humanities and social sciences)—a typical choice for Chinese students. Among international college students, the rate was over 80 per cent.[11] As one informant explained, 'In Japanese colleges, it does not really matter which specific major in arts you are in... If you study arts, mostly your career future is in marketing and sales'.

Chinese students tend to choose arts over sciences because, on the one hand, they recognise the nature of labour market demand. They see their predecessors entering Japanese companies, working in marketing and sales, and doing business with China; they aspire to do the same. On the other hand, it is a choice shaped by constraints. International students are a diverse population with various credentials and aspirations. Most Chinese students who arrive in Japan for education have already graduated from high school in China. Some fail to enter college in China. Others are lured by a foreign degree to seek university education in Japan. Most Chinese students have no previous Japanese training and therefore usually spend two years in a language school in Japan. After a long break from high school, many Chinese students find taking the college entrance examinations in mathematics and science in Japanese a daunting task. In addition, besides learning a new language and passing the highest-level proficiency test, Chinese students have to work in part-time jobs in the language academy in order to pay school fees and living expenses and save for college tuition fees. Many hardly have time to spare for college entrance examinations. Unlike science and engineering subjects that require extensive testing for admission, liberal arts programmes—especially in private universities—have fewer tests, some only requiring an interview.

In addition to Chinese students' academic concentration in arts and social sciences, the part-time off-campus work is also an integral part of cultural training for Chinese student migrants in Japan. Although sometimes pushed to physical and emotional limits, most consider their work experiences absolutely necessary for understanding Japanese work ethics and social organisation—important when navigating the transnational economy between Japan and China in their future careers. As one interviewee, Anqi, explained, 'If it is a position dealing with the domestic market, why would they need you? A native Japanese speaker can do such things better than you do'.

Moreover, Chinese employees actively help to expand the labour market demand for Chinese students. For example, when Shen Chao, a law-school graduate, started his career at a Japanese technology marketing firm, he was an advisor working in the field of intellectual property. He was initially hired for his legal expertise and English ability and, for the first few years, travelled mostly to Europe and North America. In the late 1990s, Chao reminded his boss of the potential market for patented technologies in China. Very soon, as the only Chinese person in the company of 50 employees, Chao found himself immersed in transnational business between Japan and mainland China, and the company had to hire more Chinese workers to develop this new business.

The existence of such an occupational niche in Japan's corporate labour market has meant that the economic incorporation patterns of contemporary Chinese migrants look drastically different to those of previous generations of Chinese immigrants in Japan. Commenting on these career patterns between the new and old generations of Chinese immigrants in Japan, the President of the Overseas Chinese Association in Japan, Zeng Deshen, a restaurateur, explained:

> The first generation of overseas Chinese could only take up the restaurant business because Japanese companies did not recruit Chinese. I graduated from a college in Japan, majoring in science and engineering. At that time the diplomatic relationship between Japan and China had not been normalised. The employment situation was difficult. I couldn't find a job so I had to help my parents with their restaurant business. Our generation is like this. Only after the normalisation of diplomatic relationship in 1972 did economic communications increase between the two countries. Japanese firms needed people who had Chinese skills, and started employing our Chinese sons and daughters. As long as the younger generations of Chinese have ability and competency, they are not worried about jobs.[12]

However, although the occupational niche is expanding with the transnational economy, and there seems to be increasing demand for Chinese student migrants in corporate Japan, it still begs the question: What kind of, and how much, career mobility do immigrants experience in this occupational niche? The next section takes a closer look at Chinese immigrants' career experiences and strategies within the occupational niche in Japanese firms. How do they fare compared to native Japanese employees?

## Career Mobility in the Occupational Niche

Several characteristics distinguish Chinese student migrants' employment patterns and career experiences in the occupational niche from those of Japanese employees: they are more likely to enter small firms than their newly graduated Japanese counterparts, they are more mobile, and they actively pursue a transnational career that leads them to become 'expats' at home. This section explores the reasons for such patterns of Chinese student migrants' career mobility.

*Entering Small Firms*

International students have better employment chances in small Japanese firms than in large. Among the 10,262 foreign students who obtained work visas in 2007, 50.1 per cent were employed in firms with fewer than 100 people. The proportion is much higher than among Japanese natives. If measured by the capital investment of the employer, 5,521 of the 10,262 foreign students, or 53.8 per cent, found employment in firms with a capital investment of less than 50 million yen.[13] In comparison, in 2006, only 26.3 per cent of the total population of newly graduated students with post-secondary education in Japan entered firms with fewer than 100 people.[14] Among the 60 interviewees represented in my study, with 13 missing cases, 35 of them worked for firms with fewer than 100 people.[15] In fact, the increase in employment visas in recent years is mostly due to the increase of students employed in small firms.

Chinese students' tendency to enter small firms is a consequence of the particularly acute labour demand in these firms. In Japan, there is a discrepancy between the reality of labour demands and job-seekers' employment expectations. Labour demand from the large firms has declined sharply since the early 1990s and has not significantly rebounded. Instead, the medium and small firms are the mainstay of the Japanese economy, and are where the labour demand is highest. However, newly graduated university students still mostly aspire to enter large firms. Among firms with over 1,000 workers, there were twice as many job aspirants as job vacancies, while small and medium-sized firms had two and a half times as many jobs as aspirants (Ohara Institute of Social Research 2004). By mostly entering small and medium-sized firms, therefore, Chinese students are helping to fill the vacancies passed over by the natives, their employment niche in fact resulting from a general labour shortage in positions less desirable to the natives.

However, this view is too simplistic. Both official statistics and my own research show that Chinese student migrants predominantly work in positions that require their specific linguistic and cultural skills. They are not just meeting the general labour shortage in small firms. Instead, while the labour demand of large firms is relatively stable as they have gone transnational in an earlier phase and already have an established transnational work force, small and medium firms are rapidly expanding their demand for skilled immigrants as they have just begun to seek opportunities overseas. As offshore production and global trading become important business strategies for cutting costs and developing markets, struggling small firms look toward China and other Asian countries for opportunities. In this context, Chinese students who have Japanese educational credentials, speak Japanese, Chinese and sometimes English as well, and have knowledge of both Japanese work culture and Chinese ways, become ideal agents to assist in firms' transnational businesses. By 2006, there were so many small and medium firms in Shanghai alone that a business association called Japan Small and Medium Enterprises Network at Shanghai was established (http://sme.shanghai.or.jp/entry/index.php). Of the 1,455 Japanese firms listed in JAPIT (2007) which currently have businesses in China, 861 firms, or 63 per cent of the total, had fewer than 100 company employees.

In short, the educational credentials of Chinese students in Japan often lead to careers in sales and marketing in corporate Japan, especially in transnational business with China or the Chinese-speaking world. The upside of this niche is that, with transnational economic practices spreading in the Japanese business sector and as more and more small players enter the market, Chinese students can easily find employment opportunities in Japan. In these corporate positions, Chinese students have a clear advantage over Japanese students. The downside of such an occupational niche is that, instead of working in a slick high-rise in Marunouchi, they find themselves the only foreigners among a dozen native Japanese in a crowded room in the middle of a rundown building that doubles up as a residential apartment building. This employment reality shapes the characteristics of Chinese student migrants' career mobility.

*Job Mobility*

Chinese student migrants' career experiences in the occupational niche are marked by high job turnover rates and relatively stagnant upward mobility. Among the 60 cases I used for this study, the topic of job turnover was discussed in 52 interviews. Among these 52, only eight people had never changed jobs in Japan, including two who had worked for less than a year. High job turnover is symptomatic of Chinese students' strategy to better their careers by constantly looking for opportunities. Among my informants, several did not intend to pursue a lifetime career in Japan. Instead, they saw their employment as an opportunity for accumulating business experience and financial capital. In fact, one informant turned down an offer of a permanent position in a big firm after working there for a year and chose to stay on as a contract employee because the latter received more cash payment—the company did not have to pay their social security or health insurance, or contribute to their pension fund.

The high turnover is also a result of two other factors: the low level of job security among Chinese student migrants, and the obstacles to upward career mobility they frequently confront.

Chinese students' lack of job security results from the characteristics of both the institutions they work for and the career tracks they are employed in. As explained in the previous section, Chinese employees tend to work for small and medium-sized firms. One disadvantage of small firms is the lack of job security. With the prolonged economic recession, many smaller firms find it increasingly difficult to survive. They turn to the Chinese consumer and labour market for hope, and hire Chinese students in Japan in order to launch business with China. However, these struggling firms can offer little job security. For example Zheng Jia, from central China, found that she had little choice but to work for a small Japanese trading firm despite long hours and low pay:

> I was lucky even to find this job. You see, this was my second job. The first company went bankrupt a year after I began working there. And it happened so suddenly. I was not prepared. My visa was expiring in two weeks! A friend of mine who had been in Japan for 12 years introduced me to interview at a company. But then I needed to go in for a second and a third interview. I didn't have time for that. I went to an employment agency. As it happened, my current company had just sent in the job vacancy notice. I was introduced to them immediately. It was a hot summer day. I went wearing a suit. The company owner was a woman. She saw me like that and was delighted. She said she would let me know about the result the next week. But as soon as I arrived home, I received a phone call from her asking me to work there the next day. I accepted it without hesitation. I really had no choice. Later the other company called me for a second interview. I said I had already found a job. I couldn't wait for their decision.

Job security is not guaranteed in big firms either. While regular employees in big firms in Japan tend to have low turnover,[16] Chinese students are often contract workers when they are initially employed. Some become tenured employees after several years, but most do not have the opportunity. Zhang Tian thought he was lucky to have taken the job he had instead of joining a bigger electronic appliances company like his friend:

> He went to work for S Electronics. But S only recruits foreigners as contract workers. The contract has to be renewed every year. When I graduated, he recommended me to the company, and they wanted me. S had a lot of projects in China. But then the situation became bad. About four years ago, he was called to the boss, and was told that the project he was on was cancelled. The company gave him three months' salary and did not renew the contract.

The second reason for Chinese employees' high turnover rate is the blocked vertical career ladder. In small and medium-sized firms, the career mobility chain is short. If a company consists of a few dozen people, there is little room for promotion. Hired for the business with China, Chinese employees can at best be promoted to lead the team that deals with China. According to my informants, it is unusual to make a foreigner the head of the entire department. Chen Lan explained, 'One carrot occupies one hole (*yige luobo yige keng*). As a foreigner, you have little chance to be promoted to a department leadership role managing the Japanese employees'. Lacking job security and promotion in Japanese firms, Chinese immigrants rarely feel the need to commit to one employer; the flourishing transnational economy creates enough vacancies for them to keep moving.

There are Chinese student migrants who *do* get promoted. In the occupational niche there are also mobility channels, from sales assistants to sales representatives and then on to supervisors of sales teams. Among the few people who actually had a title other than a generic 'overseas representative', one worked for a small company whose entire business was with China. He had been with the company for 16 years, and was relied upon for most business deals. He was given a title of division leader (*buchou*). Zhang Tian, after working for a trading company for eight years, was given a position of group leader (*kachou*). He earned the title by actively developing clients in China independently, so if he left, the company would lose most of their Chinese clients. It seems that those truly indispensable Chinese employees with outstanding records may have a chance for promotion, especially if they show true commitment by actually becoming a Japanese citizen. Shen Chao, who expanded his firm's business into China, was asked by his boss to naturalise in order to be entitled to a leadership role. 'Only by naturalisation, I showed them the kind of commitment they needed'. Among the technical people, corporate titles are less important than actual tasks and whether they have a leadership role in a project. IT people accumulate licences and work experience. The important career milestone for Chinese IT people in Japan is to become a 'BSE', a leadership role that is both demanding and in great demand in the transnational IT business.

## *Pseudo-Expats*

Among most Chinese corporate employees in Japan, nothing is more attractive than being sent back to China as a manager in a local branch. Going home represents a pinnacle in a Chinese employee's transnational corporate career. However, for most Chinese in Japan, home means a big Chinese city, not necessarily the town they grew up in. Chinese employees, especially family men, change jobs in order to be sent back. The aforementioned Zhang Tian negotiated with his company to be sent back to manage one of their Chinese branches. Although he had grown up in northern China, he bought an apartment in Shanghai with the hope of moving there within two or three years. When his boss told him that the company's headquarters in Tokyo needed him more than the branch did, he started interviewing with other Japanese firms with branches in Shanghai or the surrounding areas. He was willing to accept a lower salary if he could be sent back to China. In fact, a salary cut is a common experience among homecoming Chinese expatriates. Japanese companies usually apply the logic that, because it is cheaper to live in China, Chinese employees should expect less pay than in Japan. This logic does not apply to their Japanese counterparts. Instead, Japanese employees usually receive a better package than they would have in Japan because they expect to maintain the same lifestyle—eating the same food and using the same bathroom cleaner imported from Japan. Such a difference in logic has consequently created a niche opportunity for Chinese employees who have both work experience in corporate Japan and cultural familiarity with both countries. In short, they are *pseudo-expats*, holding a status somewhere between Japanese expats and local employees. The following case illustrates their in-between position.

Dai Minghua's husband used to work for one of the biggest manufacturing companies in Japan. After being in Japan for 12 years, the family was looking for an opportunity to go back to Shanghai. Through work relationships, he met his current boss who sent him to work for their branch in Shanghai. The company was in the telecommunications business, and was moving into the Chinese market:

> The boss was delighted. My husband worked very hard for them. Having worked for a Japanese company for so many years, he knows the Japanese way of management, and has learnt to work as a Japanese employee. He never complains about workload, and never asks for overtime pay. He often has to work on Sundays. The Japanese boss also needs him to deal with the Chinese employees and other Chinese staff. So he not only serves as a role model for the Chinese, but also works as a mediator and a local know-how. The Japanese was smart to pick him. Because he can do what a Japanese employee can do and better, but the company does not have to provide the expatriate package, such as providing free housing and other compensatory fees. They know he has a home in Shanghai.

Most corporate male employees I interviewed did not see themselves staying in Japan for the rest of their lives despite their permanent residency status and in some cases Japanese spouses and citizenship. They hoped, firstly, to escape the stressful work environment and feeling of constraint (*yayi*) in Japan. Stress and constraints characterise Japanese social life in general, according to my informants. In addition, they were foreigners in a country they perceived to be 'exclusive' and 'narrow-minded'. Zhang Tian, who had majored in Japanese language since high school and was a self-proclaimed 'lucky Chinese' in Japan, still remarked that 'Japan is for the Japanese'. He did not consider Japanese people particularly discriminatory towards foreigners, but believed China to be a more natural living environment for the Chinese. The second reason for Chinese employees' desire to be sent back to China is economic. The salary of even a pseudo-expat would allow them a much more comfortable life in China and a higher social status. Finally, the decision often involved children. Many of my interviewees, for various reasons, did not consider Japanese society academically and morally suitable for their own children.

**Corporate Chinese Women**

Corporate Chinese women in Japan shared many of the same advantages and constraints as Chinese men working in the occupational niche. However, the mobility patterns of Chinese women are further complicated by the structural and cultural constraints faced by women employees in corporate Japan. On the one hand, Chinese women in some sense transcend the gender barriers in Japanese firms. Because of the demand for their cultural and linguistic skills, many Chinese women take up the so-called *sogoshoku*—a professional career track that has mobility potential instead of *ippanshoku*—the administrative career track in which many Japanese women are situated (Brinton 1992). Chinese women are frequently sales representatives, travelling internationally and independently. Anqi, a sales representative at a Japanese manufacturing company, undertook business trips by herself to Taipei and Shanghai almost every month. She said she was the only woman in her company who did not have to wear a pink uniform, and she was also the only woman in the marketing department. In fact, Anqi thought the possibility for Chinese women to occupy a 'feminine' career track in Japan was relatively small because they were not suited to such jobs. First, Chinese women are not native speakers and are not socialised into gendered cultural norms. They are not equipped with the cultural skills demanded by such a labour market and are therefore not competitive. Second, brought up in socialist China, they embrace the concept of gender equality—a norm constantly brought up by my female interviewees. To show deference to men and serve them is inconceivable. Most Chinese women interviewees said they were considered 'too tough' (*qiang* in Chinese, or *tsuyoi* in Japanese) by their Japanese male colleagues. Ailing, who came to Japan in 1986 at the age of 19, had been in Japan for almost half her life when I met her. She described herself as a cultural hybrid. However, she was indignant when asked about the way women were treated at the workplace:

> I think my personality and my toughness are not like Japanese girls. . . . . . . In a Japanese company, women used to be mostly office assistants, waiting on men. Men say, 'Copy this', and they will run to copy it. It is so pathetic. M (her previous employer) was horrible (*kepa*). There was this girl who graduated from Ochanomizu University, a prestigious women's college, and who also went to study English a year in the United States and spoke very good English. She was just an assistant there, serving men. Another lady, already in her 50s, had been waiting on men all her life. She graduated from junior college a long time ago. And every morning, she would prepare tea for every man, to the degree that she remembered every man's cup. Those men were so used to it, and wouldn't even say 'Thank you'. She was used to it, too. She had always been the lowest person in the office, and any new male employee could manage her.

Although situating themselves in the occupational niche allows most Chinese women to escape the fate of serving tea to their male colleagues, their employment benefits are discounted and mobility prospects are constrained because of their gender. The Japan Institute of Labour Policy and Training's data in 2006 show that Japanese women are more likely to be employed in part-time positions and in smaller firms. Between 1989 and 2004, women's wages were 60 to 65 per cent of men's. Even after controlling for occupational and industrial properties, firm size, academic backgrounds and length of employment, female employees' wages were still between 75 and 80 per cent of those of male employees'.[17] Most Chinese women recognised the gendered wage differences, and accepted such conditions as part of Japanese corporate culture. As Zheng Jia explains:

> Women who came before me are also like this (working long hours with less pay). When we just entered (the firm), we didn't make the same. Two years later, the gap (between men and women) became even larger. In Japan, a woman quits job after getting married and having a baby. You will leave. So when there are opportunities for promotion or salary increase, they give them to men. It is almost like an unwritten rule. Nobody can say anything about it.

Compared to the lower pay, the lack of prospects for upward mobility seems to be more upsetting for some women. Chen Lan believed Chinese women were doubly disadvantaged by being both Chinese and women.

> Although I am in charge of an important part of the company business, I can never become an office manager, let alone a branch manager. Japanese men would be horrified if a Chinese woman were appointed above them.

Still others resent the gendered career expectation in corporate Japan. Yao Lin left the trading firm where she worked for five years when she turned 30. She complained,

> Japanese men are so very narrow-minded. Guess what the men in my company had always said to me? '*Toshimo soro soro, kekkon mo soro soro deshou*' (You are about the age. Get married soon.) I couldn't stand it and had to quit.

Because of these perceived disadvantages of being both a woman and a foreigner in corporate Japan, career-minded women like Yao Lin chose to become self-employed. In 2002 when I interviewed her she was 32, still single and the owner of a small trading firm. In 2005, Chen Lan also quit the trading firm and started her own business in the same trade, partnering with her former boss, the office manager. Others, however, resign from career pursuits and quit jobs upon having their first child, as many Japanese women do. The last time I spoke to Ailing, she was getting married. Although she finally made a team-leader (*shunin*) after years of struggle, she was contemplating quitting her job soon. 'A *shunin* is nothing', she said, 'I am just taking on more responsibilities'. The only woman boss she had was single, and worked 14-hour days. 'She is the last to go home, always! It is not worth it'.

## Conclusion

Chinese student migrants' employment patterns clearly suggest that an occupational niche has emerged for skilled Chinese immigrants in corporate Japan, created by a flourishing transnational economy between Japan and China as well as the supply of a skilled labour force with bilingual and bicultural competence. This study shows how the transnational economy has changed the opportunity structure for immigrants' economic incorporation and created the conditions for the emergence of an occupational niche in the Japanese labour market.

However, such an occupational niche by no means lifts Chinese student migrants into the category of 'transnational elites'. Although the global economy provides channels for upward and transnational mobility, the majority of Chinese employees are not truly mobile. Chinese skilled migrants in Japan are subject to the constraints of ethnic and gender hierarchies. Despite being white-collar workers and corporate employees, their employment situations are reminiscent of a secondary labour market in a capitalist economy (Piore 1979). They are mostly employed in small and medium-sized firms. The occupational niche is limiting and the mobility channel within it narrow and short. Chinese student migrants are constantly looking out for new opportunities because of the lack of job security and upward mobility. Their actual transnational mobility is often a result of negotiation and compromise.

Nonetheless, Chinese students' occupational characteristics in Japanese firms are different from those of the more traditional immigrant niche. Instead of filling jobs abandoned by natives, or competing with native workers by cutting wages and prolonging work hours, Chinese immigrants are taking up new types of position created in contemporary economic contexts. For these positions, they have skill advantages over locals. Moreover, as in the case of Lawson, the expanding transnational economy is increasing the demand for skilled immigrant workers with linguistic skills and cultural competencies. With the sweeping force of globalisation, it is not too far-fetched to say that, in the future, transnational business will expand and more corporations will become transnational. International migrants will then become an integral and substantial part of Japan's labour pool. The boundaries of the niche may even gradually dissolve.

## Notes

[1] 'Lawson, one third of new graduate hires going to the foreigners'. *Nikkeinet*, 22 April 2008. Online at: http://woman.nikkei.co.jp/career/news/article.aspx?id =20080422ax017b1, last accessed 1 September 2008.

[2] See the blog on J-cast. 'Lawson hiring a large number of Chinese students because (they) are better than the Japanese? Online at: http://www.j-cast.com/2008/04/26019361.html?ly =cm&p = 2, last accessed 1 September 2008.

[3] Full-time white-collar employment is to be distinguished from part-time jobs working as waiters at restaurants, as construction day-labourers, or as cashiers at convenience stores. Almost all Chinese student migrants take on part-time jobs while in school (Liu-Farrer 2009).

[4] In 2004, 28,903 foreign students were expected to graduate. However, JASSO had data on only 24,961 cases; 3,942 were labelled 'unclear'.

[5] A further 17 per cent were listed in the 'other' category, which could mean marriage or other arrangements, including losing legal status.

[6] I have not found data on the nationality breakdown of post-secondary vocational-school students.

[7] This number is the number of student-to-employment visa changes published annually by the Japanese Ministry of Justice.

[8] The English-speaking migrants who hold this visa include English-language teachers at commercial language schools; a few are students-turned-labour-migrants. They mainly enter Japan with this visa, though some enter as tourists then find employment and change over to 'Specialist in humanities/International services'. In fact, of all employment visas falling in this category, 97.3 per cent were granted to former students from Asian countries.

[9] See 'About foreign students who entered Japanese enterprises in 2007' from the Ministry of Justice website at: http://www.moj.go.jp/PRESS/080729-1.pdf, last accessed 30 August 2008.

[10] They are not necessarily labelled as 'sales representatives' in the visa applications. According to the most recent data released in July 2008, 33.4 per cent of work-visa grantees fall in the occupational category of translators/interpreters (*honyaku, tsuyaku*), which demonstrates their specialist characteristics. However, during my fieldwork among Chinese immigrants in Japan, I received numerous name-cards. 'Interpreter' or 'translator' was an extremely rare title, although translation and interpretation is taken for granted as part of the job.

[11] Based on statistics published by Ministry of Education, Culture, Sports, Science and Technology. Online at: http://www.mext.go.jp, last accessed 31 October 2006.

[12]  'Six hundred Chinese in Japan all have worries: the younger ones about careers, the older ones about family business', *China News Net*, 4 February 2007. Online at: http://www.chinanews.com.cn/hr/yzhrxw/news/2007/02-04/867497.shtml, last accessed 14 February 2007—original text in Chinese.

[13]  See 'About foreign students who entered Japanese Enterprises in 2007' from the Ministry of Justice website at: http://www.moj.go.jp/PRESS/080729-1.pdf, last accessed 30 August 2008.

[14]  The number is calculated from 'Reports on Employment Trends' by the Japanese Ministry of Health, Labour and Welfare. The specific data used are from Table 8 of the Heisei 18 statistics. Online at: http://wwwdbtk.mhlw.go.jp/toukei/kouhyo/indexkr_14_8.html, last accessed 30 August 2008. The number does not include new high- and middle-school graduates because the data on foreign students only include graduates from higher education.

[15]  I consider the cases as missing when the data do not include a rough estimation of the firm size or when the employer is an educational institution, kindergarten or university.

[16]  'Course full labour statistics—processed labour statistics—2006'. Japanese Institute for Labour Policy and Training. Online at: http://www.jil.go.jp/kokunai/statistics/kako/documents/2-11.pdf, last accessed 13 February 2007.

[17]  'Course full labour statistics—processed labour statistics—2006'. Japanese Institute for Labour Policy and Training. Online at: http://www.jil.go.jp/kokunai/statistics/kako/documents/2-11.pdf, last accessed 13 February 2007.

## References

Beaverstock, J.V. (2005) 'Transnational elites in the city: British highly skilled inter-company transferees in New York City's financial district', *Journal of Ethnic and Migration Studies*, 31(2): 245–68.

Brinton, M.C. (1992) *Women and the Economic Miracle: Gender and Work in Postwar Japan*. Berkeley, CA: University of California Press.

Cranford, C.J. (2005) 'Networks of exploitation: immigrant labour and the restructuring of the Los Angeles janitorial industry', *Social Problems*, 52(3): 379–97.

Duan, Y. (1998) *Fu Ji Dong Ying Xie Chun Qiu*. Shanghai: Shanghai Education Press.

Hawthorn, L. (2005) '"Picking winners": the recent transformation of Australia's skilled migration policy', *International Migration Review*, 39(3): 663–96.

JAPIT (2007) *2007 Data on Enterprises with Japan and China Relations (2007 nen Chūnichi Kankei Kigyō De-ta)*. Tokyo: Japanese Association for the Promotion of International Trade.

Kim, I. (1981) *The New Urban Immigrants: The Korean Community in New York*. Princeton: Princeton University Press.

Kyle, D. (2001) *Transnational Peasants: Migrations, Networks, and Ethnicity in Andean Ecuador*. Baltimore: John Hopkins University.

Landolt, P., Autler, L. and Baires, S. (1999) 'From "Hermano Lejano" to "Hermano Mayor": the dialectics of Salvadoran transnationalism', *Ethnic and Racial Studies*, 22(2): 290–315.

Liu-Farrer, G. (2009) 'Educationally channelled international labour migration: post-1978 student mobility from China to Japan', *International Migration Review*, 43(1): 178–204.

McLaughlan, G. and Salt, J. (2002) *Migration Policies Towards Highly Skilled Foreign Workers: Report to the Home Office*. Online at: http://www.homeoffice.gov.uk/rds/pdfs2/migrationpolicies.pdf, last accessed 1 September 2008.

Min, P.G. (1984) 'From white-collar occupations to small business: Korean immigrants' occupational adjustment', *The Sociological Quarterly*, 25(3): 333–52.

Min, P.G. (1988) *Ethnic Business Enterprise: Korean Small Business in Atlanta*. New York: Center for Migration Studies.

Ministry of Justice, Japan (2008) *Statistics on Registered Foreigners in 2007*. Online at: http://oohara.mt.tama.hosei.ac.jp/rn/2004/index-2004.html, accessed 22 December 2010.

Ohara Institute of Social Research (eds) (2004) *Labour Year Book of Japan 2004*. Tokyo: Junpousha.

Piore, M.J. (1979) *Birds of Passage: Migrant Labour and Industrial Societies*. Cambridge: Cambridge University Press.

Rangaswamy, P. (2007) 'South Asians in Dunkin' Donuts: niche development in the franchise industry', *Journal of Ethnic and Migration Studies*, 33(4): 671–86.

Sanders, J., Nee, V. and Sernau, S. (2002) 'Asian immigrants' reliance on social ties in a multiethnic labour market', *Social Forces*, 81(1): 281–314.

Sasatani, H. (2007) 'Kanan de no nihonjin genchisaiyou no tokushou', *Whenever Shanghai*, July, 124.

Saxenian, A.L. (2002) 'Brain circulation: how high-skill immigration makes everyone better off', *The Brookings Review*, 20(1): 28–31.

Saxenian, A.L. (2005) 'From brain drain to brain circulation: transnational communities and regional upgrading in India and China', *Studies in Comparative International Development*, 40(2): 35–61.

Saxenian, A.L. (2006) *The New Argonauts: Regional Advantage in a Global Economy*. Cambridge, MA: Harvard University Press.

Siu, P.C.P. (ed.) (1987) *The Chinese Laundryman: A Study of Social Isolation*. New York: New York University Press.

Sklair, L. (2001) *The Transnational Capitalist Class*. Oxford: Blackwell.

Waldinger, R. (1986) 'Immigrant enterprise: a critique and reformulation', *Theory and Society*, 15(1/2): 249–85.

Waldinger, R. (1994) 'The making of an immigrant niche', *International Migration Review*, 28(1): 3–30.

Waldinger, R. (1996) *Still the Promised City? New Immigrants and African-Americans in Post-Industrial New York*. Cambridge, MA: Harvard University Press.

Waldinger, R. and Lichter, M. (2003) *How the Other Half Works: Immigration and the Social Organization of Labour*. Berkeley, CA: University of California Press.

Waldinger, R. and Fitzgerald, D. (2004) 'Transnationalism in question', *American Journal of Sociology*, 109(5): 1177–95.

Waters, M. (1999) *Black Identities: West Indian Immigrant Dreams and American Realities*. New York: Russell Sage Foundation; Cambridge, MA: Harvard University Press.

Ziguras, C. and Law, S.F. (2006) 'Recruiting international students as skilled migrants: the global "skills race" as viewed from Australia and Malaysia', *Globalisation Societies and Education*, 4(1): 59–76.

# 'The Moon Back Home is Brighter'?: Return Migration and the Cultural Politics of Belonging

Sin Yih Teo

*Focusing on return migration, this paper draws out the tensions between integration and transnationalism, flexibility and rootedness, and citizenship and nationalism. I argue that the recognition of transnationalism necessitates a conceptual re-examination of return migration. Substantively, the paper is based upon my research on the flow of skilled migration between Canada and the People's Republic of China (PRC). Since 1998, China has been the top source country of skilled immigrants to Canada. In recent years, however, a counter-current has emerged with the return movement of PRC immigrants back to China. I examine how the cultural politics of identity play out amongst PRC immigrants in Canada in light of this reverse migration. Drawing on focus groups and interviews, I suggest that not only the act of return, but its very discourse, has influenced the ways in which the politics of identity and belonging are evolving amongst PRC immigrants in Canada. Ultimately, hybridised forms of cultural identification become the norm for migrants whose homes are no longer tied to one place.*

## Introduction

> When living in one culture, you always dream of another, more ideal one than your own. However, after you have experienced this other culture, your dreams of it are broken by a strange, new-found reality. Losing the comforts of your inherent culture, you wander back and forth between the two, not knowing which you belong to, unable to establish roots in either (Gu Xiong[1] quoted in Zacharias 2003).

In the summer of 2002, Haiwen, a recent immigrant in Vancouver, returned to China—not to his native Beijing, but instead to Shanghai—where, upon arrival, an

American company affiliated with his former employer recruited him. There was a geographical caveat to this apparently simple narrative of return: Vancouver was the 'third space' (Bhabha 1994) in a strategic career move involving physical relocation to avoid the complexities of workplace *guanxi* (human relationships) that would otherwise be implicated had Haiwen moved directly from Beijing to Shanghai. My intention here is not only to highlight the social embeddedness of immigration (Ley 2003) but, more fundamentally, to question the very meaning of migration in an age of rapid global flows. As such, I am more interested in how Haiwen's return fits within a wider framework of migration than in the fact of his return *per se*. Similarly, this paper focuses on return migration to draw out the tensions between integration and transnationalism, between flexibility and rootedness, and between citizenship and nationalism. Firstly, I argue that the recognition of transnationalism necessitates a conceptual re-examination of return migration. Secondly, I consider both the structural contexts of migration and the cultural dynamics underlying human responses. Thirdly, I suggest that the changing realities wrought by migration have further complicated the cultural politics of belonging.

I begin with a consideration of the myth of return and its relationship with transnationalism. Next, I adopt a more substantive focus on migrants from the People's Republic of China (PRC) by first looking at state and media constructions of the 'flexible citizen' (Ong 1999), and then examining in greater detail the everyday dilemmas and practices of migrants caught between the decision to either stay in Canada or leave for China. Finally, I consider how return migration has revealed the limitations of formal citizenship as an indicator of a migrant's sense of belonging even as it carries significant material ramifications.

## Transnationalism and the Myth of Return

The 'myth of return,' also known as the 'ideology of return' or the 'return illusion', makes return an important part of the migration ethos (Anwar 1979; Brettell 1979; Guarnizo 1997; Hoffmann-Nowotny 1978; Rubenstein 1979). No matter how settled, it is believed that migrants still dream that they will eventually return to their homeland. While migrants may genuinely believe it to be true, the myth of return also provides migrants with a legitimate cognitive framework within which they can simultaneously maintain membership in both home and diaspora (Cohen and Gold 1997). The notion of transnationalism, however, raises new questions for return migration and, by extension, the myth of return. Since the 1990s, the recognition of transnationalism by scholars has revitalised the study of migration in a profound fashion, challenging the very tenets of traditional theories of immigration that assumed a linear trajectory of migrants adapting to the 'receiving' country and gradually settling down over time. Instead, transnationalism emphasises the process by which migrants, through their daily life activities and social, economic and political relations, create social fields that cross national boundaries (Basch *et al.* 1994), thereby highlighting the relationships *between* 'sending' and 'receiving' countries, rather than the former one-directional flow. This raises an important question for return migration: What is the significance of return when immigrants already 'forge and sustain multi-stranded social relations between societies of origin and settlement' (Basch et al. 1994: 7)? Furthermore, where *is* home for migrants?

I argue that the study of return migration has the potential to sharpen our understanding of transnationalism as a process. After all, the direction of flows factors into our everyday, and policy, consideration of who a migrant is. Inevitably, there is an equation drawn between reaching a new place and the idea of migration. By re-examining reverse migration within the conceptual context of transnationalism, my intention is to draw out the complex decisions, rationales and emotions underlying return. Specifically, I emphasise that not only the act of departure, but the very discourse surrounding return migration, have influenced the ways in which the politics of identity and belonging are evolving amongst migrants. In the next section, I turn to the wider context in China.

## Flexible Yearnings: The PRC State, Media and the Changing Meaning of 'Migrant'

### State Constructions of the 'New Migrant'

Departing from its policies on Chinese overseas prior to 1978, the PRC state is now actively reaching out and incorporating Chinese overseas. The first major political change emerged in the late 1970s when Chinese citizens abroad were recognised as a patriotic force to the PRC (Thunø 2001). To win Chinese migrants' faith in the PRC, relatives of migrants living in China and returned migrants became politically rehabilitated, and were by law granted special social, economic and political privileges. By the mid-1980s, however, it was clear to the state that donations and remittances from Chinese overseas were no longer adequate avenues in pursuing foreign revenues and economic development. Globalisation and the surge of emigrants from China further meant that a new policy direction was needed. The state thus adopted a new strategy, changing its policies to focus on ethnic Chinese and especially 'new migrants' (*xin yimin*) who left China after 1978.[2]

Most recently, the PRC state has targeted 'new migrants', specifically overseas students, scholars and other skilled labour, as potential returnees. Since 1990, various state efforts have been put in place—including the establishment of a number of 'science parks' and 'special development zones' in Beijing and most provincial cities to attract this 'overseas talent' (Luo et al. 2002), and through the organising of large conventions in major cities in China aimed at recruiting overseas Chinese professionals (Xiang, this issue). At the same time, the Chinese state has promoted its incentive programmes—through recruitment fairs—to PRC migrants in countries such as the United States, Canada, Europe and Australia (*Ming Pao* 2002). From these developments, it appears that PRC migrants are now enjoying a new state-sanctioned flexibility, a status which is tied inextricably with their perceived role as *homo economicus* (Ley 2003; Ong 1999). Aihwa Ong (1999) has powerfully depicted the way

Hong Kong migrants respond fluidly to changing political-economic conditions, terming their practice 'flexible citizenship'. Are PRC migrants acting in a similar fashion? Before continuing this line of inquiry, I examine how the media, too, play a role in constructing migrants as 'flexible citizens'.

*Media and the Resurgence of Nationalism*

> The story of mass migrations (voluntary and forced) is hardly a new feature of human history. But when it is juxtaposed with the rapid flow of mass-mediated images, scripts, and sensations, we have a new order of instability in the production of modern subjectivities (Appadurai 1996: 4).

For Appadurai (1996), the creation of diasporic public spheres implies that the state can no longer be regarded as the key arbiter of important social changes. In the context of China I argue that, while the Chinese in the diaspora have the agency to negotiate their own subjectivities, the very existence of these diasporic public spheres is made possible, to quote Sun (2002: 208), 'not in spite of, but precisely because of, the power of the Chinese state and the strength of a collective memory of the Chinese nation'. For instance, the Chinese Central Television (CCTC) now has satellite transmission in many parts of North America, Europe and Oceania (Sun 2002). Electronic versions of Chinese newspapers too are accessible via the Internet to overseas readers. The availability of these resources has facilitated the formation of new 'imagined communities' (Anderson 1991) amongst diasporic Chinese. The breadth of their reach is suggested by how nearly every Chinese person to whom Nyíri (2001) spoke in Hungary regularly watches CCTV and Chinese Channel, the first Chinese satellite station broadcasting specifically for Europe.

With respect to 'new migrants', features on the 'success stories' of Chinese overseas are part of the popular media discourse about the rise of China. In the widely popular television drama series *A Beijing Native in New York*, there is a poignant scene where a group of PRC migrants rise spontaneously at a party to sing: 'Beijing, you are the heart of my motherland and symbol of our nation'. Here, the revolutionary flavour of the song is deliberately ignored and, in an ahistorical time, it articulates a specific kind of yearning borne out of displacement—a function irrelevant to the original text (Sun 2002). In another version, the 2002 Olympic Games in Sydney provided an opportunity for Chinese television to generously transmit images of patriotic Chinese overseas, which portrayed the centrifugal power of the PRC (Sun 2002). Most strikingly, many Chinese spectators in the Homebush Stadium of the Olympic Games wore T-shirts bearing the logo of the *Wuliangye* product, a hard liquor.[3] In exchange for wearing these shirts, the Australian Chinese received free tickets to the stands, cheered for the Chinese athletes, and became signifiers of diasporic Chinese patriotism.

From these accounts of the state and the media, it seems that emphasis is placed not so much on the *formal* citizenship of these 'new migrants' as on their *cultural* identity, one which is able to traverse borders *flexibly*.

## Rooted Realities: The Everyday Lives of PRC Immigrants

> We live between two cultures. We are building a new identity—a hybrid (Gu Xiong, quoted in Zacharias 2003).

*Profile and Methodology*

Since 1998, China has been the top source country of skilled immigrants to Canada. The growth of PRC immigrants has been phenomenal, increasing from 13,309 in 1995—the year when complete immigration processing to Canada started in China—to 40,365 in 2001, essentially more than tripling in six years (CIC 2004). Likewise, PRC immigrants have ranked first in Vancouver since 1998 (CIC 1999, 2002). Recent PRC skilled immigrants tend to be relatively young, with a modal range of 25 to 39 years of age; in 2000, 1,528 arrivals were 25–29 years old, 2,220 were 30–34 years old and 1,547 were 35–39 years old, representing 70.6 per cent of the total PRC skilled immigrants in that year.[4] Their children are mainly younger than 14 years old, with 457 under four years old in 2000, 635 between five and nine, and 378 between 10 and 14, collectively making up another 19.6 per cent. There are twice as many married skilled immigrants as singles. The native language of PRC skilled immigrants is commonly Mandarin. One third indicated that they had English-language ability, while only a minority were bilingual or spoke French.[5] The percentage of skilled immigrants with no 'Canadian language ability' has climbed steadily from 32 per cent in 1996 to 47 per cent in 1999, and 66 per cent in 2000, a statistic which intimates possible language integration difficulties.

Since one of the main criteria for skilled immigration is the educational qualification of the principal applicant, it is unsurprising that skilled immigrants are very well educated, with a majority holding Bachelor's degrees or above. Such a high proportion also means that it is not only the principal applicant who is highly educated, but quite frequently the spouse too. As a skilled immigrant, the principal applicant tends to have been in an occupation—usually a profession—that is considered desirable for the Canadian economy. The spouses of the principal applicants are often also professionals themselves. These points are reflected in Table 1, where the top three occupations—all of a professional nature—are in natural and applied sciences, business and finance, and social science, education, government services and religion. In 2000, the landed immigrant cohort in Canada was dominated by the category 'Professional Occupations in Natural and Applied Sciences', which includes engineers, computer professionals and other technological and scientific occupations (Couton 2002). So, too, in Vancouver, the same category represented an overwhelming 77.3 per cent of occupations indicated by PRC skilled immigrants who landed in 2000. The most common problem is the non-recognition of foreign credentials which, although not unique to PRC immigrants, is one that is causing them particular hardship.[6]

**Table 1.** Professional occupations

| Occupations | Year of landing | | | | |
|---|---|---|---|---|---|
| | 1996 | 1997 | 1998 | 1999 | 2000 |
| Senior management | 26 | 10 | 18 | 40 | 53 |
| **Professional—business and finance** | **153** | **172** | **144** | **183** | **195** |
| Skilled administrative and business | 173 | 205 | 250 | 146 | 97 |
| Clerical | 26 | 18 | 8 | 6 | 6 |
| **Professional—natural and applied sciences** | **792** | **943** | **1115** | **2130** | **2782** |
| Technical—related to natural and applied sciences | 68 | 87 | 95 | 105 | 63 |
| Professional—health | 25 | 28 | 17 | 15 | 15 |
| Technical and skilled—health | 43 | 36 | 34 | 53 | 25 |
| Assisting—in support of health services | 3 | 3 | 1 | | |
| **Professional—social sciences, education, govt services, religion** | **92** | **90** | **94** | **108** | **105** |
| Paraprofession—law, social services, education, religion | 6 | 10 | 7 | 5 | 5 |
| **Professional—art and culture** | **82** | **80** | **82** | **97** | **91** |
| Technical and skilled—art, culture, recreation, sport | 23 | 17 | 14 | 13 | 18 |
| Skilled sales and service | 108 | 123 | 163 | 145 | 85 |
| Intermediate sales and service | 26 | 39 | 33 | 50 | 28 |
| Elemental sales and service | 1 | 2 | 1 | 1 | |
| Trades | 15 | 9 | 8 | 18 | 17 |
| Skilled transport and equipment operators | 38 | 44 | 38 | 20 | 9 |
| Intermediate—transport, equipment ops, installation, maintenance | 3 | 3 | 3 | 1 | |
| Trades helpers, construction labourers and related | | 1 | | | 1 |
| Skilled—primary industry | | 1 | | | |
| Processing, manufacturing, utilities supervisors, skilled operators | 1 | 3 | 1 | 1 | |
| Labourers in processing, manufacturing, utilities | 6 | 17 | 17 | 32 | 3 |

*Source:* LIDS 1996–2000.

In recent years, a counter-current has emerged with the return movement of PRC immigrants back to China. The following section—based on focus groups and in-depth interviews with 78 PRC skilled immigrants in Vancouver from 2001 to 2002—examines how the cultural politics of identity play out amongst PRC immigrants in Canada in light of this reverse migration. The participants had immigrated to Canada—from 1996 to 2001 inclusive—through the 'point system' of the skilled worker programme, and were either principal applicants or their spouses. Half were recruited through an immigration service agency and the other half through snowball sampling, with particular care taken to ensure as much diversity amongst the respondents as possible in terms of gender, year of landing, number of household members, province of origin, and occupation in China. Elsewhere, I have discussed my research methodology in greater detail (Teo 2003, 2007).

*Between Leaving and Staying*

During the course of my research with PRC immigrants in Vancouver I realised that, even as I was considering how previous circumstances in China had influenced their initial decision to immigrate to Canada, the contemporary context of China was also shaping their present experiences in Canada. In other words, to fully understand their integration in Canada, I had to look *beyond* Canada. Respondents frequently contrasted the quick pace of change in China, particularly Shanghai, with the stagnation they perceived in Canada. 'With change', Cheryl enthused, 'there are opportunities. If things remain the same, there won't be any opportunities, right?' Huiling concurred, 'There are so many job opportunities in China, with the WTO, Olympics and so many other good opportunities. Rather than wasting their time here, the PRC immigrants might as well go back for development. Many people have returned'. To appreciate their sentiments, it is useful to remember that many recent PRC skilled immigrants have faced considerable settlement difficulties in Canada—especially in finding professional employment—presenting a common scenario of former engineers, teachers and doctors working as dishwashers, factory-workers and janitors, earning the minimum wage of CA$8/hour (Teo 2007). When asked about their future plans, a common refrain was that they would 'take one step at a time' (*zouyibukanyibu*) or 'wait and see'. After describing the plight of several Canadian immigrants who reluctantly remained in Canada, a reporter for *Nanfang Dushibao* (a Southern China newspaper) wrote:

> From these different stories, we can see each person's dilemma. On the one hand, they are facing a better overall environment abroad, and finding it difficult to completely relinquish their hopes for, and pursuit of, a better life. On the other hand, they cannot help but face their roots and networks. Thus between the two choices of 'leaving' and 'staying', more people are choosing 'not to choose': 'we will see; we will talk about it again; who knows what may happen in the future?' (Zhang 2002).

While finding that a sizeable number of respondents were indeed choosing 'not to choose', the dilemma that they had sketched for me—which I will discuss later—was somewhat different. It is useful to note that Nyíri's (2001) observation of discursive patriotism in the media is reflected in the tone of the reporter's conclusion:

> If it is good, stay on; if not, then return immediately! After all, we have the same ethnic blood flowing through our veins no matter whether we are working hard together in the same place or looking across at each other from different shores. There will always be an inviolable bond between us (Zhang 2002).

At times, I detected echoes of official discourse in the speech of a few respondents, especially those who were slightly older and had worked in the state unit. Orina, 40, declared:

> Now China is more open-minded. It is more supportive of talent moving around for in fact when *zhongguoren* (Chinese nationals) walk towards the world, no matter whether it is to study abroad or to immigrate, it is beneficial for China. Now there is talent mobility, eventually there will be talent returning. This is an exchange between Eastern and Western culture, and will bring new dynamism back to China.

> After studying and working for a few years and getting the *shenfen* (status), then they have both educational qualifications and work experience. They will certainly bring Western thinking and the Western way of solving problems to China. I think this is beneficial to China.

While Orina presented a state-sanctioned picture of new migrants as patriots (and an internalised form of Orientalism *and* Occidentalism), many migrants, such as Ruhao, told me that, with regard to immigration, 'The state doesn't encourage or disapprove. It doesn't interfere'. This contradicts Nyíri's (2001): 639) assertion—based on examining public narratives, and hence raising the issue of reception—that 'migrants go abroad with the sense that their project is in line with the values of the dominant discourse of Chineseness'. My research also concurs with Xiang's (this issue) finding that 'only a very limited number of overseas Chinese professionals, including those who have been considering returning to China on a permanent basis, have detailed knowledge about the policies'. On the whole, respondents' consideration of return migration stemmed from a confluence of their settlement difficulties in Canada and their perception of better career opportunities in China. While the thought of return might have crossed the respondents' minds, they were quick to point out their mitigating concerns, of which the foremost was their children's welfare. Huiling, a mother of two, revealed:

> From my understanding, there are many who wish to return, at least in their hearts. Some people have indeed returned. Others are here physically although their hearts are still not stable. They think of going back to China but because of their children, family and other reasons, they may not necessarily be able to leave. [...] Now my daughter is in grade 7. She likes the life here very much. She said, 'Mama, even if you are going back, I'm not going with you'.

Boyang, a father of two, was more explicit:

> I will definitely stay here. The children cannot possibly go back [laughed]. We had intended to let the children stay there for three months for the summer, but after staying for one month, both the children fell ill, and I brought them home. They also said that they don't ever want to go back so we have no choice. I have even filled in 'permanent' on your survey form.

Often, respondents were concerned that their children, after being in the Canadian education system—which was perceived to be less rigorous at the elementary level—would be unable to 'catch up' with their peers in China. Moreover, there was a difference in the primary language of instruction. Some respondents also wished their children to receive a Canadian university education ultimately, a goal that was more cost-effective if achieved through immigration rather than sending them as international students later. Another important reason was that, having devoted much time, money, and emotional commitment to the immigration process, many respondents were reluctant to abandon their original intentions without a hard fight.

Caught between leaving and staying, the pathos of their situation is a sobering reminder that, despite the celebratory tones attached to the 'age of migration' (Castles and Miller 1993), migration is after all, a *human* flow, filled with all the complexities of choice and decision-making, sacrifice and commitment, thoughts and emotions. Zhehui confided:

> Before I immigrated, I had to quit my job. I had to cancel all my *shenfen* (status) and *guanxi* (interpersonal relationships) so that I can come here. When you are here, if you go back with nothing, you can't account for it from all aspects because you are not coming here to tour and see whether it is good before you come again. When you come, you have pulled all your roots; you have pulled your roots in China to come to Canada. But you realise that the water and soil are not suitable and the roots are not able to grow. There has to be a process. At this juncture, you have contradictory feelings.

A third reason was the desire to *yijinhuanxiang* (return to their hometown in silken robes). To Evelyn, this meant 'you only dare to go back to your hometown when you are grand or rich. You will have more face among your kin and relatives'. Zhiyang, originally from Taiyuan, mentioned a further concern about return migration:

> If you are returning to your country, you won't want to return to a small city. Then you will just be going back to the original place. If you go to a big city, it will be just like an immigrant. When you go to Shanghai, you will be discriminated by others, and that won't do. If you put the discrimination issue aside, you still have to integrate into the local society. You are a new migrant again. It is the same.

For some migrants, a constant battle rages in their minds as these attenuating reasons are pitted against the challenges encountered in everyday life. Indeed for many, as Gerald commented, 'the immigration decision is not a one-time affair; it is a continuous process'. Zhiyang, who had been in Vancouver for nearly three years, admitted:

> I have all along planned to stay but recently, these few days, I have thought that is not necessarily the case. I can't say. It's hard to say...

Iris, on the other hand, had already made a decision:

> Since we have decided to move our family over and to be transplanted here, then our concern is how our roots should be grown here, how to flower, and how to grow joint by joint, like a bamboo. Thus we don't think on the bitter side, we are quite optimistic.

At the time of interview, seven of the 36 households in my research were astronaut families, with the wives in all except one case staying in Vancouver while the husband worked in China, and shuttled to Vancouver every four months on average.[7] All emphasised that this was only a temporary arrangement, and one that eventually needs to be resolved (Teo 2007). Indeed, at least two of the seven families have returned to China, including Haiwen, the Beijing native who had left for Shanghai, and Huiling—whose daughter had wanted to remain in Vancouver. For these transnational families, almost invariably, 'It is *still the family* that is important'. These dilemmas are echoed by the transnational childcare arrangements of some PRC immigrant families. When interviewed, 11 of the 29 households with children had sent their offspring back to China to be looked after by the grandparents or babysitters. Again, the long-term goal is for the family to be reunited. The phenomena of astronaut families and transnational families have brought to light the painful tolls of transnationalism. Arrangements that appear to be flexible initially turn out to have a more rooted goal of family reunion.

*Between Citizenship and Nationality*

When asked about whether they have applied for, or intended to apply for, Canadian citizenship, or *ruji* (be naturalised), as was the preferred term, there was a spectrum of views ranging from 'We will definitely *ruji* because we have no plans to leave', through 'When we *ruji*, we can move freely, can go to the US or to other countries' and 'We will see', to 'What's the use of getting the citizenship?'. These replies have to be understood in light of a variety of factors, including their—possibly evolving—goals with regard to immigration, settlement experiences in Canada, attitude towards return migration, and their particular professional circumstances. Jiansheng, a social scientist in a state research institute, divulged:

> I'm very pragmatic. If a university or a Canadian governmental department is recruiting and I really want the job, then I may *ruji*.[8] Otherwise, it does not matter to me whether I *ruji* as there is not a difference economically. If I can't find a job here and I return to China to find a job, then having the [Canadian] citizenship is instead troublesome because you can't go back to find a job since the job you can find is restricted to those in foreign companies and not in China's state enterprises or its government departments.

In contrast, Cheryl—formerly employed in a Canadian company in China—perceived a strategic advantage in possessing Canadian citizenship in China:

> I am still *zhongguoren* [Chinese national]. I am still me [laughs]. I don't have anything different. I only have an additional three years of Canadian experience. Working in Canada these three years, I have Canadian working experience. Second, I have acquired Canadian citizenship, my status (*shenfen*) changes. Do you know? It equals changing my status (*shenfen*). Were I to go back to China, the opportunities I have are: firstly, if I were to return to a foreign company for employment, people may feel that, since I have returned from overseas, since I have worked overseas, then I must have overseas experience, my ability, thinking and experience must be more advanced, it must be higher. Another point is that it may have a more direct advantage—my income may be different from the locals [Chinese citizens].

Haojie further pointed out:

> The Chinese government is cleverer now. No matter what, if you are rich or you have a high degree, then they will accept you as residents. If so, then why don't you *ruji* since you can go back to be *zhongguoren* if you do return to China. You are giving yourself an additional option. Thus I will definitely *ruji* when the time comes, I will not dwell further on it. I have many friends who dwell on it. Because after you *ruji*, if your financial ability or other areas are not adequate, that is, they are still unsure, still thinking of going back, if you *ruji*, it will bring you a lot of trouble. China's dual residence is not open to everyone; you have to have either talent or money. If not, when you go back, your child has no *hukou* [household registration status], and will be considered as a foreign national's child, and will have to pay very high education fees.

Reflecting a concern that several other respondents held, Gerald remarked:

> Giving up [Chinese citizenship] forces them to become Canadians. Actually, if you recognise dual citizenship, then I am still *zhongguoren*, just that I have two passports. If I want to return to China, I can. If I want to stay here, I can. That is, I have two homes, right? If you do not have such political permission, then one is forced to be 'non-Chinese'. Of course, there is a historical basis for this, but now there should be consideration as to which policy should be amended to be more suitable for current trends.

To date, China does not recognise dual citizenship. Presently, the issue of citizenship is still a dilemma for a number of respondents. On a few occasions, it was apparent that there were distinct differences within the families as to whether they should apply for citizenship. While one couple openly debated with each other the utility of *ruji*, another couple's disagreement grew apparent when the wife asked me repeatedly 'Have you met others that have different feelings within a family?'. In both cases, it was the wife who preferred to apply for citizenship. Some respondents attributed the differences—from their observations (and what they heard from others)—to the gendered nature of settlement experiences. Women were commonly perceived to 'adapt' better to Canada than men. It is pertinent to note, too, that women were more likely to be the initiators in the case of PRC migration (Teo 2003). Overall, though, it is individual experiences that shape the migrants' perspective of their realities in Canada, as Haojie, a technician, illustrated:

> Maybe because I have been working with Canadians, I find that when I am talking to my friends, I feel that my change is greater than theirs. Really [laughed]. I feel that I am gradually having feelings for Canada. Indeed, I have found a job in Canada. Canada has given my family and me good benefits. It really varies for individuals. If you are still doing rotten work after seven years, working in a Chinese Richmond factory and being paid hourly, then I think the feeling would definitely be different. The feeling would definitely not be to treat Canada as your mother. I really do have the feeling that Canada is like my mother [laughed]. My second mother.

When asked whether they saw themselves as *zhongguoren* [Chinese nationals], *huaqiao* [overseas Chinese] or Canadians, participants in both the male and female focus groups unanimously declared that they were *zhongguoren*. For them, national identity was not so much an issue of citizenship as of feelings of attachment to a country they grew up in. Peixian, who expressed a desire to apply for Canadian citizenship, perceived time as a significant factor in her identification:

> I have been here for more than one year. The time is not that long. All the while I have been feeling that I'm a *zhongguoren*. Whenever I talk about Canada, I would say 'their' Canada, 'their' place, 'their' Canadian government, 'they' Canadians, etc., but I think as time gets longer, and I have stayed here for years, this kind of feeling may fade...and I won't say 'their' Canada [laughed].

In contrast, Kaiyang, who has lived in Canada for five years, demonstrates that the passage of time or even adaptation to Canadian society does not necessarily mean a straightforward identification with Canada:

> We are not citizens of China anymore [smiled]. We are already citizens of Canada. To return to China to stay for the long term? But we have already adapted here. [...] We are Canada's *zhongguoren*. Because we have pledged loyalty to our motherland [China]. Actually we also quite identify with this country Canada.

Postmodern notions of ambivalence, hybridity and 'in-between' spaces, which are celebrated by cultural theorists such as Bhabha (1990, 1994) and Gilroy (1993), help to illuminate Kaiyang's feelings of belonging—of being simultaneously a Canadian citizen and a Chinese national. Hybridised forms of cultural identification hence become the norm for migrants whose homes are no longer tied to one place. Yet identity, *because* it is so important, cannot remain only at the level of cultural politics. Lanxin, reacting to her husband's attempts to be upbeat about their prospects as immigrants in Canada, exclaimed:

> At least our house needs to look like a home! Look at our place—does it look like a home? How do you expect me to like this place?! I don't have this feeling at all now [half-laughs as she gestures at her house]. When the condition is better...when the condition...and it has the look of a home, the feeling of a home.

Identity is thus also deeply rooted in the materiality of everyday life. The flexibility of PRC migrants' identification with China and/or Canada relies ultimately on how they perceive their practical experiences.

## Conclusion

In Chinese poetry, legends and folk songs, the moon is a recurring metaphor for a migrant's longing for his or her hometown. Since it is the same moon that shines in both the homeland and the foreign land, an imaginary connection is drawn between the two when the migrant gazes at the moon. Hence it is perhaps no surprise that autobiographical and semi-fictional writings by PRC migrants feature titles such as *The Bright Moon of Another Land* and *The Moon Back Home is Brighter*, as noted by Yang (1997: 313). In this paper, I have focused on the structural forces and human agency involved in producing and consuming images of the moon back home being brighter. While I am conscious of the active role played by the PRC state in creating political discourses to draw migrants back into the fold of the nation-state and the very real attraction that the growing economy of contemporary China holds for migrants, my emphasis has been on the 'cultural logics that inform and structure border crossings' (Ong 1999: 5).

Following Ien Ang (2001), I have tried to revive notions of 'experience' and 'emotion' for theorising, in the process uncovering the complexities of their emotional geographies (Davidson *et al.* 2005). After all, at a basic level, migration is a human link between different places (King 1995). Moreover, as we move, 'so too do our personal and social boundaries shift; in this sense, migration involves a constant process of reinvention and self-redefinition' (Gardner 1995). This approach enables me to provide a quite different face to the *homo economicus* that Haiwen—the immigrant I described in the introduction—initially appeared to be. He, too, had been a member of a transnational household during his time in Vancouver, leading him to conclude that 'Immigration is almost always very painful. Why? Even though it is a good path for development, the change is too drastic; it decides the way you live for the rest of your life. It is not easy to take this step'. Likewise, despite discursive constructions of the 'flexible citizen' by the state and the media, foregrounding the migrants' voices has led me to emphasise the material ramifications of border crossings for their everyday lives.

I further suggest that exploring the possibility of return migration has opened up notions of 'citizenship' and 'nationality' to further complicate the cultural politics of identity and belonging. In my view, formal citizenship may not necessarily reflect the layered nuances of a migrant's identity yet it may account for significant impact on a migrant's life such as when deciding his or her length of stay in order to fulfil the three years' residency requirement to obtain Canadian citizenship (Teo 2006). However, from listening carefully to my respondents, I would emphasise that, even though citizenship may become an objective *after* an immigrant's arrival in Canada, it is quite often not the key motivation for their initial immigration decision. Instead, the hope for personal development, the chance to give their children a better education, and a desire for a different environment—whether social or natural—were the main reasons for their immigration (Teo 2003). One reason for being mindful of these actual factors is exactly to critique the over-liberating powers attached to diasporic identity. Here, I adopt Ang's (2001) argument that, by focusing on the imagined community of others elsewhere, diaspora, as a concept, tends to de-emphasise, and even diminish, the importance of living *here*. This is a particularly salient point with regard to the PRC migrants, who face considerable settlement difficulties that are very much *here*, for now.

## Acknowledgements

I would like to thank David Ley, Brenda Yeoh, Shirlena Huang and an anonymous *JEMS* reviewer for their helpful comments on an earlier version of this paper. I am grateful to the Vancouver Metropolis Centre (RIIM) for funding this research. My deepest thanks go to my respondents for sharing their stories with me.

## Notes

[1] A multi-media artist from China, Gu Xiong now lives in Canada.
[2] Apart from other forms of liaison work, the promotion of Chinese education and culture overseas expanded greatly in the 1990s (Thunø 2001). The PRC supported the establishment of local Chinese schools and exported educational schemes by compiling 20 different sets of teaching materials now used in 78 countries worldwide. One hundred and fifty teachers were sent to teach Chinese in 20 countries, and several thousand teachers from overseas have received Chinese teacher-training in the PRC. Summer camps were also set up for second- and third-generation ethnic Chinese.
[3] This is an example of a collusion between capitalism and nation-building.
[4] The data in this section are based on statistics derived from the Landed Immigrant Data System (LIDS) of the Department of Citizenship and Immigration Canada (CIC) for the years 1996–2000 and include both principal applicants and their dependants.
[5] Note that the 'point system' for the skilled workers programme was fundamentally revised in 2002. An important change was the tightening of English- (or French-)language requirements for skilled immigrants. The language profile of PRC skilled immigrants who applied from 2002 onwards is hence likely to be different from that of the present group.
[6] This has been a notoriously persistent problem faced by new immigrants in Canada. There is growing evidence that a substantial proportion of immigrants to Canada are not able to convert their foreign qualifications into jobs that match their training and experience (Basran and Li 1998).
[7] According to my respondents, this practice was far more common among business investor immigrants.
[8] Jiansheng is under the impression that Canadian citizenship is preferred for these positions.

## References

Anderson, B. (1991) *Imagined Communities: Reflections on the Origin and Spread of Nationalism.* London: Verso.
Ang, I. (2001) *On Not Speaking Chinese.* London and New York: Routledge.
Anwar, M. (1979) *The Myth of Return: Pakistanis in Britain.* London: Heinemann.
Appadurai, A. (1996) *Modernity At Large: Cultural Dimensions of Globalization.* Minneapolis and London: University of Minnesota Press.
Basch, L.G., Schiller, N.G. and Szanton Blanc, C. (1994) *Nations Unbound: Transnational Projects, Postcolonial Predicaments and Deterritorialized Nation-States.* Amsterdam: Gordon and Breach.
Basran, G.S. and Li, Z. (1998) 'Devaluation of foreign credentials as perceived by visible minority professional immigrants', *Canadian Ethnic Studies*, 30(3): 6–23.
Bhabha, K.H. (1990) *Nation and Narration.* London and New York: Routledge.
Bhabha, K.H. (1994) *The Location of Culture.* London and New York: Routledge.

Brettell, C.B. (1979) 'Emigrar para voltar: a Portuguese ideology of return migration', *Papers in Anthropology*, 20(1): 1–20.
Castles, S. and Miller, M. (1993) *The Age of Migration: International Population Movements in the Modern World*. Basingstoke: Macmillan.
CIC (1999) *Facts and Figures 1999: Immigration Overview*. Ottawa: Strategic Policy, Planning and Research. Online at: http://www.collectionscanada.gc.ca/webarchives/20060119022109/http://epe.lac-bac.gc.ca/100/201/301/facts_figures_immigration_overview/mp43-333-2000e.pdf, last accessed 24 October 2009.
CIC (2002) *Facts and Figures 2002: Immigration Overview*. Ottawa: Strategic Policy, Planning and Research. Online at: http://www.collectionscanada.gc.ca/webarchives/20060303204353/http://www.cic.gc.ca/english/pub/facts2002/index.html, last accessed 24 October 2009.
CIC (20040) *Facts and Figures 2004: Immigration Overview: Permanent and Temporary Residents*. Ottawa: Research and Evaluation Branch. Online at: http://www.collectionscanada.gc.ca/webarchives/20061026001451/http://www.ci.gc.ca/english/pub/facts2004/index.html, last accessed 24 October 2009.
Cohen, R. and Gold, G. (1997) 'Constructing ethnicity: myth of return and modes of exclusion among Israelis in Toronto', *International Migration*, 35(3): 373–94.
Couton, P. (2002) 'Highly skilled immigrants: recent trends and issues', *ISUMA: Canadian Journal of Policy Research*, 3(2): 114–23.
Davidson, J., Bondi, L. and Smith, M. (eds) (2005) *Emotional Geographies*. Aldershot: Ashgate.
Gardner, K. (1995) *Global Migrants, Local Lives: Travel and Transformation in Rural Bangladesh*. Oxford: Clarendon Press.
Gilroy, P. (1993) *The Black Atlantic: Modernity and Double Consciousness*. London: Verso.
Guarnizo, L.E. (1997) '"Going home": class, gender and household transformation among Dominican return migrants', in Pessar, P. (ed.) *Caribbean Circuits: New Directions in the Study of Caribbean Migration*. New York: Center for Migration Studies, 13–60.
Hoffmann-Nowotny, H.J. (1978) 'European migration after WWII', in McNeil, W.H. and Adams, R.S. (eds) *Human Migration*. Bloomington: University of Indiana Press, 85–105.
King, R. (1995) 'Migrations, globalization and place', in Massey, D. and Jess, P. (eds) *A Place in the World*. Oxford: Oxford University Press, 6–44.
Ley, D. (2003) 'Seeking Homo Economicus: the Canadian state and the strange story of the Business Immigration Program', *Annals of the Association of American Geographers*, 93(2): 426–41.
Luo, K., Fei, G. and Huang, P. (2002) 'China: government policies and emerging trends of reversal of the brain drain', in Iredale, R., Fei, G. and Rozario, S. (eds) *Return Skilled and Business Migration and Social Transformation*. Wollongong: University of Wollongong, APMRN, 71–90.
*Ming Pao* (2002) 'Fifty-two Shenchuanese organisations recruit talents from North America', *Ming Pao*, 15 July.
Nyíri, P. (2001) 'Expatriating is patriotic? The discourse on "new migrants" in the People's Republic of China and identity construction among recent migrants from the PRC', *Journal of Ethnic and Migration Studies*, 27(4): 635–53.
Ong, A. (1999) *Flexible Citizenship: The Cultural Logics of Transnationality*. Durham NC: Duke University Press.
Rubenstein, H. (1979) 'The return ideology in West Indian migration', *Papers in Anthropology*, 20(1): 21–38.
Sun, W. (2002) *Leaving China: Media, Migration and Transnational Imagination*. Maryland: Rowman & Littlefield.
Teo, S.Y. (2003) 'Dreaming inside a walled city: imagination, gender and the roots of immigration', *Asian and Pacific Migration Journal*, 12(4): 411–38.
Teo, S.Y. (2006) 'Circular migration between China and Canada: a focus on the return segment', *Around the Globe*, 3(2): 45–7.

Teo, S.Y. (2007) 'Vancouver's newest Chinese diaspora: settlers or "immigrant prisoners"?', *GeoJournal*, 68(2–3): 211–22.
Thunø, M. (2001) 'Reaching out and incorporating Chinese overseas: the trans-territorial scope of the PRC by the end of the 20th century', *The China Quarterly*, 168: 910–29.
Yang, M. (1997) 'Mass media and transnational subjectivity in Shanghai: notes on (re)cosmopolitanism in a Chinese metropolis', in Ong, A. and Nonini, D.M. (eds) *Ungrounded Empires: The Cultural Politics of Modern Chinese Transnationalism*. New York: Routledge, 287–323.
Zacharias, Y. (2003) 'We live between two cultures', *The Vancouver Sun*, 16 October: B 1–2.
Zhang, N. (2002) 'Immigration stories: to leave or to return, foreign identity, Chinese heart', *Nanfang Dushibao*. Online at: http://www.tigtag.com/community/immigration/16788_0_6.html, last accessed 24 October 2009.

# A Ritual Economy of 'Talent': China and Overseas Chinese Professionals
Xiang Biao

*Since the Guangzhou municipality in south China organised the first Overseas Students Fair in 1998, large conventions aimed at recruiting overseas Chinese professionals (OCPs) have become a regular scene in major cities in China. These conventions constitute one of the most visible means of the Chinese government's engagement with the 800,000 OCPs who remain overseas after receiving tertiary education abroad. Characteristic of the conventions, and OCP policies in general, is a highly 'materialistic' thinking: it is argued that OCPs deserve generous financial rewards because they are economically and technologically beneficial to China, and that financial reward is the most feasible means to attract them back. My ethnographic data, however, reveal that the language of economism is communicated in a highly ritualistic manner and, conversely, political rituals serve as a crucial part of the conventions. The ritualised economic- and technological-determinist discourse appears apolitical, yet acquires strong mobilising and legitimating power, and is thus particularly effective in accommodating OCPs into the established political order. The concept 'ritual economy' denotes such deep intertwining between the economic, the ritualistic and the political.*

When I landed in Changchun, the capital city of Jilin Province in North-East China, in early June 2004 I was immediately embraced by a festival atmosphere. In the sky flew colourful balloons, on the ground lay carefully arranged flowers. The main road from the airport to downtown Changchun was densely dotted by banners of different shapes: the vertical, narrow ones hung on lamp-posts and the horizontal ones covered the sides of flyovers; huge boards were erected from the ground up in strategic places such as roundabouts or in the middle of squares.

'North-East Rejuvenation, Win–Win Cooperation' (*dongbei zhenxing, yingying hezuo*)—the key line highlighted in the banners and boards—was firmly planted in my mind by the time I arrived at the hotel.

The Convention for Cooperation and Exchange among Overseas Chinese Enterprises in Scientific and Technological Innovation was taking place, organised by the Overseas Chinese Affairs Office (OCAO) of the State Council and three provincial governments in the north-east (Heilongjiang, Jilin and Liaoning) in response to central government's call for 'rejuvenating the North-East'. The main target group of the convention were 'new overseas Chinese' (*xin huaqiao*, also referred to as *xin yimin* or 'new migrants'; see Teo, this issue)—who left China after the Cultural Revolution—and particularly overseas Chinese professionals (OCPs). The slogan 'Win–Win Cooperation' was novel. Official discourses in China about overseas Chinese have long been dominated by such notions as patriotism and contributions (to the development of homeland), and overseas Chinese are typically depicted as the 'wandering sons' (*youzi*) who yearn for mother's hug. But 'win–win cooperation' clearly puts the motherland and OCPs in the position of a mutually beneficial, equal partnership.

The convention started with a gala banquet for 500 guests. In the middle of the hall, at a table twice the size of the others, sat almost all the top leaders of the province, a deputy minister of OCAO, and a couple of OCP representatives. As an observer I was placed on a peripheral table with drivers, bodyguards, reporters and photographers. After a session of effusive speeches made by officials and OCP representatives in hierarchical order, the officials proposed toasts. They started with the table next to the central one, and officials above a certain level stopped toasting at certain tables as it is regarded as inappropriate for senior officials to propose a toast to those more junior. My table waited for more than 20 minutes before we were approached by an enthusiastic but slightly nervous local cadre. Following the toasts, a dramatic tenor who earned his name for a song celebrating the first Liberation truck manufactured in China in the 1950s[1] sang a song about motherhood written by a US-based OCP specialising in industrial lubricants. The lubricants specialist was so emotional after hearing the song that he ran to the stage and improvised a speech. Tears, hugs, handshaking and long applause followed.

The real business started the next day. At numerous concurrent panels, OCPs presented their technological innovations, highlighted market potential and projected astonishing profits for investors. Mr Yang, a middle-ranking official in the State Council OCAO in charge of OCP affairs told me that this part of the convention was modelled on the investment seminars organised by venture capitalists in Silicon Valley. At the same time, local firms and institutes, including government departments, set up stalls in the hall to recruit employees and collaborative partners for the projects they had in mind. Official hierarchy was temporarily suspended for these Silicon Valley days. Middle-ranking officials roamed around, sneaked into seminar rooms in the middle of presentations, sat down and observed quietly.

The convention was concluded on the fourth day with a grand ceremony of signing agreements for collaboration. Starting with a few selected representatives of OCPs and local companies reporting how much they had achieved at the meeting, officials from OCAO and the province then made brief speeches to confirm that the convention had been a great success. Officials from Beijing retreated. Local officials stood on the stage in line, wine glasses in hand, overseeing batches of OCPs and local companies coming on stage to sign agreements. A press conference followed immediately. Detailed information about the achievements of the convention—in terms of the number of contracts signed and the amount of investment committed—was readily available in printed material. Given that almost all the business deals had been signed just minutes earlier, the outcomes of the convention were obviously ensured even before it started.

The convention was thus at once commercial, technological, political and theatrical. I argue that, although seemingly contradictory, the political rituals and calculative business activities mutually enhance and legitimise each other. It is through endorsing and even encouraging the uncompromisingly pragmatic business endeavours that the political establishment projects itself as progressive, scientific, forward-looking and capable of delivering concrete achievements. At the same time, the political rituals glorify business interests, provide OCPs with special political clout and social prestige, and effectively incorporate them into the established political order.

Conventions like this, which have become regular events in major Chinese cities, present a 'ritual economy' about OCPs. First, the conventions are *rituals about economy* in the sense that economic calculations are regarded as the most powerful, reasonable and realistic rationality. Second, there is an *economy of rituals*. The convention in Changchun cost the local government RMB 0.7 million, excluding subsidies from central government. Every year the Ministry of Education invests about RMB 300–400 million (US$40–53 million) in OCP programmes, and the Ministry of Personnel allocated nearly RMB 200 million (about US$27 million) in the first half of the 2000s for the same purpose. Most was spent on sponsoring OCPs' visits; a substantial part also went towards ritual activities (indeed, many visits are themselves symbolic and ritualised). Third and most importantly, the conventions present *economy as a ritual*. The conventions are, on the one hand, relentlessly outcome-oriented and aimed at maximising the number of commercial contracts but, on the other, the investments may never prove to have paid off economically, and the government is certainly not concerned with this when they allocate the budget. In other words, the conventions are premised on and promote an economistic ideology, but are themselves run 'uneconomically'. This paradox is reflective of a larger contradiction in the mainstream discourse in China about OCPs. It is believed that OCPs deserve generous financial rewards because they are economically and technologically beneficial to China; in return, China has to offer material benefits in order to attract them (thus 'win–win') as the OCPs are construed as *homo economicus* (Ley 2003; Ong 1999). But even if it becomes evident that OCPs contribute less to Chinese society than they receive, the state may well continue deploying current OCP discourse and carry on with the investment because the economic- and technological-determinist discourses are *apolitical* and are thus most effective in facilitating a strong relation between the state and OCPs, a connection which is itself politically important for the Chinese state in the era of globalisation. In contrast, a global convention of Chinese journalists, for example, would be too politically sensitive and thus unproductive for the state and other stakeholders to invest in. Economic rationalities and business activities are ritualised in order to serve other agendas.

The ritual economy is certainly not uniquely Chinese. India's enthusiasm about its Information Technology (IT) workers overseas, Singapore's strong interest in closer ties with its overseas professionals and South Korea's courtship of its diaspora are all couched in the language of remittances, investment and technology transfer. But this language is communicated in a highly ritualistic manner. For example preferential policies are announced on occasions such as Pravasi Bharatiya Divas (Overseas Indians' Day) in India, and evidence of the diaspora's contributions is circulated through emotionally touching stories. In return, the materialistic language serves much broader political and ideological purposes, be it the religious agenda of the Bharatiya Janata Party of India, the Singapore government's concern about identity, or South Korea's ethnonationalist ideology.[2]

Such a ritual economy of talent is also implicitly buttressed by globally dominant academic discourses. In studying diaspora in general, and overseas professionals in particular (normally under the rubrics of 'brain drain' and 'brain gain'), academic publications tend to rationalise state–diaspora relations in narrowly defined economic and technological terms. It is widely assumed that states are interested in educated diasporas primarily because of their potential economic and technological contributions. By depriving the state of its political, social and moral concerns, and by presenting it as a pure, cold and naked economic agent, this academic discourse has not only simplified realities, but has also itself become part of the ritual economy—one that privileges and even fetishises economic rationality.

In this paper I examine the relations between the Chinese state and OCPs in a more nuanced manner, demonstrating that the strategies and calculations behind OCP programmes go far beyond the investment–return equilibrium and are instead shaped by social–political structure. I pay special attention to the connections and differences between central and local government. The ritual economy, although presented in a universal, homogenising language, is practised by actors with differentiated intentions and strategies.

The paper is based on my field research conducted in China and the UK in 2004 and 2005. I collected government policy documents issued between 1986 and 2003; conducted in-depth interviews with 36 government officials, staff at research institutes and OCPs, and organised focus-group discussions in Beijing and Leeds (UK). Furthermore, a questionnaire survey was carried out in Changchun, Shenyang (China) and Leeds (UK), with 55 valid returns. This project also utilised 130 OCPs' detailed *curriculum vitae*, randomly selected from the government database of more than 20,000 CVs.

I first review the history of the formation of the OCP group after the Cultural Revolution—directly shaped by both domestic politics in China and prevailing international relations. The second section looks at OCP programmes and teases out how central government manages the ritual economy by balancing 'soft' policies and statements with 'hard' (concrete) activities. The third section describes local government initiatives based on my participatory observation of two major OCP events in North-East China. Local government typically adopts a strategy of 'government sets the stage, business runs the opera'; they encourage OCPs to invest in commercial projects and are keen to see immediate business outcomes. Although it is questionable whether the initiatives achieve what they are meant to achieve, they are certainly successful operas.

## The Making of '*haiwai xuezi*'

There are in total 1.6 million OCPs (known in China as *haiwai xuezi*, literally meaning 'overseas students/scholars')—the main target of the ritual economy—including 600,000 who left before 1949[3] and more than 1 million who left after 1978, who form the current policy focus. Among those who left after 1978, about 200,000 have completed their tertiary education.[4] Despite the media hype, it is important not to overestimate the number of OCPs. According to an official who has worked in the field since the 1980s, fewer than 1,000 new OCPs (who left after 1978) worldwide have obtained tenured position in universities or have attained a comparable achievement (Zhao 2003).[5] The head of the Association of International Personnel Exchange in London, an office of the National Bureau of Foreign Experts in Beijing, told me that fewer than 1,000 OCPs have obtained degrees and have started working in the UK. Indeed, the possibly very limited number of 'real talents' has raised debates in China on the worthiness of government investment in OCPs. The discrepancy between the enormous resources dedicated to OCP programmes, and the relatively small number of OCPs whom the programmes target, once again highlights the ritual aspect of state–diaspora relations.

The typical image of *haiwai xuezi* is that they are technologically advanced, socially progressive and transcend political interest and ideological debates commonly regarded as wasteful. OCP representatives are regularly invited for government-organised activities and popular social events. The state is not the only institution that appropriates OCPs as a valuable symbol. China Soul for Christ Foundation, a California-based Christian organisation whose website is banned in China, recently released a series of VCDs titled 'As *Haiwai Xuezi* Testify' (*haiwai xuezi jianzhen xilie*). Apparently quite popular with Chinese audiences, the VCDs taped a group of OCPs lecturing about their experiences of conversion.

*Haiwai xuezi* as a special social group, a policy target and a discursive category emerged through the interplay between migration flows and state policies. Unlike in other major source countries of migrant professionals such as India, the Philippines and Ghana, studying overseas (as opposed to the migration of professionals who have completed their education) is the dominant path to the formation of OCPs. One source estimates that as many as 60 per cent of all the Chinese who emigrated through legal means after 1978, including both skilled and unskilled, were students and their families (Gao 2003: 390, 395). Studying abroad was out of the question for most Chinese during the Cultural Revolution until the end of the 1970s, when the Ministry of Education (MoE), pushed by Deng Xiaoping, started sending selected researchers to the West to pursue studies. This was further facilitated by the Sino-America Understanding on Educational Exchanges (October 1978) and the Agreement on Cooperation in Science and Technology of January 1979 (see Zweig and Chen 1995: 19).[6] In 1979, the MoE, the National Science Committee and the Ministry of Foreign Affairs jointly issued a document detailing how Chinese overseas students should be regulated. The procedure was strict and those who did not return on time would be punished.

In 1981, the State Council approved the *Temporary Regulations on Self-financed Overseas Education*. This was the first time that the Chinese government had formally recognised self-financed overseas study—going abroad for studying without the state's sponsorship—as a legitimate means of exiting China.[7] Since the early 1980s, employers could also send their staff overseas for academic exchange or even degree education. The employer covered the costs in full or in part and normally the individual was obliged to return to the same employer to work. Thus were established the three main channels of Chinese student migration: those sent by the government, those sent by the work unit, and those who were self-financing. These led to the first wave of 'fever to study abroad' by the mid-1980s (see Zweig and Chen 1995: 20).

The late 1980s saw the formation of a sizable OCP group (i.e. graduates who decided to stay on overseas) when, with the gradual relaxation in the regulations, the number of migrant students increased but the return rate dropped significantly. Although this triggered much concern about 'brain drain', the top leadership seemed not to be alarmed. In 1987, Zhao Ziyang, the then secretary general of the Chinese Communist Party, argued that brain drain should be regarded as a case of 'storing brainpower overseas' that would be used in the future (see Zweig and Chen 1995: 17). Similarly, the State Commission for Science and Technology suggested in 1988 that OPCs should be regarded as an overseas reservoir (Zweig and Chen 1995).

The Tian'anmen Square incident in 1989 was a crucial turning point in the history of OCPs. The United States issued an executive order to grant PRC students permanent residency in 1990, followed by the 1992 Chinese Students Protection Act. Other major Western countries followed suit. As a result, 70,000 Chinese students and scholars in the US (including 20,000 family members), 10,000 in Canada (through the OM-IS-399 policy, see Zweig and Chen 1995: 7) and 28,500 in Australia (Mackie 1997: 47) obtained permanent residency almost overnight. This laid down the basis for a large OCP pool.

The Tian'anmen incident was especially important not only because it rapidly enlarged the number of OCPs, but also because it signalled a new relationship between them and the Chinese state. How would the Chinese government deal with the OCPs who have openly 'betrayed' them? The Chinese government, surprisingly, not only continued sending students out, but made a significant policy shift—from preventing and punishing student overstayers, to encouraging return regardless of whether they had ever broken agreements with the state. In 1992, the State Council issued a special circular emphasising that all returned overseas students would be welcomed no matter what their past political attitudes were:

> No further investigation shall be made about those who had made incorrect statements or committed incorrect activities when they were overseas. Even those who had participated in organisations that are against the Chinese government, and had damaged the state's security, interests and honour shall also be welcomed as long as they have withdrawn from these organisations and no longer commit unconstitutional and illegal anti-governmental activities (State Council 1992).

This was clearly referring to those who left China or refused to return due to the Tian'anmen incident. For those who were sent to study overseas, the circular urged their employers to keep in touch with them. Originally, overseas students had to apply for approval from their employers in China to extend their stay overseas. If they stayed on without permission, their salary would be suspended for the first year, and subsequently the employer could fire them. In the early 1990s, the rule was changed and those who stayed overseas without permission could pay compensation to the employer and terminate the employment relationship as a normal arrangement, in contradistinction to the fact that this was previously recorded as a violation of rules. Returned OCPs were also allowed to quit their jobs in the public sector if they preferred to work in private or foreign-owned enterprises. The liberalised policy is summarised as the 'Twelve-Characters Approach', the twelve characters in Chinese being *zhi chi liu xue, gu li hui guo, lai qu zi you,* meaning 'support study overseas, encourage returns, guarantee freedom of movement'. OCPs' autonomy was further stressed when central government proposed the slogan *weiguo fuwu* (serve the motherland) in the late 1990s.[8] As compared to the earlier slogan of *huiguo fuwu* (return and serve the motherland), the new notion indicated that staying overseas is just as patriotic as physically returning. This led to 'a new state-sanctioned flexibility' as Teo (this issue) aptly calls it.

These policy changes were presented as driven by a concern for 'individual choice'. It is argued to be ethically problematic and practically unfeasible to force OCPs to return. Talents are scarce human capital and should be given the freedom to choose any country in which to work and reside. To do otherwise would be to act against the global law of reality. When I asked whether current OCP policies attach too much importance to financial rewards, Mr Yang from the state OCAO looked surprised: '*You* should know what their living and working conditions are like overseas. We are still offering too little. Otherwise why should they come to China?'. In this regard, the

Chinese state has transformed from a despotic regime that treated OCPs (as well as other populations) as its subjects, into a regulatory system that sees OCPs as free individuals and citizens. The state no longer tries to maintain its authority and power by claiming 'possession' over the OCPs; instead it encourages OCPs to accumulate wealth in the global market, before attempting to win their allegiance through economically termed contractual relations.

This approach is set to perpetuate itself further with the overwhelming trend towards the commodification of international education. Since 2000, more than 100,000 students have left China each year to study overseas, and an increasing portion of them pay for their education out of their own (or rather, their parents') pockets. Chinese students are commonly identified as major customers by overseas universities. The number of international education agents, who work as commercial brokers assisting self-financing students, has also mushroomed. First appearing in China at the end of the 1990s, by early 2001 there were at least 309 in operation in Beijing alone. For these students who embark on international education as an investment, neoliberal governmentality is the most, and possibly only, feasible way for the state to establish meaningful relations with them. It is precisely in order to capture nuanced governmental strategies in this new context that I focus on how government cultivates delicate relations with OCPs who may or may not return, instead of examining actual return migration, which has attracted much attention for recent studies on returnees (see Cao 2004; Chen X.F. *et al.* 2003; Chen Y.C. 2008; Cheng 2002; Iredale *et al.* 2003; Wang *et al.* 2006; Xiao 2001; Zweig *et al.* 2006).

## Central Government: One Hand Soft, One Hand Hard

The central government manages the ritual economy of OCPs by balancing 'soft' efforts targeting general OCPs with 'hard' activities targeting selected individuals. The 'soft' actions include issuing policies, opening new avenues of communication—particularly websites—and conferring honours. They are 'soft' in the sense that they do not require large amounts of investment and are aimed at creating symbolic effects in the larger society. Following an index provided by the MoE, I collected 180 government policies issued during the period from 1986 to 2003, including eight general policies issued by the State Council, 90 general policies by local government, 34 regarding industrial parks exclusively for returned overseas students, seven on education for returnees' children, 27 on personnel policy, nationality, household registration and even marriage of returnees, and 14 on customs regulations. Indeed, since so many ministries individually promulgated favourable policies, the MoE decided to issue special ID cards for selected OCPs which enable them to enjoy all the benefits provided by the different ministries—from buying cars to sending children to kindergarten.

These policies, however, may have more symbolic than substantive significance. As our interviews and focus-group discussions reveal, only a very limited number of OCPs—including those who have been considering returning to China on a permanent basis—have detailed knowledge about the policies. The Research Team on the Motivations and Rules of the Return of Overseas Talents and the Strategies to Encourage the Return (2003) indicates that many returned OCPs in Shanghai, ranging from 98.4 per cent to 44.8 per cent depending on the particular policy, do not know about policies promulgated by Shanghai municipality government aimed at offering them special benefits. This was confirmed by the research conducted by Chen X.F. *et al.* (2003). But what is also interesting is that, according to a recent survey conducted by the Department for Overseas Scholars of the Chinese Youth Federation and the newspaper *Digests for Youth*, nearly 41 per cent of those surveyed who had never studied or worked overseas regard favourable government policies for OCPs as necessary, only slightly lower than the percentage of returned OCPs who held the same view (43 per cent). This indicates that public opinion is strongly in favour of OCPs, who probably benefit more from the effects of the policies on domestic opinion than from the policies themselves.

A similar slippage between intended and actual effects can be observed in official websites dedicated to OCPs. Acknowledging the importance of the Internet for transnational network-building, almost all government departments related to OCPs have set up websites, or created special sections under their general portals. The most notable example is *China Scholar Abroad* (www.chisa.edu.cn) set up by the MoE. First appearing as a conventional magazine in May 1987, *China Scholar Abroad* became the first Chinese e-magazine in January 1995. Other ministries, most provinces and even municipalities have also launched OCP websites.[9] However, according to our survey, the most popular website—*China Scholar Abroad*—was visited only occasionally by most informants, and many other websites were hardly known. We also found that the younger the OCPs, the less likely they are to visit these websites, in exact opposition to the general pattern of website usage. Our informants stated that there are too many, rather than too few, websites for and about OCPs, which is sometimes confusing.

A more important reason for OCPs' lack of interest in the websites is because they do not provide the information they need. Most is about government policies, experiences of studying overseas, successful stories of returnees, and the general situation of major receiving countries. The most suitable audience seems to be students in China who plan to study overseas. Indeed, the websites are meaningful and interesting only when they are read from a China-centred perspective about how OCPs *as a group* live and work in various countries. Why should an OCP living in Singapore be particularly interested in what an OCP in London is doing? OCP as a category is fundamentally a construct by China, and members are lumped together simply because of their connections with China. In this sense the websites are important because they establish the category of OCPs symbolically, particularly in the domestic arena.

The government also resorts to its time-honoured working method—'setting up models' (*shu dianxing*)—in making *haiwai xuezi*, awarding a total of 939 returned outstanding OCPs (the 'models') in 1991, 1997 and 2003 through high-profile formal meetings in Beijing that were broadcast nationwide, thus creating minor state spectacles. While the first two honouring conferences (*biaozhang dahui*) were organised by the MoE and the Ministry of Personnel, the third was organised jointly by the ministries and three departments (of Organisation, of Propaganda and of the United Front) of the Central Committee of the Communist Party. The action remains 'soft', but gains much more weight.

Whenever I mention these awards ceremonies to OCPs, both during this fieldwork and on other occasions, the responses are always either indifferent or cynical. 'Who cares?' they ask. But these state spectacles are not intended to be consumed by OCPs only. Equally as, or even more important than, honouring OCPs, they mobilise staff within the state and make OCPs a professionalised 'sphere of work' (*gongzuo lingyu*). In selecting who is to be honoured, recommendations from local government are the most important considerations. The discretion of recommending certain candidates and not others immediately provides local government with authority among OCPs. Furthermore, these events also reward individuals and institutes who have performed well in working with OCPs. For those employed by government and public institutes, awards from the central government are of the utmost importance for their career development. Mobilising and reorganising apparatus *within* the state are thus essential for the successful construction of *haiwai xuezi* and the effective development of new relations between them and the state.[10]

At the same time as carrying out 'soft' activities, central government also spends hard cash and establishes concrete programmes, the large number of which, implemented by the different ministries, renders a comprehensive overview or an exhaustive categorisation impossible. I will instead provide a brief comparison of two of the best-known programmes—the Chunhui Plan and the Cheung Kong Scholar Program. In so doing, I illustrate the general art of managing the ritual economy.[11]

The Chunhui Plan targets relatively junior OCPs and aims to develop wider ties. It supports OCPs' short-term visits for the purposes of academic exchange, the provision of training, the joint supervision of PhD students, technology transfer to underdeveloped regions in China, and participation in R&D at large and medium state-owned enterprises.[12] Since its inception in 1996, the programme has sponsored about 7,000 OCP short-term visits to China. The central committee of the Plan, located at the MoE, identifies annual priorities (in terms of occupations and places to visit) for funding, and forwards the list to education attachés in foreign missions. At the same time, OCPs submit their applications, which are processed by the foreign missions—except for group applications or requests for full sponsorship which need to be approved by the MoE in Beijing. Local government is also heavily involved. Funding priorities are often identified according to needs expressed by local government and, while the MoE subsidises international trips, local governments who want the OCPs to visit normally cover all the costs of travel and accommodation in China.

The Chunhui Plan launched a sub-programme in 2001 to enable OCPs to work in China during their sabbaticals. According to the scheme, universities in China advertise their short-term positions internationally, and interested OCPs submit applications for the positions to the foreign missions in the country of residence; the embassy, after processing the application, passes it on to the university. When the university decides to accept an OCP, the application is sent to the MoE for final approval. When approved, the MoE covers the international airfare. The university decides on the remuneration rate for the OCPs, which can be five to eight times higher than the norm in China. The MoE subsidises the university RMB 5,000, 7,000 and 8,000 (US$667; US$933 and US$1,067) monthly for assistant, associate and full professorships respectively. The university also provides free accommodation or an allowance, medical insurance and some financial support for academic activities (MoE 2002).

In contrast to the Chunhui Plan, the Cheung Kong Scholar Program recruits leading researchers in strategic areas. In 1998, the Hong Kong-based company Cheung Kong Holdings and the MoE allocated RMB 60 million (US$8 million) each as the initial fund to set up the programme. In addition the Lee KC Foundation donated HKD 10 million (US$1.3 million) to set up the Cheung Kong Scholar Achievement Award. The Cheung Kong Scholar Program sponsors OCPs to work in China either as a Specially Invited Professor for three years (extendable for another two) or a Chair Professor for one year. A professor is paid an annual stipend of RMB 100,000 (US$13,000), and some are also given a Cheung Kong Achievement Award of RMB 1 million (US$133,000). Scholars are selected through a strict procedure. Firstly, universities apply to the MoE to set up Cheung Kong Scholar chairs, which the university then advertises internationally. Applications are reviewed by a committee of 60 Fellows of the Chinese Academy of Science and Fellows of the Chinese Academy of Engineering, and the final list needs to be approved by six pre-eminent scientists. Academic and administrative staff in the universities and the Chinese Academy of Science whom we interviewed unanimously agreed that the programme has attracted truly leading figures, and has therefore significantly contributed to academic research in China.

There are a few other initiatives similar to the Cheung Kong Scholar Program, though of a smaller scale. The Distinguished Young Scholars Program set up by the National Science Foundation, for example, grants four-year research funding of RMB 550,000–800,000 (US$73,000–107,000) to scientists below 45 years of age. The One Hundred Talent Program of the Chinese Academy of Sciences offers each selected scientist RMB 2 million (US$267,000) over three years. These programmes target senior scientists and are individual- instead of group-oriented.

There is a general trend that an emphasis on the soft glove is shifting to a focus on the hard grip. The state OCAO for example, has largely focused on soft activities in its engagement with OCPs in past years. But Mr Yang, the official at OCAO, told me that, in the future, the OCAO will consider placing more emphasis on top OCP individuals in order to achieve more concrete results. When I mentioned that I may not be able to help with the individual targeted programmes because, as a sociologist,

I can only carry out structural and institutional analysis, Yang assured me that my research would still be relevant:

> We need to understand the group as well. The work about top individuals still needs to be based on the work about the whole group... Policies must be about groups, the work about individuals must be guided by policies.

Yang's comment and the government's effort to balance the soft and the hard provide a solution to a deep contradiction built into the ritual economy of talent. On the one hand, the term 'talent' is intrinsically individualistic. It implies that some individuals possess more 'human capital' than others and are thus more valuable and desirable, and also that 'individual merits' can defy structural constraints. On the other hand government policies, in order to be legitimate and mobilise sufficient social support, must present their target as groups and collectives. In economic calculation, talent must be distinct individuals; in political consideration, talent must be collective. The ritual economy on the one hand accommodates economic calculation into a political framework through ritual, soft and group-oriented performance; on the other hand, through ritualised economic rationalities, it legitimates and practically facilitates the political agenda of forging close relations with OCPs.

## Local Government: Government Sets the Stage, Businesses Run the Opera

The ritual economy of talent manifests itself quite differently in the activities initiated by local government, whose policies—as it is not in a position to articulate the relation between OCPs and the Chinese state through general policies—are more specific and thus even more materialistic. For example, as early as August 1993 the Shanghai municipality issued The Notification on Special Treatment on Installing Telephones, Gas and Air Conditioning for Overseas Students Who Are to Work in Shanghai. Guangzhou municipality hands out RMB 100,000 (US$13,000) as the 'golden hello' (*jianmianli*) to returnees who decide to work in Guangzhou. Even poor provinces such as Shanxi and cities such as Xi'an provide OCPs with a free office and facilities, seedcorn funds for research, and housing. Liaoning Province, one of the places facing the most severe unemployment, invested RMB 78.5 million (US$10.5 million) to attract OCPs by 2003 (Mu 2003). These material and financial offers make the policies sensational in local society. It should be noted, however, that their implementation is subject to various conditions. In many cases, the money is merely intended rather than actually allocated. Two Masters graduates from Singapore whom I interviewed, for example, returned to their respective home cities, Fuzhou and Guangzhou—capitals of the two most famous provinces for overseas Chinese and among the economically most developed—but were denied the benefits promised in policies. It turned out that, while the government stipulates the policies and provides some money to the employer (local universities in both cases), it is at the universities' discretion to decide whether they forward the funds to the individuals concerned.

As joint commercial projects are the main intended outcome of local government's engagement with OCPs, fairs have been the most common activity. The Guangzhou Overseas Students Fair (*liujiaohui* in Chinese abbreviation), that started in 1998, is probably the earliest of this type. An initiative of the Guangzhou municipal government, it is held jointly by a few ministries. The Guangzhou government shoulders most of the costs. The fair takes place annually during the Christmas break to cater to the time schedule of most OCPs. Covering the full expenditure of travel and accommodation, the fair welcomes anyone who has studied or worked overseas, and normally attracts more than 200,000 participants (including both OCPs and representatives of China-based institutes). Mr Yang at the state OCAO called Guangzhou Fair a 'Rome gathering', a term the origin of which I cannot identify (possibly something to do with Catholic masses that are open to everyone?), and commented that its main functions are 'creating momentum' (*zaoshi*) and 'forming influence' (*zaocheng yinxiang*).

Some local governments started emulating Guangzhou in the early 2000s, but few could allocate as much funding; instead they developed more focused working methods. The Jilin Convention of Consultation and Cooperation between Overseas Chinese Professionals and Domestic Enterprises, in which I participated in 2004, provides a typical example of the 'less-but-better' strategy. The organiser, the Jilin Provincial Office for Overseas Chinese Affairs and Foreign Affairs, starts preparations six months before the event. As the first step, the Office sends out calls for proposals to 300–400 OCPs through the state OCAO, organisations such as the Jilin University Alumni Association in the USA, and the contacts that the provincial government has accumulated. After receiving the proposals from OCPs, the organiser invites departments such as the provincial Bureaux of Science and Technology, Information Technology, Environment Protection, Commerce, and Small and Medium Enterprise Development to evaluate the proposals. Selected proposals are forwarded to local enterprises. If three or more local firms express interest in a particular proposal, the OCP will be invited. All the invitees must have PhDs and a minimum of three years' work experience, or Masters degrees with a minimum of five years' work experience. The provincial Office for Overseas Chinese Affairs as well as the state OCAO helps local enterprises establish contacts with OCPs and encourages them to communicate with each other prior to meeting at the Convention. The Convention in 2003 attracted 59 OCPs from 14 countries and regions and 288 enterprises from China. In the end they signed 79 agreements with a total investment of RMB 3,520 million (US$469 million), including 530 million from overseas.

There are good reasons for the emphasis on commercial projects. From the organisers' point of view, 'deliverability'—the concrete results they can yield—is essential for the sustainability of their work. This is particularly true for local OCAOs which need specially allocated budgets from the provincial and municipal government to support their work; it would be difficult to justify the constant requests for soft money without hard achievement. Demonstrable results are also important for government departments because they serve as the most convincing evidence of performance. For this reason a government department is eager to have a large number of agreements, no matter how tentative, signed on the spot at the event they organise.

But this outcome-oriented method is often at odds with the larger goal, as stated by the government, which is to encourage technology transfer. First, this method excludes those whose ideas and innovations cannot immediately be turned into commercial projects. The head of a social science department of a top university in Beijing told me that they were badly handicapped in engaging OCPs despite the university's prestige because there were hardly any resources they could tap into to invite social science and humanities researchers. The department can only apply for less than RMB 20,000 (US$2,600) a year from the university for inviting scholars from overseas—barely enough for food and local transport. Second, local governments strive to maximise the numbers of joint project deals, a large number of which, at least as I witnessed at the two conventions, are not necessarily innovative. I came across plans such as establishing business consultancies to help Chinese traders enter the foreign market, and running immigration and tourism agencies. Another unintended result of the strong desire to maximise output is the appearance of a group of OCPs sometimes dubbed 'conference worms' (*hui chongzi*), so called because it is said that they almost live on the conferences and events in China. One participant in a convention had met almost one third of the participants before and felt that the project proposals all sounded familiar. Finally, paradoxically enough, the emphasis on commercial projects, when ritualised as a political project, does not mean that the existing OCP programmes link themselves to the dynamism of the global economy or domestic industry, as evidenced by a comparison between the Chinese and Indian experiences that I detail elsewhere (Xiang 2007).

Nevertheless, although many OCP participants agreed that such conventions are to some extent only 'shows', they maintain that such activities are beneficial to them. Ms Hua, who runs trading companies in both the USA and Hungary, was one such participant. She was purchasing a certain type of stone for construction projects, which had nothing to do with high technology. She had sealed a deal with the seller in Jilin Province, but decided to sign the agreement at the convention when she learned about it accidentally. For Ms Hua, the convention gave much publicity and legitimacy to the project, and she expected that this would 'make things easier in dealing with government'. For the government organisers, commercial joint projects are symbolic of their programmatic and developmental approach that is celebrated and even obligatory in a time of neoliberal globalisation. It is through the intertwining of the ritual and the economy that a mutually productive relationship between OCPs and the state is established.

## Discussion

This paper has demonstrated multiple paradoxes in relations between the Chinese state and OCPs. First, historically, in making *haiwai xuezi* into a new social category and policy target, the state relaxed its control over OCPs significantly and accorded full recognition to their individual autonomy. At the same time, the state developed an unprecedented number of policies and programmes to aggressively forge new relations with OCPs. Although aimed at benefiting the entire society—including the private sector—the state remains the major, or even the only, investor in and organiser of, these programmes. Furthermore, the engagement with OCPs does not follow a single principle. On the one hand material rewards are regarded as the primary incentive for both OCPs and their domestic counterparts to engage with each other, and many programmes are solely aimed at facilitating business deals. On the other hand, these activities are carried out through carefully performed political rituals. For ordinary OCPs (except for a very small number of top individuals), these political rituals serve as the most efficient vehicle to obtain material rewards, which together thus form inseparable packages. These paradoxes, I suggest, can be understood through a single analytical lens—the ritual economy. Underpinning the rituals is an unmistakably economic- and technological-determinist ideology. The ritual economy in turn serves much larger projects of producing new subjectivities and developing new social and political relations across national borders.

The combination of the ritual and the economic effectively mainstreams certain social groups and ideologies, and marginalises others. Those who are less valuable in the global market tend to be politically marginalised, and those who do not conform to the political order may be economically ousted. As both political rituals and economic calculation in their current formats are highly masculine, the ritual economy has clear gender implications. Of the 130 CVs from the OCAO database (with whom the OCAO has regular contacts), over 95 per cent are male. Of those who were honoured as 'outstanding returned overseas students' by central government in 2003, 91 per cent were male.

There are deeper reasons for such a ritual economy to emerge in this particular historical juncture. It is part of the new configuration of how the economic and the political intersect in China since the late 1990s. Chinese reform has been predominantly perceived, by both policy-makers and academics, as a process whereby the market expands and the state withdraws. This is no longer the reality. It is increasingly evident that the state, particularly the communist party, has reinforced its influence or even control in almost all arenas of social and economic life. OCPs as agents of globalisation are eager to tap into economic opportunities in China (many OCPs working in academic or education institutes develop ties with China precisely for the purpose of turning their research results into commercial projects), but they know only too well that a 'proper' relation with the state is essential. Friction does exist but, by and large, they are incorporated into the system.

Although hailed as one of the most progressive and innovative groups, OCPs are probably more domesticated than many inside China. The earlier anticipation that OCPs would act as powerful agents outside the establishment to transform China looks ever more doubtful.

## Acknowledgements

This paper is based on a project which was funded by the Asian Development Bank and carried out in close association with the Overseas Chinese Affairs Office (OCAO), State Council, People's Republic of China. I am grateful to staff at OCAO for sharing with me their insights and offering me the rare opportunity to conduct participatory observation.

## Notes

[1] The first Liberation truck, manufactured in 1956 in Changchun, was widely hailed in China as a symbol of the country's economic independence and socialist industrialisation. Mao Zedong showed a strong personal interest in the truck.

[2] Discourses and activities about the overseas populations are more 'ritualised' than those about domestic ones precisely because the relationship between the state and the diaspora is contentious and unstable. Rites serve as a site for defining, negotiating and managing such relationships.

[3] A report by OCAO in early 2002 indicates that, among the estimated 30 million 'old' overseas Chinese as opposed to those who left after the Reform, there are about '600,000 overseas Chinese technology personnel in Western developed countries. There are 450,000 in the USA alone, including 30,000 world-class professionals, making up about one quarter of the 130,000 first-rank scientists and technology personnel in the USA' (OCAO 2002: 2). We cannot identify the exact basis of this estimate, but it is a consensus that the number of 30 million is a gross underestimate and that 600,000 is also a fairly conservative estimate.

[4] By the end of 2006, more than 1 million students in total had gone overseas for study and about 270,000 had returned to China on a long-term basis (Ministry of Education 2009).

[5] This group includes those who have reached the position of principal investigator in a research institute or branch manager in a large corporation, have important research achievements or have published significant papers in influential international journals, or are appointed to certain positions in government or non-government organisations. Two-thirds are based in the USA.

[6] Educational exchanges with the West began before that, in 1972–73, with the UK, Australia, France, Italy, New Zealand, Canada and other countries with which China had established diplomatic relations. But the numbers of students involved were very small.

[7] In Chinese, studying abroad without state sponsorship is called *zifei liuxue*, literally meaning 'self-financed overseas education'. But most Chinese students who moved abroad to study without government funding are supported by scholarships from the receiving universities or other international foundations.

[8] The term *weiguo fuwu* was formally articulated for the first time in the document Suggestions on Encouraging Overseas Students to Serve Countries by Various Means, jointly issued by five ministries on 14 May 2001.

[9] The *China Diaspora Web* (www.hslmw.com), run by the state OCAO, is another major domain for the diaspora. The websites *Liuxue.net* (www.liuxue.net), managed by the MoE,

China Overseas Talents (MoP— www.chinatalents.gov.cn) and CAS Overseas Study and Continuing Education (www.castalents.ac.cn) tend to be more focused, primarily providing OCPs with policy-related information. Other major websites are *China Human Resource Network* (http://www.hr.com.cn/), *China International Employment Net* (http://www.chinajob.cc/), and *Chinese Service Centre for Scholarly Exchange* (http://www.cscse.edu.cn/); examples of province- and municipality-based websites are *Nanjing International Talent Networks* (www.wininjob.com) and *Liaoning Overseas Chinese Scholar Innovation Engineering Network* (http://www.ocs-ln,gov.cn).

[10] For a discussion of how holiday celebrations and national conferences in post-apartheid South Africa serve to instil a sense of unity and pride within the African National Congress party, see Jensen (2001: 106).

[11] For a fuller review of central government's initiatives regarding OCPs, see Xiang (2005).

[12] Chunhui literally means 'the spring sunlight'. The expression originates from a well-known poem: 'How can the soul of small grass, repay the sunlight of the spring', which refers to a child's gratitude to his or her parents.

# References

Cao, C. (2004) *China's Efforts at Turning 'Brain Drain' into 'Brain Gain'.* Singapore: National University of Singapore, East Asian Institute Background Brief No. 216.

Chen, X.F. et al. (2003) *The Cost and Benefits of Studying Overseas: A Research on the Performance of China's State-Sponsored Overseas Education.* Beijing: Educational Science Press.

Chen, Y.C. (2008) 'The limits of brain circulation: Chinese returnees and technological development in Beijing', *Pacific Affairs*, 81(2): 195–215.

Cheng, X. (2002) *Studies on Contemporary Chinese Overseas Students.* Hong Kong: Hong Kong Social Science Publications.

Gao, W.N. (2003) *Chinese New Migrants in the Context of International Migration.* Beijing: Zhongguo Huaqiao Chubanshe.

Iredale, R., Guo, F. and Rozario, S. (eds) (2003) *Return Migration in the Asia Pacific.* Cheltenham: Edward Elgar.

Jensen, S. (2001) 'The battlefield and the prize: ANC's bid to reform the South African state', in Hansen, T. and Stepputat, F. (eds) *States of Imagination.* Durham and London: Duke University Press, 97–122.

Ley, D. (2003) 'Seeking Homo Economicus: the Canadian state and the strange story of the Business Immigration Program', *Annals of the Association of American Geographers*, 93(2): 426–41.

Mackie, J. (1997) 'The politics of Asian immigration', in Coughlan, J. and McNamara, D. (eds) *Asians in Australia.* South Melbourne: Macmillan Education Australia, 10–48.

Ministry of Education (2002) *Notification on Setting up Chunhui Plan: Overseas Students' Return to Work during their Academic Sabbaticals.* Beijing: Ministry of Education.

Ministry of Education (2009) *News Release*, 25 March. Online at: http://www.bonoffer.com/show_detail.php?id=1718, accessed 4 May 2009.

Mu, X.S. (2003) 'Speech to Liaoning Technology Business Development Delegation—Chinese Scholars and Students Seminar', Shenyang, 9 August.

OCAO (2002) 'Importing OCPs aggressively, contributing to the industrialization of high technologies in China effectively'. Document prepared for the National Conference on Science and Technology, No. 15, Beijing, 9 January.

Ong, A. (1999) *Flexible Citizenship: The Cultural Logics of Transnationality.* Duke University Press.

Research Team on the Motivations and Rules of the Return of Overseas (2003) 'A Research on the Motivations and Rules of the Return of Overseas Talents and the Strategies to Encourage the Return'. Shanghai: unpublished manuscript.

State Council (1992) *Circular by the State Council on Overseas Students*. Beijing: State Council Office Code 44.

Wang, C.B., Wong, S.L. and Sun, W.B. (2006) 'Haigui: a new area in China's policy toward the Chinese diaspora?', *Journal of Chinese Overseas*, 2(2): 294–309.

Xiang, B. (2005) *Promoting Knowledge Exchange through Diaspora Networks: The Case of People's Republic of China*. Oxford: COMPAS.

Xiang, B. (2007) 'Productive outflow of skills: what India and China can learn from each other', *Asian Population Journal*, 3(2): 115–33.

Xiao, R. (2001) 'A study of the academic development of returned scholars in Beijing University'. Beijing: Beijing University, Advanced Education College, unpublished MA thesis.

Zhao, X.C. (2003) 'Some thoughts on improving the work on OCPs', *China Scholar Abroad*, 30 December. Online at: www.chisa.edu.cn, last accessed 11 April 2009.

Zweig, D. and Chen, C.G. (1995) *China's Brain Drain to the United States: Views of Overseas Chinese Students and Scholars in the 1990s*. Berkeley: University of California, Institute of East Asian Studies.

Zweig, D., Chung, S.F. and Vanhonacker, W. (2006) 'Rewards of technology: explaining China's reverse migration', *Journal of International Migration and Integration*, 7(4): 449–71.

# Index

Page numbers in *Italics* represent tables.
Page numbers in **Bold** represent figures.

American Club: Singapore 32
Ang, Ien 150
*angmoh* 52, 55, 56
Appadurai, A. 141
appropriate bodies 48, 50
appropriateness 51
Asian values 56
aspiration 17
Association of International Personnel Exchange 158

Babyface 85, 92
Bar Rouge 88
bar streets: Shanghai 86
Beaverstock, J.V. 27, 28, 31
Beijing 104
*A Beijing Native in New York* (TV series) 141
belonging: cultural politics of 2–4
Bhabha, K. 149
Bourdieu, P. 10, 23
brain drain 122, 157, 159
British Club: Club Membership 39; members view of role 36–9; membership and British National Identity 40; membership as a social survival strategy 40–1; personal characteristics of members *37–8*; reasons for joining *39*
British expatriate communities: ordinary experiences 29
British women: China 72
Britishness 53, 55, 73; Hong Kong 74
Brits Abroad in Shanghai 71
The Bund 110, 111
Bund Three 88

career mobility: occupational niche 127–32
career paths 29–30
Castells, M. 112, 113
Castles, S. 115, 116
Chang, C.F. 103
Chang, Eileen 109, 111
Chang, T.C. 31, 43
Chatterton, P. 89

Chen, X.F. 162
Cheung Kong Holdings 164
Cheung Kong Scholar Program 163
Chicago 82
childcare 147
children 132; education 145; stability 113
China 4; Agreement on Cooperation in Science and Technology 159; British living in 67; British women 72; citizenship 102; Cultural Revolution 72; culture 70; dual citizenship 148; identity 57; Japan trade 125; masculinity 95; media and resurgence of nationalism 141; OCPs after Tian'anmen 160; pubs 84; recruitment fairs 140; returnees 83; sending researchers overseas 159; Singapore relationship 76; Singaporean and British Transmigrants 66–7; Singaporeans living in 67; social interaction 71; state constructions of the new migrant 140–2; Taiwanese migration 102–3; Temporary Regulations on Self-financed Overseas Education 159; western divide 71; work permits 102
*China Scholar Abroad* (website) 162
China Soul for Christ Foundation 158
Chinese Academy of Science and Engineering 164
Chinese Central Television (CCTC) 141
Chinese migrants: everyday lives 142–9
Chinese migrants in Canada: between Citizenship and Nationality 147–9; between leaving and staying 143–7; conclusion 149–50; everyday lives 142–9; flexible yearnings 140–1; introduction 138–9; professional occupations *143*; profile and methodology 142–3; transnationalism and myth of return 139–40; women 148
Chinese patriotism: Sydney Olympics 141
Chinese student migrants: conclusion 134–5; employee turnover 130; employment patterns 124; employment reality 129; entering small firms 128–9; job mobility 129–31; marketing and sales 126; numbers

# INDEX

in Japan 123, **124**; occupations of interviewees *125*; problems for 120; pseudo-expats 131–2; study data 122–3
Chinese Students Protection Act 159
Chinese Women: corporate 132–4
Chinese Youth Federation: Department for Overseas Scholars 162
Chunhui Plan 163–4
circulation 2
citizenship 147–9
citizenship (dual): recognition of 148
city-sensitive migration 101
class 49
class stratification: Shanghai nightscapes 88
Cohen, R. 10, 14, 27
colonialism 59, 72; transnational elites 70–3
community: sense of 113
conformity 22
Conradson, D. 27, 28, 29, 41, 50
consumption 95–6
contact zones 2, 65, 66, 77, 112; constructing 67–76; global nightscapes 83
Convention for Cooperation and Exchange among Overseas Chinese Enterprises in Scientific and Technological Innovation 155
cosmopolitan encounter: research as 15–16
cosmopolitan society 50
cosmopolitanism 47, 76; concept 9–11; financial services 16–22; old and new 113–15; in recruitment process 17
cosmopolitans: inside/outside international workplace 50–3
Council of Cross-Strait Affairs in Taiwan 103
Court, G. 19
Crazy Horse nightclub 14
Credit Suisse 16
cultural capital 115
cultural competence 77
cultural experience: transnational elites 77
cultural habits 55
cultural identification: hybrid 149
cultural identity: class 23
cultural metropolis: creation 101
cultural policy: Singapore 13
Cultural Revolution: China 72
cultural skills 128
culture shock 72; Singaporean transmigrants in London 50–1
culture-contact 68

dance clubs: Shanghai 85
Deng, Kun-Yan 110
Deng, Xiaoping 159
design 106
destination 101
dialectical identity 52

difference 50, 59, 73
*Digests for Youth* 162
Dikec, M. 53
disco plazas 85
The Distinguished Young Scholars Program 164
diversity 22
Dragon's diaspora 75
dress codes 20–1
drinking culture: London 52, 53, 55
Duan, Y. *Writing Histories in Japan* 122
Dubai 29, 82, 84, 94
Dunkin' Donuts 120

economic development: cultural policy 13
economic niches 121
education: all-English 115; children 145; international schools 36, 114
Ehrkamp, P. 52
*Emigrate to Shanghai Magazine* 110
employment rights 129
enclaves 112
English language 57; ability 18
entrepreneurship: ethnic 120–1
Erwin, K. 95
ethnic entrepreneurship 120, 121
ethnic networks 121
ethnicity: nationality 58
ethnosexual contact zones 82, 95
Eurocentric diffusionism 68
Europe: free movers 101
expatriate transnational social space 42
expatriates: categories of 68; wives 71
expatriation 27–30; ordinary transnationalism 41–2
expatriatisation: City 42–3; Holland Village 31, 43

Fallow, James 110
family 147
fantasy city 101
Farrer, James 4, 5, 6
Favell, A. 101, 107, 115
female migrants: Shanghai 105
femininity 19
feminism: geographers 1
financial services: cosmopolitanism 16–22
flexible citizens 139, 141, 150
Florida 101
Florida, R. 43
foreign capital investments 103
foreign talent: Singapore 12
foreign workers: global talent 13
free movers: Europe 101
frictionless space 120

gated communities 113

# INDEX

gender 49; global spaces 5; workplace 1
gendered dimensions 19–20
Gilroy, P. 149
glass ceiling: racialised 55
Global Chinese 5
global nightscapes 81–4; race and sexuality 96; socially structured spaces of consumption 95–6
global talent: attracting 16; foreign workers 13
global talent magnet 13
*Global Views Monthly* 109
Global Whiteness 5
globalisation 5, 121, 140
globalising careers: roots 108
Goh, Chok Tong 12, 76
Greater China schemes 105
Guangzhou Overseas Students Fair 166
Guangzhou Women's International Committee 71
*guanxi* 3
Gubei community 112

*haigui* 83
*haiwai xuezi* 168; making of 158–61
Hannerz, U. 28, 77
Hannigan, J. 101
Harvey, David 9, 10, 23, 65
headhunters 100
Ho, E. 3, 5, 13, 116
Ho, Kee Tong 75
Ho, P.S.Y. 95
Holland Village: expatriatisation 31, 43
Hollands, R. 89
*homo economicus* 140, 150, 156
homogeneity: workforce 18
Hong Kong 29, 70, 141; Britishness 74; interracial gay relationships 95
hospitality 53
HSBC Bank International 16
Huang, M.T.Y. 108
Hui, W.T. 30
human flow 146
hybridisation 149

identity 60, 149, 157; British 40; cosmopolitan 17; cultural politics of 4–6; national 57; self and other 70
identity-making 59
imagined communities 141
immigration: social embeddedness 139
inclusion 22
India: ritual economy 157
inequality 22
intolerance 22

Japan: China Team 124; China trade 125; Chinese residents in 123; use of Chinese students 120
Japan Institute of Labour Policy and Training 133
Japan Small and Medium Enterprises Network: Shanghai 128
Japanese Students Support Organisation (JASSO) 123
Jilin Convention of Consultation and Cooperation between Overseas Chinese Professionals and Domestic Enterprises 166
Jinjiang Hotel 85
job security 107, 129, 130
Jurong Industrial Estate 75

Kant, Immanuel 9
Kelly, P.F. 15, 41, 51
Kelsky, Karen 95
Kipnis, B.A. 100
Kmart 107
knowledge: arbitrage 75; nomads 2; tacit 107
Kobayashi, A. 3
Kong, L. 57
Koolhaas, Rem 99
Koshy, Susan 95

labour: low-wage 121
language skills 18, 73, 128, 135, 142
Latham, A. 27, 28, 29, 41, 50
Lawson 135; recruitment policy 119
Lee, Ang 109
Lee KC Foundation 164
Lee, L.O.F.: *Shanghai Modern* 113
Ley, David 2, 3, 10, 27, 29
Liu-Farrer, G. 3, 5
London 3, 82; clubs 86; drinking culture 52
*A Love Story between Taipei and Shanghai* (musical) 111
*Lust, Caution* (film) 109

McDowell, L. 19, 48, 51
management style 52
Mandarin 75; learning 73
Maoming clubs 86, 87
Massey, D. 48
migrant (new) 140–2
migrants: change of meaning in China 140–2
migration: terminology of 2
mobility 1
Molotch, H. 101
Moskowitz, M.L. 97
moveability 1
moving: cultural politics of 2–4
multiple migration 2
myth of return: transnationalism 139–40

174

# INDEX

Nagel, J. 82
*Nanfang Dushibao* (newspaper) 144
National Bureau of Foreign Experts (Beijing) 158
national identity 74
National Science Foundation 164
National Taiwan University Student Association 111
nationalism: China 141
nationality 49, 147–9; ethnicity 58
nationality dynamics 56–9; splintering race 56–9
Nayak, A. 48
networks: ethnic 121
New York 29; clubs 86; Times Square 83
Ni, W.J. 110
nightlife genres 82
nightlife zones 83
Nyíri, P. 144, 145

occupational niche: career mobility 127–32; emergence of 123–5; skilled migration 120–2; transnational economy 125–7
Old Shanghai Charm 111
Olds, K. 106
Olympic Games Sydney (2002) 141
Ong, Aihwa 140
online job sites 104
other 60, 70, 72, 73; engaging with 5, 10
outsiders 54, 58
Overseas Chinese Affairs Office (OCAO) 155, 160, 164, 166
Overseas Chinese Association in Japan 127
overseas Chinese professionals (OCPs) 3, 155; after Tian'anmen 160; award ceremonies 163; central government approach 161–5; research 157–8
Overseas Indian's Day 157

Pai, H.-Y.: *Taipei People* 110
Paris 29
Park 97 (club) 89, 92, 94
Pearl River Delta 107
physical attractiveness 19
physical impressions 19
Pines Town: Singapore 35
place: cultural politics of 4–6; politics of 2
points system: skilled worker 143
power relations 66
Pratt, Mary Louise 66
Pravasi Bharatiya Divas 157
professionalism 54; physical appearance 19
promotion: blocked 130
prostitution 86
public space 87
pubs: China 84

race 21–2, 48, 49; constructs of 54; sexuality 96; splintering 56–9
racial barriers 93
racial clustering 56
racial hierarchies 90
racial segregation: voluntary 91
racialised bodies 55
racialised cosmopolitan cultures 47–50
racialised subjectivism: embodying and negotiating 54–9
racism 22
Raffles Marina Club (Singapore) 32
relocation: Shanghai 114
relocation packages 27, 29, 33
Research Team on the Motivations and Rules of the Return of Overseas Talents and the Strategies to Encourage the Return 162
residency rights 100
return illusion: transnationalism 139–40
return migration 2, 3, 66; fears of 146; questions for 140
ritual economy 156, 168; talent 165
rooted realities: everyday lives of PRC immigrants 142–9
roots 113; globalising careers 108

Saitama Prefecture 123
salary 132
Saldanha, A. 49, 60
Salt, Bernard 1
sameness 50
Sassen, S. 104, 105, 110
schooling: international 36
schools 114
Scott, Allen 101
Scott, Sam 101
segregation 113
self 72, 73
self-conscious cosmopolitanism 47
self-fashioning 47, 50
self-identity 73
Sennett, R. 66
sexual capital 95
sexual contact zones 82, 84
sexual status 89–90
sexuality: race 96
Shanghai 3, 4; bar streets 86; career city 115; city planning and foreign corporations 114; construction as a fantasy city 110–11; dance clubs 85; female migrants 105; foreign nationals 83; global city 104; image in Taiwan's media 109; instance of the global 107–8; Japan Small and Medium Enterprises Network 128; job hub 125; the job-hub city 104–8; nightlife problems 87; regionalisation of business structures 105–6; relocation 114; rush 108–10; talent gap

106–7; transnational corporations 105; World Exposition (2010) 104
*Shanghai Culture* (journal) 113
*Shanghai Modern* (Lee) 113
Shanghai nightscapes: class stratification 88; competing racialised femininities 91–5; competing racialised masculinities 89–91; data and methodology 84–5; ethnosexual contact zones 85–9
Shanghai Paramount 111
*shili yangchang* (ten-mile-long foreign zone) 113
Singapore 5, 29; American Club 32; brand name 75; British citizens 27; British Club 33–41; as cosmopolis 11–15; cultural policy 13; economic strategy 30; expatriate clubs 27, 32; expatriate clubs surveyed *34*; expatriate workforce 30; expatriation and foreign talent 30–1; foreign talent 12; identity 57, 59, 70; international social clubs 32; international town and country recreation clubs 32; Pines Town 35; post-colonial history 12; prestige private business clubs 32; Raffles Marina Club 32; Regionalisation 2000 programme 66; social and recreational clubs 31–3; social and recreational clubs (British expatriates) 33–41; Swiss Club 35, 36; Tanglin Club 33, 36; Three Quays 83; Tower Club 32
Singapore Club 71
Singapore Cricket Club 35
Singapore-Suzhou Township model 75
Singaporean transmigrants in London 50; culture shock 50–1
skilled migration: globalizing cities 100–1
skilled worker: points system 143
skills: generic 100
Sklair, L. 43, 47, 83, 99
Smith, M.P. 1, 28
social embeddedness: immigration 139
social exclusion 53
social interaction: China 71
social space: ownership 90
socialisation 23; British Club 40
Soja, E. 101, 115
sojourning 2
South Korea 157
space of flows 2, 65; settling in 112–13
space of place 65, 112
special development zones 140
step migration 2
studying abroad 159
Swiss Club: Singapore 35

Taipei: regionalist 104
*Taipei People* (Pai) 110
Taiwan Social Change Survey 103
Taiwanese job seeker sites 104
Taiwanese Professional Women's Society (TPWS) 105
Taiwanese skilled migrants in Shanghai 102–3; data 102; indicators of interaction *103*
talent: attracting 13; ritual economy 165; shortages 106; workers 1
Tanglin Club: Singapore 33, 36
Tanglin Trust School 36
Temasek Holdings 12
Teo, S.Y. 3, 4, 160
third space 139
Three Quays: Singapore 83
Tian'anmen Square 159, 160
Times Square: New York 83
Tower Club: Singapore 32
transculturation 2, 65, 68
transnational capitalist class 83, 99; hyper-mobility 65
transnational economy: occupational niche 125–7
transnational elites 28; assumptions of 2; colonialists 70–3; cultural experience 77; culturalists 68–70; imperialists 74–6; transnational space 27–9
transnational migrants: sexual status 91
transnational space 71; transnational elites 27–9
transnational urbanism 28
transnationalism 27–30; ordinary 41–2; return illusion 139–40
Tsai, M.C. 103
Tsang, A.K.T. 95
Tseng, Y.H. 3, 4
Twelve-Characters Approach 160

United World College South East Asia 36
universalism 10

Vancouver 29; occupations of Chinese immigrants 142, *143*
Vertovec, S. 10, 14, 27

wage structures 103
Wal-Mart 107
Walsh, K. 82, 84, 94
Wang, J.L. 112
Waters, J.L. 29
Whiteness 95
Willis, K. 28, 57, 83, 112
Win-Win Cooperation 155
women (Chinese) 132–4; migrants in Canada 148
work etiquette 51
work permits 100
workforce homogeneity 18
World City 27–30

# INDEX

*Writing Histories in Japan* (Duan) 122

Xiang, B. 3, 4, 145
Xintiandi 87, 88

Yangtze River Basin 104
Yangtze River Delta 107
Ye, J. 15–16, 41, 51
Yeo, George 75
Yeoh, B.S.A. 11, 28, 30, 57, 83, 112

*yijinhuanxiang* (hometown return in silken robes) 146
Young, C. 10

Zhao, Ziyang 159
Zhongjiang High-Tech Park 113

# Journal of Ethnic and Migration Studies

2010 Impact Factor: 1.041
Ranking: 5/13 (Ethnic Studies) 13/24 (Demography)
©2011 Thomson Reuters, *2010 Journal Citation Reports*®

Editor:
**Russell King** - *Sussex Centre for Migration Research, University of Sussex, UK*

Associate Editors:
**Richard Bedford** - *University of Waikato, New Zealand*, **Michael Collyer** - *Sussex Centre for Migration Research, University of Sussex, UK*, **Adrian Favell** - *Institut d'Etudes Politiques, France* and **Peggy Levitt** - *Wellesley College, USA*

The *Journal of Ethnic and Migration Studies (JEMS)* publishes the results of first-class research on all forms of migration and its consequences, together with articles on ethnic conflict, discrimination, racism, nationalism, citizenship and policies of integration. Contributions to the journal, which are all fully refereed, are especially welcome when they are the result of comparative research, for example within Europe or between one or more European country and the countries of North America and the Asia-Pacific.

**Recent and Forthcoming Articles**

The Effect of Classroom Diversity on Tolerance and Participation in England, Sweden and Germany
*Jan Germen Janmaat*

Exploring the Demands of Assimilation among White Ethnic Majorities in Western Europe
*Marco Antonsich*

Borders Behind the Border: An Exploration of State-Level Differences in Migration Control and their Effects on US Migration Patterns
*Arjen Leerkes, Mark Leach and James Bachmeier*

Who Needs Migrant Workers? Labour Shortages, Immigration and Public Policy
*Nigel Harris*

**Visit www.tandfonline.com/cjms to:**
- view free articles, news & offers
- register to receive quarterly eUpdates
- register to receive table of contents alerts
- read a free online sample copy
- subscribe to the journal
- submit your research
- order back issues

www.tandfonline.com/cjms

Routledge
Taylor & Francis Group

www.routledge.com/9780415503662

### Related titles from Routledge

## The New Expatriates

Postcolonial Approaches to Mobile Professionals

**Edited by Anne-Meike Fechter and Katie Walsh**

While scholarship on migration has been thriving for decades, little attention has been paid to professionals from Europe and America who move temporarily to destinations beyond 'the West'. In many ways, these are the modern-day equivalents of colonial settlers and expatriates, yet the continuities in their migration practices have rarely been considered. This volume advances our understanding of contemporary mobile professionals by engaging with postcolonial theories of race, culture and identity. It evaluates the significance of the past in shaping contemporary expatriate mobilities and highlighting postcolonial continuities in relation to people, practices and imaginations. *The New Expatriates* explicitly examines the way in which whiteness and imperial relationships continue to shape the migrations experiences of Euro-American skilled migrants as they seek out new places to live and work.

This book was originally published as a special issue of the *Journal of Ethnic and Migration Studies*.

July 2012: 246 x 174: 192pp
Hb: 978-0-415-50366-2
£80 / $125

For more information and to order a copy visit
www.routledge.com/9780415503662

**Available from all good bookshops**

www.routledge.com/9780415594509

### Related titles from Routledge

## Innovation and Learning Experiences in Rapidly Developing East Asia

**Edited by Rajah Rasiah, Thiruchelvam and Keun Lee**

Technology and technical change is sector- and industry-specific, embedded by locational institutions and organizations, and integrated in global networks. It is non-linear in its emergence and movement, and subsumed in the nature of micro, meso and macro interactions. Using evolutionary theory and its methodological complement of inductive research, this collection showcases selected examples of innovation and learning experience in the rapidly evolving developing economies of East Asia.

Consistent with evolutionary postulations of technology and technical change, this volume provides a range of empirically rich articles that elucidate innovation and learning experiences in East Asia. The case studies range from the dramatic movement of button manufacturing in China, to the globe's technology frontier. The rich selection of industry-based national case studies provide a comprehensive account of technological catch-up experiences that will be very useful for both scholars and policy makers.

This book was originally published as a special issue of *Asia Pacific Business Review*.

November 2011: 246 x 174: 144pp
Hb: 978-0-415-59450-9
**£80 / $125**

For more information and to order a copy visit
www.routledge.com/9780415594509

**Available from all good bookshops**

www.routledge.com/9780415674836

**Related titles from Routledge**

# International Business in China
## Understanding the Global Economic Crisis

**Edited by Robert Taylor**

This volume discusses dramatic innovation and learning experiences in East Asia. It explores Chinese management as China emerges as a global economic player, with a greater role in international business during a global economic crisis. Since the 1980s, Chinese management has benefited from an infusion of capital, technology and managerial expertise through inward direct investment via joint and wholly-owned foreign ventures.

As the so-called 'workshop of the world', China and its exports, face protectionism in the United States and the European Union. To avoid this, Chinese leaders are emphasising domestic consumption, itself dependent on rising personal income levels and an improved national social insurance system.

The creation of a knowledge economy, in addition to outward investment in manufacturing, could lead to a distinctive independent style of Chinese management and China's participation in intra-regional trade underlines the nation's role in Asian regional business networks. Such developments present a challenge to Western and global business.

This book was originally published as a special issue of *Asia Pacific Business Review*.

May 2012: 246 x 174: 152pp
Hb: 978-0-415-67483-6
£80 / $125

For more information and to order a copy visit
www.routledge.com/9780415674836

Available from all good bookshops